Te

SRA
Spelling Through
Morphographs

Robert Dixon

Siegfried Engelmann

A Division of The McGraw-Hill Companies

Columbus, Ohio

SRA/McGraw-Hill

A Division of The **McGraw·Hill** *Companies*

Send all inquiries to:
SRA/McGraw-Hill
8787 Orion Place
Columbus, OH 43240

Printed in the United States of America.

ISBN 0-02-684869-4

6 7 8 9 0 MAZ 05 04

Contents

EXERCISE 1

Word and Spelling Introduction

1. (Write on the board: **graph, phone, photo, shape, fry,** and **physic.**)
   These words are made up of only one morphograph.

2. (Point to **graph.**)
   What word? (S) *Graph.*
   Spell **graph.** Get ready. (S)
   (Repeat this procedure for each word.)

3. (Erase the words.)
   Spell the words again.
   First word: **fry.** Get ready. (S)
   (Repeat until firm.)

4. (Repeat step 3 for **phone, photo, physic, shape,** and **graph.**)

5. Find part **A** on your worksheet.
   Get ready to write the words you just spelled.

6. First word: **photo.**
   What word? (S) *Photo.*
   Write **photo.**
   (Repeat for **graph, physic, fry, shape,** and **phone.**)

7. You'll find the spellings of the words we're going to check in appendix **G,** section **B.**

8. (Call on a student.)
   Look up the spelling of the word **photo.**

9. (Assign each of the remaining words to different students.)

10. Get ready to check part **A.**
    Put an **X** next to any word you missed and write that word correctly.

11. (Call on the student who looked up **photo.**)
    Spell **photo.**
    (Write **photo** on the board.)

12. (Repeat step 11 for each remaining word.)

EXERCISE 2

Word Building

Get ready to spell some words that have more than one morphograph.
These words are made up of morphographs that cannot stand alone.

1. First word: **misconception.**
   What is the first morphograph in **misconception**? (S) *mis.*
   What is the next morphograph in **misconception**? (S) *con.*
   What is the next morphograph in **misconception**? (S) *cept.*
   What is the next morphograph in **misconception**? (S) *ion.*
   Spell **misconception.** Get ready. (S)

2. Next word: **deception.**
   What is the first morphograph in **deception**? (S) *de.*
   What is the next morphograph in **deception**? (S) *cept.*
   What is the next morphograph in **deception**? (S) *ion.*
   Spell **deception.** Get ready. (S)

3. (For **regression, except, projected, detecting, injected,** and **congress,** have students identify each morphograph and spell each word.)

4. Find part **B** on your worksheet.
   You are going to write the words you just spelled.

5. First word: **except.** Write it.

6. Next word: **congress.** Write it.

7. (Repeat step 6 for **misconception, injected, deception, detecting, regression,** and **projected.**)

8. (Check spellings and have students rewrite any missed words.)

Spelling Review

1. I'll spell some words quickly.
   Then I'll call on different people to spell each word.
   When I call on you, spell the word quickly.
2. My turn: **t - e - n - t.**
   Everybody, what word? (S) *Tent.*
3. Next word: **m - a - i - n.**
   What word? (S) *Main.*
4. (Repeat step 3 for **unsure, storage, some, pausing, ruin, cloudy, painlessly, given, exclaim, straightest, contract, friendly,** and **pure.**)
5. Your turn.
   (Call on a student.)
   Spell **pausing.** Go.
6. (Praise students who respond correctly.)
7. (Call on a student.)
   Spell **main.** Go.
8. (Repeat step 7 for **some, painlessly, contract, tent, given, friendly, unsure, ruin, exclaim, pure, storage, cloudy,** and **straightest.**)

Rule Discrimination

I'll say words.
Figure out whether the doubling rule, the **y**-to-**i** rule, or no rule applies.

1. The first word begins with **try.**
   Spell **try.** Get ready. (S)
   Could a rule apply? (S) *Yes.*
   Which rule? (Call on a student.)
   The rule about changing y to i.
   Everybody, how do you know the **y**-to-**i** rule could apply? (S)
   Try ends with a consonant-and-y.
2. The word is **trying.**
   Does the **y**-to-**i** rule apply? (S) *No.*
   How do you know? (Call on a student.)
   Ing begins with an i.
   Spell **trying.** Get ready. (S)

3. The next word begins with **drop.**
   Spell **drop.** Get ready. (S)
   Could a rule apply? (S) *Yes.*
   Which rule? (Call on a student.)
   The rule about doubling a letter.
   Everybody, how do you know the doubling rule could apply? (S)
   Drop is a short cvc word.
4. The word is **dropper.**
   Does the doubling rule apply? (S) *Yes.*
   How do you know? (Call on a student.)
   Er begins with v.
   Spell **dropper.** Get ready. (S)
5. The next word begins with **stay.**
   Spell **stay.** Get ready. (S)
   Could a rule apply? (S) *No.*
   Why not? (Call on a student.) *Stay does not end with cvc or a consonant-and-y.*
6. The word is **stayed.**
   Spell **stayed.** Get ready. (S)
7. The next word begins with **glory.**
   Spell **glory.** Get ready. (S)
   Could a rule apply? (S) *Yes.*
   Which rule? (Call on a student.)
   The rule about changing y to i.
   Everybody, how do you know the **y**-to-**i** rule could apply? (S)
   Glory ends with a consonant-and-y.
8. The word is **glorious.**
   Does the **y**-to-**i** rule apply? (S) *Yes.*
   How do you know? (Call on a student.)
   Ous does not begin with i.
   Spell **glorious.** Get ready. (S)

Morphograph Analysis

Everybody, find part **C** on your worksheet.

1. You are going to fill in the blank to show the morphographs in each word. But the blank doesn't show how many morphographs there are. So you have to write the morphographs and put plus signs between them.
2. The first word is **reporting.**
   How many morphographs is **reporting**? (S) *Three.*

3. Write them on the blank with plus signs between the morphographs. (Pause and check.)
4. The next word is **photograph.**
   How many morphographs is **photograph**? (S) *Two.*
5. Write them on the blank with a plus sign between the morphographs. (Check.)
6. You will finish part **C** later.

Independent Work

1. Complete the rest of the worksheet on your own.
   Be sure to read the instructions carefully.
2. (Check and correct all work.)

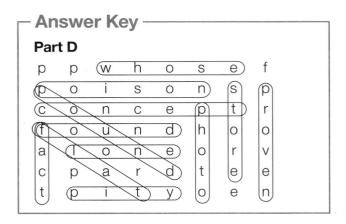
Supplemental Blackline Masters

Supplemental blackline masters 27 and 28 provide additional practice on material covered in Lessons 66 through 70. You may assign any or all of the activities, and you may award bonus points.

Word and Spelling Introduction

1. (Write these words on the board: **hero, base, prime, tin, spin,** and **win.**)
   These words are made up of only one morphograph.
2. (Point to **hero.**)
   What word? (S) *Hero.*
   Spell **hero.** Get ready. (S)
   (Repeat this procedure for each word.)
3. (Erase the words.)
   Spell the words again.
   First word: **tin.** Get ready. (S)
   (Repeat until firm.)
4. (Repeat step 3 for **base, prime, spin, win,** and **hero.**)
5. Find part **A** on your worksheet.
   Get ready to write the words you just spelled.
6. First word: **prime.**
   What word? (S) *Prime.*
   Write **prime.**
   (Repeat for **hero, win, tin, spin,** and **base.**)
7. You'll find the spellings of the words we're going to check in appendix **G**, section **B**.
8. (Call on a student.)
   Look up the spelling of the word **prime.**
9. (Assign each of the remaining words to different students.)
10. Get ready to check part **A**.
    Put an **X** next to any word you missed and write that word correctly.
11. (Call on the student who looked up **prime.**)
    Spell **prime.**
    (Write **prime** on the board.)
12. (Repeat step 11 for each remaining word.)

Nonword Base

1. (Write on the board: **tain.**)
   Here is a new morphograph that cannot stand alone.
   It is pronounced **tain.**
   What morphograph? (S) *tain.*
2. Everybody, spell **tain.** Get ready. (S)
   (Repeat until firm.)
3. Get ready to spell words that have the morphograph **tain.**
   First word: **retaining.**
   What is the first morphograph in **retaining**? (S) *re.*
   What is the next morphograph in **retaining**? (S) *tain.*
   What is the next morphograph in **retaining**? (S) *ing.*
   Spell **retaining.** Get ready. (S)
4. Next word: **contain.**
   What is the first morphograph in **contain**? (S) *con.*
   What is the next morphograph in **contain**? (S) *tain.*
   Spell **contain.** Get ready. (S)
5. (Repeat step 4 for **detain** and **maintain.**)

Spelling Review

1. I'll spell some words quickly.
   See if you can figure out each word.
2. Listen: **e - x - p - l - a - i - n.**
   Everybody, what word? (S) *Explain.*
3. Listen: **t - r - a - c - t - i - o - n.**
   What word? (S) *Traction.*
4. (Repeat step 3 for **photograph, resent, surely, furious, frying, extent, shaping, shapely, phone, physics, painful, passion,** and **edit.**)

5. Find part **B** on your worksheet.
Get ready to write some of those words.

6. First word: **photograph.** Write it.

7. Next word: **explain.** Write it.

8. (Repeat step 7 for **resent, furious, frying, shaping, physics,** and **painful.**)

9. I will spell each word.
Put an **X** next to any word you missed and write that word correctly.
(Write each word on the board as you spell it.)

<hr>

EXERCISE 4

Word Building

Get ready to spell some words that have more than one morphograph.
These words are made up of morphographs that cannot stand alone.

1. First word: **project.**
What is the first morphograph in **project**?
(S) *pro.*
What is the next morphograph in **project**?
(S) *ject.*
Spell **project.** Get ready. (S)

2. Next word: **conjecture.**
What is the first morphograph in **conjecture**? (S) *con.*
What is the next morphograph in **conjecture**? (S) *ject.*
What is the next morphograph in **conjecture**? (S) *ure.*
Spell **conjecture.** Get ready. (S)

3. (For **deceptive, exception, rejection, contain, detained,** and **progressive,** have students identify each morphograph and spell each word.)

4. Find part **C** on your worksheet.
You are going to write the words you just spelled.

5. First word: **progressive.** Write it.

6. Next word: **project.** Write it.

7. (Repeat step 6 for **detained, conjecture, contain, deceptive, exception,** and **rejection.**)

8. (Check spellings and have students rewrite any missed words.)

<hr>

EXERCISE 5

Study for Spelling Contest

Find appendix **G,** section **B.**

1. During Lesson 73, we're going to have a spelling contest.

2. Most of the contest words will come from appendix **G,** section **B.**

3. When you've completed your worksheet, study those words.

Note. Students may study in pairs or independently.

<hr>

EXERCISE 6

Independent Work

1. Complete the rest of the worksheet on your own.
Be sure to read the instructions carefully.

2. (Check and correct all work.)

EXERCISE 1

Spelling Contest

Note. There is no student worksheet for Lesson 73.

Today we're going to have a spelling contest.

1. We'll make up two teams.
    (Assign students to each team.)
2. (Make a scorebox on the board.)

Team A	Team B

3. Here are the rules for the contest.
    a. I will dictate words to the teams.
    b. Every time a team spells a word correctly, it gets a point.
    c. If a team misses a word, the other team gets to try that word.
    d. The first team to get 30 points wins the spelling contest.
4. (Praise correct spellings and mark them in the scorebox.)

To correct misspellings:
a. That's not how the word _____ is spelled.
b. (Call on a member of the other team to spell that word.)

5. (Call on teams alternately to spell words from the following list.)

rainy	protected	lengthy
nightly	photograph	physics
contain	winner	snappy
progression	pleasure	preside
unprotected	cloudy	furious
injection	sure	blower

famous	regain	gainfully
exception	retention	purely
restore	richest	glorious
pressure	strengthen	reception
shiniest	poison	thoughtless
surely	tracing	straight
painfulness	wonderful	couldn't
graph	author	
unproven	deceptive	

First team to get 30 points . . . . 10 bonus points.

If the other team has 27–29 points . . . . 8 bonus points.

If the other team has 24–26 points . . . . 5 bonus points.

If the other team has less than 24 points . . . 0 bonus points.

Crossword Puzzles

The crossword puzzles are made up exclusively of the words presented in the review lessons. Every word in these lessons has been used. For each review lesson, there are two or three sets of puzzles, depending on how many words are in the lesson. A set is made up of two puzzles—an original and an alternate. The alternate uses the same words and clues as the original, but in a different arrangement. This gives you a good deal of flexibility in how you use the puzzles.

The crossword puzzle blackline masters are located at the back of this Teacher Presentation Book.

Bingo

Find part **A** on your worksheet.

1. We're going to play bingo.
   I'll dictate words for you to write in the boxes.
2. Remember:
   a. A row may go across, or down, or corner to corner.
   b. The first student or students to get four words in a row earn four bonus points.
   c. If you have misspelled any words in your row, that row won't count for bonus points.
3. First word: **light.**
   Write **light** in one of the boxes.
4. Next word: **author.**
   Write **author** in one of the boxes.
5. (Repeat step 4 for **whether, please, civil, equal, wonder, wander, poisonous, protect, concept, rejection, physics, sure, fluid,** and **where.**)
6. Now we'll mark the boxes.
7. (Spell each word quickly.)
   First word: **p - r - o - t - e - c - t.**
   Mark an **X** in the box containing that word.
8. Next word: **f - l - u - i - d.**
   Mark an **X** in the box containing that word.
9. (Repeat step 3 for as many of the following words as necessary: **light, physics, concept, whether, civil, wonder, equal, wander, sure, author, where, please, rejection,** and **poisonous.**)
10. (When one or more students get a bingo, stop the game and award the bonus points.)

Word Building

Find part **B** on your worksheet

Get ready to write some words that have more than one morphograph. Some of these words follow the rule you have learned about adding **es** to words that end with a **consonant-and-y.**

1. Word one: write **baby** in the first column. (Check.)
   Write **s** or **es** in the second column. (Check.)
   Now write **babies** in the last column.
2. (Repeat step 1 for **flies, hurries,** and **plays.**)
3. (Check work and have students rewrite any misspellings.)
4. Everybody, turn your worksheet over and get ready to spell the words from the last column without looking.
5. Word one: **flies.** (Pause.)
   Spell **flies.** Get ready. (S)
6. (Repeat step 5 for **hurries, plays,** and **babies.**)
7. (Repeat each word until firm. Give individual turns.)

Nonword Base

1. One morphograph that cannot stand alone is **cept.**
   What morphograph? (S) *cept.*
   Spell **cept.** Get ready. (S)
   (Repeat spelling of **cept** until firm.)
2. Get ready to spell words that have the morphograph **cept.**
   First word: **concept.**
   What is the first morphograph in **concept**? (S) *con.*
   What is the next morphograph in **concept**? (S) *cept.*
   Spell **concept.** Get ready. (S)

3. Next word: **exception.**
   What is the first morphograph in **exception**? (S) *ex.*
   What is the next morphograph in **exception**? (S) *cept.*
   What is the next morphograph in **exception**? (S) *ion.*
   Spell **exception.** Get ready. (S)
4. (Repeat step 3 for **receptive** and **deception.**)

EXERCISE 4

Vowel-Consonant

When is **w** a vowel letter? (S)
At the end of a morphograph.
(Repeat until firm.)

EXERCISE 5

Homonyms

1. Everybody, spell the **feat** that means: **doing something great.**
   Get ready. (S)
2. Everybody, spell the **feet** that means: **the things you walk on.**
   Get ready. (S)
3. (Repeat steps 1 and 2 until firm. Give individual turns.)

EXERCISE 6

Independent Work

1. Complete the rest of the worksheet on your own.
   Be sure to read the instructions carefully.
2. (Check and correct all work.)

Affix Introduction

1. (Write on the board: **dislike, disarm,** and **disease.**)
   Each of these words has a morphograph **dis** at the beginning.
   What morphograph? (S) *dis.*
2. Read these words. (Point to **dislike.**)
   What word? (S) *Dislike.*
   What is the first morphograph in **dislike**?
   (S) *dis.*
   What is the next morphograph in **dislike**?
   (S) *like.*
3. (Point to **disarm.**)
   What word? (S) *Disarm.*
   What is the first morphograph in **disarm**?
   (S) *dis.*
   What is the next morphograph in **disarm**?
   (S) *arm.*
4. (Point to **disease.**)
   What word? (S) *Disease.*
   What is the first morphograph in **disease**?
   (S) *dis.*
   What is the next morphograph in **disease**?
   (S) *ease.*
5. (Erase the board.)
   Everybody, spell the word **like.**
   Get ready. (S)
   Now spell the word **dislike.** Get ready. (S)
6. Everybody, spell the word **arm.**
   Get ready. (S)
   Now spell the word **disarm.** Get ready. (S)
7. Everybody, spell the word **ease.**
   Get ready. (S)
   Now spell the word **disease.** Get ready. (S)
8. (Repeat spelling of **dislike, disarm,** and **disease** until firm. Give individual turns.)

Spelling Review

Find part **A** on your worksheet.

You are going to write some words made up of morphographs you have spelled before.

1. First word: **famous.**
   What word? (S) *Famous.*
   Write **famous.**
2. Next word: **spinning.**
   What word? (S) *Spinning.*
   Write **spinning.**
3. (Repeat step 2 for **fuzzy, furious, feature, fluid, prime, fried, painlessness, ruin, thoughtless,** and **nervous.**)
4. I'll spell each word.
   Put an **X** next to any word you missed and write that word correctly.
   (Write each word on the board as you spell it.)

Word Building

Get ready to spell some words that have more than one morphograph.
These words are made up of morphographs that cannot stand alone.

1. First word: **retained.**
   What is the first morphograph in **retained**? (S) *re.*
   What is the next morphograph in **retained**? (S) *tain.*
   What is the next morphograph in **retained**? (S) *e-d.*
   Spell **retained.** Get ready. (S)

2. Next word: **progression.**
   What is the first morphograph in
   progression? (S) *pro.*
   What is the next morphograph in
   progression? (S) *gress.*
   What is the next morphograph in
   progression? (S) *ion.*
   Spell **progression.** Get ready. (S)
3. (For **except, retaining, projection,
   detain, protective,** and **contained,** have
   students identify each morphograph and
   spell each word.)
4. Find part **B** on your worksheet.
   You are going to write some of the words
   you just spelled.
5. First word: **detain.** Write it.
6. Next word: **projection.** Write it.
7. (Repeat step 6 for **protective** and **except.**)
8. (Check spellings and have students rewrite
   any missed words.)

EXERCISE 4

Homonyms

1. (Write on the board: **cent.**)
   This word is **cent.** What word? (S) *Cent.*
2. This **cent** does not mean: **moved
   somewhere.**
   This **cent** means: **one hundred.**
   What does this **cent** mean? (S) *One
   hundred.*
3. And how is it spelled? Get ready. (S)
4. (Erase the board.)
   Spell **cent** again. Get ready. (S)
5. Remember that word.

EXERCISE 5

Rule Review

Let's go over some of the spelling rules you
have learned.

1. Tell me when you drop the **e** from a word.
   (Pause 2 seconds.)
   Get ready. (S)
   *When the next morphograph begins with a
   vowel letter.*

2. Tell me when you change the **y** to **i** in
   a word.
   (Pause 2 seconds.)
   Get ready. (S)
   *When the word ends consonant-and-y, and
   the next morphograph begins with
   anything except i.*
3. (Repeat steps 1 and 2 until students are
   firm on both rules.)

EXERCISE 6

Independent Work

1. Complete the rest of the worksheet on
   your own.
   Be sure to read the instructions carefully.
2. (Check and correct all work.)

┌─ **Answer Key** ─────────────

Part E
1. prove
2. starless
3. phone
4. couldn't

└──────────────────────────────

Lesson 76

EXERCISE 1

Word and Spelling Introduction

1. (Write these words on the board: **quote, quest, quick,** and **quart.**)
   These words are made up of only one morphograph.

2. (Point to **quote.**)
   What word? (S) *Quote.*
   Spell **quote.** Get ready. (S)
   (Repeat this procedure for each word.)

3. (Erase the words.)
   Spell the words again.
   First word: **quick.** Get ready. (S)
   (Repeat until firm.)

4. (Repeat step 3 for **quest, quart,** and **quote.**)

5. Find part **A** on your worksheet.
   Get ready to write the words you just spelled.

6. First word: **quest.**
   What word? (S) *Quest.*
   Write **quest.**
   (Repeat for **quote, quart,** and **quick.**)

7. You'll find the spellings of the words we're going to check in appendix **H,** section **B.**

8. (Call on a student.)
   Look up the spelling of the word **quest.**

9. (Assign each of the remaining words to different students.)

10. Get ready to check part **A.**
    Put an **X** next to any word you missed and write that word correctly.

11. (Call on the student who looked up **quest.**)
    Spell **quest.**
    (Write **quest** on the board.)

12. (Repeat step 11 for each remaining word.)

EXERCISE 2

Sentence Dictation

Find part **B** on your worksheet.

Get ready to write sentences made of words you know.

1. Remember, the first letter of the first word is capitalized, and you put a period at the end of the sentence.

2. Listen. I have worried about misspellings that are confusing.
   Everybody, say that sentence. Get ready. (S)
   I have worried about misspellings that are confusing.
   (Repeat until firm.)

3. Write that sentence by number one on your worksheet.
   Remember to spell every word correctly.
   (Repeat the sentence as students write.)

4. Listen. You shouldn't carelessly unwrap that package.
   Everybody, say that sentence. Get ready. (S)
   You shouldn't carelessly unwrap that package.
   (Repeat until firm.)

5. Write that sentence by number two on your worksheet.
   Remember to spell every word correctly.
   (Repeat the sentence as students write.)

6. (Check and correct misspellings. Underlined words—I, that, and you—have not been taught. If any of those words are missed, include them in the next Word and Spelling Introduction.)

Proofreading

Everybody, find part **C** on your worksheet.

1. Some words in these sentences are misspelled.
    Look carefully at each word.
2. Underline any word that is misspelled and write it correctly in the right-hand column.
    You have some extra spaces.
3. You have three minutes to complete part **C.** (Pause.)
4. Get ready to check part **C.**
    Put an **X** above any word in the sentences that you missed.
5. What is the first word that is misspelled? (S) *Boxes.*
    Everybody, spell **boxes.** Get ready. (S)
    Put an **X** above **boxes** if you didn't write it correctly.
6. What is the next word that is misspelled? (S) *Poison.*
    Everybody, spell **poison.** Get ready. (S)
    Put an **X** above **poison** if you didn't write it correctly.
7. (Repeat step 6 for **place, sprayed,** and **motor.**)

Oral Spelling Review

You are going to spell some words made up of morphographs you have spelled before.

1. First word: **hero.**
    What word? (S) *Hero.*
    Spell **hero.** Get ready. (S)
    (Repeat until firm.)
2. Next word: **physics.**
    What word? (S) *Physics.*
    Spell **physics.** Get ready. (S)
    (Repeat until firm.)
3. (Repeat step 2 for **content, consent, resent, giving, straight, relate, prime, photograph, mistaken,** and **fittest.**)

Rule Review

Let's go over some of the spelling rules you have learned.

1. Tell me when you double the final **C** in a short word.
    (Pause 2 seconds.)
    Get ready. (S)
    When the word ends cvc and the next morphograph begins with v.
2. If a word ends **consonant-and-y,** you add **es** to make the plural word.
    Everybody, tell me the rule.
    (Pause 2 seconds.)
    Get ready. (S)
    If a word ends consonant-and-y, you add es to make the plural word.
3. (Repeat steps 1 and 2 until students are firm on both rules.)

Independent Work

1. Complete the rest of the worksheet on your own.
    Be sure to read the instructions carefully.
2. (Check and correct all work.)

Supplemental Blackline Masters

Supplemental blackline masters 29 and 30 provide additional practice on material covered in Lessons 71 through 75. You may assign any or all of the activities, and you may award bonus points.

EXERCISE 1

Nonword Base

1. (Write on the board: **pel.**)
   Here is a new morphograph that cannot stand alone.
   It is pronounced **pel.**
   What morphograph? (S) *pel.*

2. Everybody, spell **pel.** Get ready. (S)
   (Repeat until firm.)

3. Get ready to spell words that have the morphograph **pel.**
   First word: **propel.**
   What is the first morphograph in **propel**?
   (S) *pro.*
   What is the next morphograph in **propel**?
   (S) *pel.*
   Spell **propel.** Get ready. (S)

4. Next word: **expel.**
   What is the first morphograph in **expel**?
   (S) *ex.*
   What is the next morphograph in **expel**?
   (S) *pel.*

5. (Repeat step 4 for **repel** and **dispel.**)

EXERCISE 2

Affix Introduction

1. (Write on the board: **realist, artist,** and **harpist.**)
   Each of these words has a morphograph **ist** at the end.
   What morphograph? (S) *ist.*

2. Read these words. (Point to **realist.**)
   What word? (S) *Realist.*
   What is the first morphograph in **realist**?
   (S) *real.*
   What is the next morphograph in **realist**?
   (S) *ist.*

3. (Point to **artist.**)
   What word? (S) *Artist.*
   What is the first morphograph in **artist**?
   (S) *art.*
   What is the next morphograph in **artist**?
   (S) *ist.*

4. (Point to **harpist.**)
   What word? (S) *Harpist.*
   What is the first morphograph in **harpist**?
   (S) *harp.*
   What is the next morphograph in **harpist**?
   (S) *ist.*

5. (Erase the board.)
   Everybody, spell the word **real.**
   Get ready. (S)
   Now spell the word **realist.** Get ready. (S)

6. Everybody, spell the word **art.**
   Get ready. (S)
   Now spell the word **artist.** Get ready. (S)

7. Everybody, spell the word **harp.**
   Get ready. (S)
   Now spell the word **harpist.** Get ready. (S)

8. (Repeat spelling of **realist, artist,** and **harpist** until firm. Give individual turns.)

EXERCISE 3

Word and Spelling Introduction

1. (Write on the board: **heavy, breath, head, flat,** and **bet.**)
   These words are made up of only one morphograph.

2. (Point to **heavy.**)
   What word? (S) *Heavy.*
   Spell **heavy.** Get ready. (S)
   (Repeat this procedure for each word.)

3. (Erase the words.)
   Spell the words again.
   First word: **flat.** Get ready. (S)
   (Repeat until firm.)

4. (Repeat step 3 for **breath, head, heavy,** and **bet.**)

5. Find part **A** on your worksheet.
   Get ready to write the words you
   just spelled.
6. First word: **head.**
   What word? (S) *Head.*
   Write **head.**
   (Repeat for **heavy, bet, flat,** and **breath.**)
7. You'll find the spellings of the words we're
   going to check in appendix **H,** section **B.**
8. (Call on a student.)
   Look up the spelling of the word **head.**
9. (Assign each of the remaining words to
   different students.)
10. Get ready to check part **A.**
    Put an **X** next to any word you missed and
    write that word correctly.
11. (Call on the student who looked up **head.**)
    Spell **head.**
    (Write **head** on the board.)
12. (Repeat step 11 for each remaining word.)

EXERCISE 4

Spelling Review

1. I'll spell some words quickly.
   See if you can figure out each word.
2. Listen: **h - u - r - r - i - e - s.**
   Everybody, what word? (S) *Hurries.*
3. Listen: **h - o - p - e - l - e - s - s - l - y.**
   What word? (S) *Hopelessly.*
4. (Repeat step 3 for **quickly, what's,
   quarts, carrier, deception, contract,
   refuse, hero, given, various, shopping,
   misquoted,** and **quest.**)
5. Find part **B** on your worksheet.
   Get ready to write some of those words.
6. First word: **carrier.** Write it.
7. Next word: **hopelessly.** Write it.
8. (Repeat step 7 for **deception, contract,
   refuse, various, shopping,** and
   misquoted.)
9. I will spell each word.
   Put an **X** next to any word you missed and
   write that word correctly.
   (Write each word on the board as you
   spell it.)

EXERCISE 5

Word Building

Get ready to spell some words that have more
than one morphograph.

1. First word: **repel.**
   What is the first morphograph in **repel**?
   (S) *re.*
   What is the next morphograph in **repel**?
   (S) *pel.*
   Spell **repel.** Get ready. (S)
2. Next word: **contained.**
   What is the first morphograph in
   contained? (S) *con.*
   What is the next morphograph in
   contained? (S) *tain.*
   What is the next morphograph in
   contained? (S) *e-d.*
   Spell **contained.** Get ready. (S)
3. (For **except, protect, progress, reject,
   propel,** and **expel,** have students identify
   each morphograph and spell each word.)
4. Find part **C** on your worksheet.
   You are going to write the words you
   just spelled.
5. First word: **except.** Write it.
6. Next word: **protect.** Write it.
7. (Repeat step 6 for **repel** and **reject.**)
8. (Check spelling and have students rewrite
   any missed words.)

EXERCISE 6

Independent Work

1. Complete the rest of the worksheet on
   your own.
   Be sure to read the instructions carefully.
2. (Check and correct all work.)

┌─ **Answer Key** ──────────────

Part D

1.	poisonous	5.	equip
2.	blissful	6.	distract
3.	portable	7.	hottest
4.	phone	8.	hopefulness

Lesson 78

EXERCISE 1

Homonyms

1. (Write on the board: **tail.**)
   This word is **tail.** What word? (S) *Tail.*
2. This **tail** does not mean: **story.**
   This **tail** means: **the end.**
   What does this **tail** mean? (S) *The end.*
3. And how is it spelled? Get ready. (S)
4. (Erase the board.)
   Spell **tail** again. Get ready. (S)
5. Remember that word.

EXERCISE 2

Word and Spelling Introduction

1. (Write on the board: **duty, scope, fail, rail,** and **state.**)
   These words are made up of only one morphograph.
2. (Point to **duty.**)
   What word? (S) *Duty.*
   Spell **duty.** Get ready. (S)
   (Repeat this procedure for each word.)
3. (Erase the words.)
   Spell the words again.
   First word: **rail.** Get ready. (S)
   (Repeat until firm.)
4. (Repeat step 3 for **scope, fail, duty,** and **state.**)
5. Find part **A** on your worksheet.
   Get ready to write the words you just spelled.
6. First word: **fail.**
   What word? (S) *Fail.*
   Write **fail.**
   (Repeat for **scope, duty, state,** and **rail.**)
7. You'll find the spellings of the words we're going to check in appendix **H,** section **B.**
8. (Call on a student.)
   Look up the spelling of the word **fail.**
9. (Assign each of the remaining words to different students.)

10. Get ready to check part **A.**
    Put an **X** next to any word you missed and write that word correctly.
11. (Call on the student who looked up **fail.**)
    Spell **fail.**
    (Write **fail** on the board.)
12. (Repeat step 11 for each remaining word.)

EXERCISE 3

Word Building

Get ready to spell some words that have more than one morphograph.

1. First word: **detain.**
   What is the first morphograph in **detain**? (S) *de.*
   What is the next morphograph in **detain**? (S) *tain.*
   Spell **detain.** Get ready. (S)
2. Next word: **propel.**
   What is the first morphograph in **propel**? (S) *pro.*
   What is the next morphograph in **propel**? (S) *pel.*
   Spell **propel.** Get ready. (S)
3. (For **reject, dispel, detective, reception, progressive,** and **contained,** have students identify each morphograph and spell each word.)
4. Find part **B** on your worksheet.
   You are going to write some of the words you just spelled.
5. First word: **reject.**
   Write it.
6. Next word: **detective.**
   Write it.
7. (Repeat step 6 for **reception** and **contained.**)
8. (Check spellings and have students rewrite any missed words.)

EXERCISE 4

Nonword Base

1. (Write on the board: **vise.**)
   Here is a new morphograph that usually does not stand alone.
   It is pronounced **vize.**
   What morphograph? (S) *vise.*
2. Everybody, spell **vise.** Get ready. (S)
   (Repeat until firm.)
3. Get ready to spell some words that have the morphograph **vise.**
   First word: **revise.**
   What is the first morphograph in **revise**? (S) *re.*
   What is the next morphograph in **revise**? (S) *vise.*
   Spell **revise.** Get ready. (S)
4. Next word: **devise.**
   What is the first morphograph in **devise**? (S) *de.*
   What is the next morphograph in **devise**? (S) *vise.*
   Spell **devise.** Get ready. (S)
5. Next word: **vision.**
   What is the first morphograph in **vision**? (S) *vise.*
   What is the next morphograph in **vision**? (S) *ion.*
   Spell **vision.** Get ready. (S)

EXERCISE 5

Spelling Review

1. I'll spell some words quickly.
   See if you can figure out each word.
2. Listen: **r - e - a - l - l - y.**
   Everybody, what word? (S) *Really.*
3. Listen: **h - e - a - v - y.**
   What word? (S) *Heavy.*
4. (Repeat step 3 for **photograph, physics, quicken, refuse, winner,** and **babies.**)
5. Find part **C** on your worksheet.
   Get ready to write those words.
6. First word: **refuse.**
   Write it.
7. Next word: **heavy.**
   Write it.

8. (Repeat step 7 for **babies, physics, winner, really, quicken,** and **photograph.**)
9. I will spell each word.
   Put an **X** next to any word you missed and write that word correctly.
   (Write each word on the board as you spell it.)

EXERCISE 6

Rule Review

Let's go over some of the spelling rules you have learned.

1. Tell me when you double the final **C** in a short word.
   (Pause 2 seconds.) Get ready. (S)
   When the word ends cvc and the next morphograph begins with v.
2. Tell me when you change the **y** to **i** in a word.
   (Pause 2 seconds.) Get ready. (S)
   When the word ends consonant-and-y, and the next morphograph begins with anything except i.
3. (Repeat steps 1 and 2 until students are firm on both rules.)

EXERCISE 7

Independent Work

1. Complete the rest of the worksheet on your own.
   Be sure to read the instructions carefully.
2. (Check and correct all work.)

Sentence Dictation

Find part **A** on your worksheet.

Get ready to write sentences made of words you know.

1. Remember, the first letter of the first word is capitalized, and you put a period at the end of the sentence.
2. Listen. It's really loud when <u>a</u> car crashes. Everybody, say that sentence.
    Get ready. (S)
    It's really loud when a car crashes.
    (Repeat until firm.)
3. Write that sentence by number one on your worksheet.
    Remember to spell every word correctly.
    (Repeat the sentence as students write.)
4. Listen. She could have stayed later, <u>but</u> she didn't.
    Everybody, say that sentence.
    Get ready. (S)
    She could have stayed later, but she didn't.
5. Write that sentence by number two on your worksheet.
    Remember to spell every word correctly.
6. You must put a comma after the word **later.**
    (Repeat the sentence as students write.)
7. (Check and correct misspellings. Underlined words—<u>a</u> and <u>but</u>—have not been taught. If any of those words are missed, include them in the next Word and Spelling Introduction.)

──────── EXERCISE 2 ────────

Word and Spelling Introduction

1. (Write on the board: **spirit, chief, niece, grief,** and **brief.**)
    These words are made up of only one morphograph.

2. (Point to **spirit.**)
    What word? (S) *Spirit.*
    Spell **spirit.** Get ready. (S)
    (Repeat this procedure for each word.)
3. (Erase the words.)
    Spell the words again.
    First word: **grief.** Get ready. (S)
    (Repeat until firm.)
4. (Repeat step 3 for **chief, niece, brief,** and **spirit.**)
5. Find part **B** on your worksheet.
    Get ready to write the words you just spelled.
6. First word: **niece.**
    What word? (S) *Niece.*
    Write **niece.**
    (Repeat for **spirit, brief, grief,** and **chief.**)
7. You'll find the spellings of the words we're going to check in appendix **H,** section **B.**
8. (Call on a student.)
    Look up the spelling of the word **niece.**
9. (Assign each of the remaining words to different students.)
10. Get ready to check part **B.**
    Put an **X** next to any word you missed and write that word correctly.
11. (Call on the student who looked up **niece.**)
    Spell **niece.**
    (Write **niece** on the board.)
12. (Repeat step 11 for each remaining word.)

──────── EXERCISE 3 ────────

Homonyms

1. (Write on the board: **sent.**)
    This word is **sent.** What word? (S) *Sent.*
2. This **sent** means: **moved somewhere.**
    What does this **sent** mean? (S) *Moved somewhere.*
3. And how is it spelled? Get ready. (S)
    (Erase the board.)

4. Everybody, spell the **sent** that means: **moved somewhere.** Get ready. (S)
5. Everybody, spell the **cent** that means: **one hundred.** Get ready. (S)
6. (Repeat steps 4 and 5 until firm. Give individual turns.)

═══════ **EXERCISE 4** ═══════

Oral Spelling Review

You are going to spell some words made up of morphographs you have spelled before.

1. First word: **duty.**
   What word? (S) *Duty.*
   Spell **duty.** Get ready. (S)
   (Repeat until firm.)
2. Next word: **scope.**
   What word? (S) *Scope.*
   Spell **scope.** Get ready. (S)
   (Repeat until firm.)
3. (Repeat step 2 for **fail, rail, state, heavy, breath, request,** and **physical.**)

═══════ **EXERCISE 5** ═══════

Rule Discrimination

I'll say words.

Figure out whether the doubling rule, the **y**-to-**i** rule, or no rule applies.

1. The first word begins with **heavy.**
   Spell **heavy.** Get ready. (S)
   Could a rule apply? (S) *Yes.*
   Which rule? (Call on a student.) *The rule about changing y to i.*
   Everybody, how do you know the **y**-to-**i** rule could apply? (S)
   Heavy ends with a consonant-and-y.
2. The word is **heavily.**
   Does the **y**-to-**i** rule apply? (S) *Yes.*
   How do you know? (Call on a student.)
   Ly does not begin with i.
   Spell **heavily.** Get ready. (S)
3. The next word begins with **win.**
   Spell **win.** Get ready. (S)
   Could a rule apply? (S) *Yes.*

Which rule? (Call on a student.) *The rule about doubling a letter.*
Everybody, how do you know the doubling rule could apply? (S)
Win is a short cvc word.
4. The word is **winner.**
   Does the doubling rule apply? (S) *Yes.*
   How do you know? (Call on a student.)
   Er begins with v.
   Spell **winner.** Get ready. (S)
5. The next word begins with **duty.**
   Spell **duty.** Get ready. (S)
   Could a rule apply? (S) *Yes.*
   Which rule? (Call on a student.) *The rule about changing y to i.*
   Everybody, how do you know the **y**-to-**i** rule could apply? (S)
   Duty ends with a consonant-and-y.
6. The word is **dutiful.**
   Does the **y**-to-**i** rule apply? (S) *Yes.*
   How do you know? (Call on a student.)
   Ful does not begin with i.
   Spell **dutiful.** Get ready. (S)
7. The next word begins with **sad.**
   Spell **sad.** Get ready. (S)
   Could a rule apply? (S) *Yes.*
   Which rule? (Call on a student.) *The rule about doubling a letter.*
   Everybody, how do you know the doubling rule could apply? (S)
   Sad is a short cvc word.
8. The word is **sadness.**
   Does the doubling rule apply? (S) *No.*
   How do you know? (Call on a student.)
   Ness does not begin with v.
   Spell **sadness.** Get ready. (S)

═══════ **EXERCISE 6** ═══════

Independent Work

1. Complete the rest of the worksheet on your own.
   Be sure to read the instructions carefully.
2. (Check and correct all work.)

Lesson 80

EXERCISE 1

Homonyms

1. (Write on the board: **plain.**)
   This word is **plain.** What word? (S) *Plain.*
2. This **plain** does not mean: **the thing you fly in.**
   This **plain** means: **ordinary.**
   What does this **plain** mean? (S) *Ordinary.*
3. And how is it spelled? Get ready. (S)
4. (Erase the board.)
   Spell **plain** again. Get ready. (S)
5. Remember that word.

EXERCISE 2

Affix Introduction

1. (Write on the board: **graphic, heroic,** and **basic.**)
   Each of these words has a morphograph **ic** at the end.
   What morpograph? (S) *ic.*
2. Read these words. (Point to **graphic.**)
   What word? (S) *Graphic.*
   What is the first morphograph in **graphic**? (S) *graph.*
   What is the next morphograph in **graphic**? (S) *ic.*
3. (Point to **heroic.**)
   What word? (S) *Heroic.*
   What is the first morphograph in **heroic**? (S) *hero.*
   What is the next morphograph in **heroic**? (S) *ic.*
4. (Point to **basic.**)
   What word? (S) *Basic.*
   What is the first morphograph in **basic**? (S) *base.*
   What is the next morphograph in **basic**? (S) *ic.*
5. (Erase the board.)
   Everybody, spell the word **graph.**
   Get ready. (S)
   Now spell the word **graphic.** Get ready. (S)

6. Everybody, spell the word **hero.**
   Get ready. (S)
   Now spell the word **heroic.** Get ready. (S)
7. Everybody, spell the word **base.**
   Get ready. (S)
   Now spell the word **basic.** Be careful. Get ready. (S)
8. (Repeat spelling of **graphic, heroic,** and **basic** until firm. Give individual turns.)

EXERCISE 3

Nonword Base

1. (Write on the board: **duce.**)
   Here is a new morphograph that cannot stand alone.
   It is pronounced **duce.**
   What morphograph? (S) *duce.*
2. Everybody, spell **duce.** Get ready. (S)
   (Repeat until firm.)
3. Get ready to spell words that have the morphograph **duce.**
   First word: **produce.**
   What is the first morphograph in **produce**? (S) *pro.*
   What is the next morphograph in **produce**? (S) *duce.*
   Spell **produce.** Get ready. (S)
4. Next word: **conducive.**
   What is the first morphograph in **conducive**? (S) *con.*
   What is the next morphograph in **conducive**? (S) *duce.*
   What is the next morphograph in **conducive**? (S) *ive.*
   Spell **conducive.** Get ready. (S)
5. (Repeat step 4 for **reducing** and **deduce.**)

Spelling Review

1. I'll spell some words quickly.
   See if you can figure out each word.
2. Listen: **t - r - a - c - t - i - o - n.**
   Everybody, what word? (S) *Traction.*
3. Listen: **q - u - i - c - k - e - n.**
   What word? (S) *Quicken.*
4. (Repeat step 3 for **richest, niece, failure, safely, painful, spirit, worried, heavy, revise,** and **strength.**)
5. Find part **A** on your worksheet.
   Get ready to write some of those words.
6. First word: **richest.** Write it.
7. Next word: **niece.** Write it.
8. (Repeat step 7 for **safely, painful, spirit, and strength.**)
9. I will spell each word.
   Put an **X** next to any word you missed and write that word correctly.
   (Write each word on the board as you spell it.)

Homonyms

1. Everybody, spell the **sent** that means: **moved somewhere.**
   Get ready. (S)
2. Everybody, spell the **cent** that means: **one hundred.**
   Get ready. (S)
3. (Repeat steps 1 and 2 until firm. Give individual turns.)

Independent Work

1. Complete the rest of the worksheet on your own.
   Be sure to read the instructions carefully.
2. (Check and correct all work.)

Answer Key

Part B

Part D

1.	friendliness	5.	berries
2.	boxes	6.	feature
3.	easy	7.	sprayer
4.	biggest	8.	wondering

Mastery Test

1. You are going to have a test today. It will help you see how well you are learning to spell.
2. Everybody, take out a sheet of lined paper and draw a line down the middle. Then number the paper from 1 through 20.
3. (Check and correct.)
4. Word 1 is **quickly.**
   We have to mop up the water **quickly.**
   What word? (S) *Quickly.*
   Write **quickly.**
5. Word 2 is **progress.**
   Are you making **progress** on your report?
   What word? (S) *Progress.*
   Write **progress.**
6. (Repeat step 5 for the remaining words on the list.)

3.	**various**	12.	**prime**
4.	**stretch**	13.	**confront**
5.	**heavy**	14.	**quote**
6.	**blissful**	15.	**other**
7.	**deny**	16.	**contract**
8.	**breath**	17.	**studied**
9.	**quart**	18.	**bet**
10.	**hopelessly**	19.	**changeless**
11.	**famous**	20.	**deception**

7. Everybody, exchange papers with your partner. (Pause.)

8. I'll spell each word. If the word is not spelled correctly on the paper you're marking, put an **X** next to it.
    If the word is spelled correctly, don't put any mark next to it.

9. Word 1 is **quickly: q - u - i - c - k - l - y.** Check it.

10. **(Repeat step 9 for each remaining word.)**

11. Return your partner's test paper.

12. Now correct any errors you made. If there is an **X** next to a word on your test, write the word correctly in the right column. Raise your hand if you don't know how to spell any words.

13. Turn your paper over when you're finished. I'll come around and check your paper.

14. If you didn't make any mistakes, raise your hand now.

15. Write the number correct at the top of your test.

Lesson 81

══════ **EXERCISE 1** ══════

Homonyms

1. (Write on the board: **tale.**)
   This word is **tale.** What word? (S) *Tale.*
2. This **tale** means: **a story.**
   What does this **tale** mean? (S) *A story.*
3. And how is it spelled? Get ready. (S)
   (Erase the board.)
4. Everybody, spell the **tale** that means: **a story.** Get ready. (S)
5. Everybody, spell the **tail** that means: **the end.** Get ready. (S)
6. (Repeat steps 4 and 5 until firm. Give individual turns.)

══════ **EXERCISE 2** ══════

Word and Spelling Introduction

1. (Write on the board: **first, thirst, hop, with, plant,** and **ship.**)
   These words are made up of only one morphograph.
2. (Point to **first.**)
   What word? (S) *First.*
   Spell **first.** Get ready. (S)
   (Repeat this procedure for each word.)
3. (Erase the words.)
   Spell the words again.
   First word: **with.** Get ready. (S)
   (Repeat until firm.)
4. (Repeat step 3 for **thirst, hop, ship, plant,** and **first.**)
5. Find part **A** on your worksheet.
   Get ready to write the words you just spelled.
6. First word: **hop.**
   What word? (S) *Hop.*
   Write **hop.**
   (Repeat for **first, ship, plant, with,** and **thirst.**)
7. You'll find the spellings of the words we're going to check in appendix **H,** section **B.**
8. (Call on a student.)
   Look up the spelling of the word **hop.**

9. (Assign each of the remaining words to different students.)
10. Get ready to check part **A.**
    Put an **X** next to any word you missed and write that word correctly.
11. (Call on the student who looked up **hop.**)
    Spell **hop.**
    (Write **hop** on the board.)
12. (Repeat step 11 for each remaining word.)

══════ **EXERCISE 3** ══════

Oral Spelling Review

You are going to spell some words made up of morphographs you have spelled before.

1. First word: **briefly.**
   What word? (S) *Briefly.*
   Spell **briefly.** Get ready. (S)
   (Repeat until firm.)
2. Next word: **tract.**
   What word? (S) *Tract.*
   Spell **tract.** Get ready. (S)
   (Repeat until firm.)
3. (Repeat step 2 for **request, heaviness, any, studying, artist, flattest, quickly, retain, protection,** and **realistic.**)

══════ **EXERCISE 4** ══════

Word Building

Get ready to spell some words that have more than one morphograph.

1. First word: **chiefly.**
   What is the first morphograph in **chiefly**? (S) *chief.*
   What is the next morphograph in **chiefly**? (S) *ly.*
   Spell **chiefly.** Get ready. (S)
2. Next word: **graphic.**
   What is the first morphograph in **graphic**? (S) *graph.*
   What is the next morphograph in **graphic**? (S) *ic.*
   Spell **graphic.** Get ready. (S)

24   LESSON 81

3. (For **joyous, dislike, cloudy,** and **regain,** have students identify each morphograph and spell each word.)
4. Find part **B** on your worksheet.
   You are going to write the words you just spelled.
5. First word: **cloudy.** Write it.
6. Next word: **dislike.** Write it.
7. (Repeat step 6 for **chiefly, graphic, regain,** and **joyous.**)
8. (Check spellings and have students rewrite any missed words.)

EXERCISE 5

Sentence Dictation

Find part **C** on your worksheet.
Get ready to write sentences made of words you know.

1. Remember, the first letter of the sentence is capitalized, and you put a period at the end of the sentence.
2. Listen. <u>The</u> heavy plant quickly flattened <u>the</u> hat <u>of</u> <u>the</u> hero.
   Everybody, say that sentence.
   Get ready. (S) *The heavy plant quickly flattened the hat of the hero.*
   (Repeat until firm.)
3. Write that sentence by number one on your worksheet.
   Remember to spell every word correctly.
   (Repeat the sentence as students write.)
4. Listen. <u>The</u> detective showed <u>the</u> photograph <u>to</u> <u>the</u> chief.
   Everybody, say that sentence.
   Get ready. (S) *The detective showed the photograph to the chief.*
   (Repeat until firm.)
5. Write that sentence by number two on your worksheet.
   Remember to spell every word correctly.
   (Repeat the sentence as students write.)
6. (Check and correct misspellings.
   Underlined words—the, of, and to—have not been taught. If any of those words are missed, include them in the next Word and Spelling Introduction.)

EXERCISE 6

Word Building

Get ready to spell some words that have more than one morphograph.
These words are made up of morphographs that cannot stand alone.

1. First word: **reduce.**
   What is the first morphograph in **reduce**? (S) *re.*
   What is the next morphograph in **reduce**? (S) *duce.*
   Spell **reduce.** Get ready. (S)
2. Next word: **detection.**
   What is the first morphograph in **detection**? (S) *de.*
   What is the next morphograph in **detection**? (S) *tect.*
   What is the next morphograph in **detection**? (S) *ion.*
   Spell **detection.** Get ready. (S)
3. (For **congress, detain, reception, injected,** and **expel,** have students identify each morphograph and spell each word.)

EXERCISE 7

Independent Work

1. Complete the rest of the worksheet on your own.
   Be sure to read the instructions carefully.
2. (Check and correct all work.)

┌─ **Answer Key** ─────────
Part E
2. ship
5. joy
└────────────────────────

Supplemental Blackline Masters

Supplemental blackline masters 31 and 32 provide additional practice on material covered in Lessons 76 through 80. You may assign any or all of the activities, and you may award bonus points.

EXERCISE 1

EXERCISE 1

Proofreading

Everybody, find part **A** on your worksheet.

1. Some words in these sentences are misspelled.
   Look carefully at each word.
2. Underline any word that is misspelled and write it correctly in the right-hand column.
3. You have three minutes to complete part **A**. (Pause.)
4. Get ready to check part **A**.
   Put an **X** above any word in the sentences that you missed.
5. What is the first word that is misspelled? (S) *Thought.*
   Everybody, spell **thought.** Get ready. (S)
   Put an **X** above **thought** if you didn't write it correctly.
6. What is the next word that is misspelled? (S) *Brother.*
   Put an **X** above **brother** if you didn't write it correctly.
7. (Repeat step 6 for **would, photograph, niece, head,** and **injection.**)

EXERCISE 2

Spelling Review

1. I'll spell some words quickly.
   See if you can figure out each word.
2. Listen: **q - u - i - c - k - n - e - s - s.**
   Everybody, what word? (S) *Quickness.*
3. Listen: **c - h - i - e - f - l - y.**
   What word? (S) *Chiefly.*
4. (Repeat step 3 for **spirit, scope, wonderful, heavy, dutiful, graphic, physics, berries, stretcher, choices, preserve,** and **neatly.**)
5. Find part **B** on your worksheet.
   Get ready to write some of those words.

6. First word: **spirit.** Write it.
7. Next word: **wonderful.** Write it.
8. (Repeat step 7 for **heavy, berries, stretcher, preserve, chiefly,** and **neatly.**)
9. I will spell each word.
   Put an **X** next to any word you missed and write that word correctly.
   (Write each word on the board as you spell it.)

EXERCISE 3

Homonyms

1. (Write on the board: **tale.**)
   This word is **tale.** What word? (S) *Tale.*
2. This **tale** means: **a story.**
   What does this **tale** mean? (S) *A story.*
3. And how is it spelled? Get ready. (S)
   (Erase the board.)
4. Everybody, spell the **tale** that means: **a story.** Get ready. (S)
5. Everybody, spell the **tail** that means: **the end.** Get ready. (S)
6. (Repeat steps 4 and 5 until firm. Give individual turns.)

EXERCISE 4

Homonyms

1. Everybody, spell the **sent** that means: **moved somewhere.**
   Get ready. (S)
2. Everybody, spell the **cent** that means: **one hundred.**
   Get ready. (S)
3. (Repeat steps 1 and 2 until firm. Give individual turns.)

Word Building

Get ready to spell some words that have more than one morphograph.

These words are made up of morphographs that cannot stand alone.

1. First word: **detain.**
   What is the first morphograph in **detain**?
   (S) *de.*
   What is the next morphograph in **detain**?
   (S) *tain.*
   Spell **detain.** Get ready. (S)
2. Next word: **dispel.**
   What is the first morphograph in **dispel**?
   (S) *dis.*
   What is the next morphograph in **dispel**?
   (S) *pel.*
   Spell **dispel.** Get ready. (S)
3. (For **retain, detective, repel,** and **reception,** have students identify each morphograph and spell each word.)
4. Find part **C** on your worksheet.
   You are going to write the words you just spelled.
5. First word: **retain.** Write it.
6. Next word: **detective.** Write it.
7. (Repeat step 6 for **detain, reception, dispel,** and **repel.**)
8. (Check spellings and have students rewrite any missed words.)

Study for Spelling Test

Find appendix **H,** section **B.**

1. During lesson **83,** we're going to have a spelling test.
2. Most of the test words will come from appendix **H,** section **B.**
3. When you've completed your worksheet, study the words.

Note. Students may study in pairs or independently.

Independent Work

1. Complete the rest of the worksheet on your own.
   Be sure to read the instructions carefully.
2. (Check and correct all work.)

Lesson 83

===== EXERCISE 1 =====

Spelling Test

Note. There is no student worksheet for Lesson 83.

1. Everybody, take out a sheet of lined paper for the spelling test.
2. I'll dictate 50 words.
   Some of them you haven't spelled before, but you have spelled all the morphographs.
   If you get 45 words or more correct, you earn 12 worksheet points.
3. Word one: **physical.**
   What word? (S) *Physical.*
   Write **physical.**
4. Word two: **realist.**
   What word? (S) *Realist.*
   Write **realist.**
5. (Repeat step 4 for the following list of words.)

3.	thirsty	21.	heavily
4.	failure	22.	disease
5.	chief	23.	expressed
6.	without	24.	nieces
7.	revise	25.	misstated
8.	propel	26.	spirit
9.	headed	27.	relative
10.	conquest	28.	station
11.	flatly	29.	plainly
12.	planted	30.	produce
13.	request	31.	quickly
14.	unheroic	32.	hopping
15.	inducing	33.	herbs
16.	quotable	34.	pleasure
17.	stately	35.	discount
18.	basics	36.	briefly
19.	duties	37.	breathless
20.	question	38.	motorist
39.	shipped	45.	rail
40.	disliked	46.	unfriendly
41.	reduce	47.	lengthen
42.	first	48.	quietly
43.	scope	49.	inhuman
44.	quart	50.	poisonous

6. I'll spell each word. Put an **X** next to any word you missed and write that word correctly.
   (Write each word on the board as you spell it.)
7. (Award points: 45–50 . . . . 13 points
   43–44 . . . . 10 points
   41–42 . . . . 7 points
   39–40 . . . . 5 points
   37–38 . . . . 3 points)

Crossword Puzzles

The crossword puzzles are made up exclusively of the words presented in the review lessons. Every word in these lessons has been used. For each review lesson, there are two or three sets of puzzles, depending on how many words are in the lesson. A set is made up of two puzzles—an original and an alternate. The alternate uses the same words and clues as the original, but in a different arrangement. This gives you a good deal of flexibility in how you use the puzzles.

The crossword puzzle blackline masters are located at the back of this Teacher Presentation Book.

EXERCISE 1

Homonyms

1. Everybody, spell the **tale** that means: **a story.** Get ready. (S)
2. Everybody, spell the **tail** that means: **the end.** Get ready. (S)
3. (Repeat steps 1 and 2 until firm. Give individual turns.)

EXERCISE 2

Word and Spelling Introduction

1. (Write on the board: **south, round, pound, ground, thousand,** and **cover.**)
   These words are made up of only one morphograph.
2. (Point to **south.**)
   What word? (S) *South.*
   Spell **south.** Get ready. (S)
   (Repeat this procedure for each word.)
3. (Erase the words.)
   Spell the words again.
   First word: **ground.** Get ready. (S)
   (Repeat until firm.)
4. (Repeat step 3 for **round, pound, thousand, south,** and **cover.**)
5. Find part **A** on your worksheet.
   Get ready to write the words you just spelled.
6. First word: **pound.**
   What word? (S) *Pound.*
   Write **pound.**
   (Repeat for **south, cover, thousand, round,** and **ground.**)
7. You'll find the spellings of the words we're going to check in appendix **I,** section **C.**
8. (Call on a student.)
   Look up the spelling of the word **pound.**
9. (Assign each of the remaining words to different students.)

10. Get ready to check part **A.**
    Put an **X** next to any word you missed and write that word correctly.
11. (Call on the student who looked up **pound.**)
    Spell **pound.**
    (Write **pound** on the board.)
12. (Repeat step 11 for each remaining word.)

EXERCISE 3

Word Building

Get ready to spell some words that have more than one morphograph.

1. First word: **heroic.**
   What is the first morphograph in **heroic**? (S) *hero.*
   What is the next morphograph in **heroic**? (S) *ic.*
   Spell **heroic.** Get ready. (S)
2. Next word: **artistic.**
   What is the first morphograph in **artistic**? (S) *art.*
   What is the next morphograph in **artistic**? (S) *ist.*
   What is the next morphograph in **artistic**? (S) *ic.*
   Spell **artistic.** Get ready. (S)
3. (For **feature, proclain, rainy,** and **request,** have students identify each morphograph and spell each word.)
4. Find part **B** on your worksheet.
   You are going to write the words you just spelled.
5. First word: **feature.** Write it.
6. Next word: **artistic.** Write it.
7. (Repeat step 6 for **heroic, request, proclaim,** and **rainy.**)
8. (Check spellings and have students rewrite any missed words.)

Oral Spelling Review

You are going to spell some words made up of morphographs you have spelled before.

1. First word: **realistic.**
   What word? (S) *Realistic.*
   Spell **realistic.** Get ready. (S)
   (Repeat until firm.)
2. Next word: **distract.**
   What word? (S) *Distract.*
   Spell **distract.** Get ready. (S)
   (Repeat until firm.)
3. (Repeat step 2 for **question, spirit, heavy, bedding, basic, grief, graphic, joyously, reduce, hopper, first, nieces,** and **failing.**)

Word Building

Get ready to spell some words that have more than one morphograph.
These words are made up of morphographs that cannot stand alone.

1. First word: **conducive.**
   What is the first morphograph in **conducive**? (S) *con.*
   What is the next morphograph in **conducive**? (S) *duce.*
   What is the next morphograph in **conducive**? (S) *ive.*
   Spell **conducive.** Get ready. (S)
2. Next word: **repel.**
   What is the first morphograph in **repel**?
   (S) *re.*
   What is the next morphograph in **repel**?
   (S) *pel.*
   Spell **repel.** Get ready. (S)
3. (For **contained, except, reduce, project, progressively,** and **induce,** have students identify each morphograph and spell each word.)
4. Find part **C** on your worksheet.
   You are going to write the words you just spelled.

5. First word: **induce.** Write it.
6. Next word: **project.** Write it.
7. (Repeat step 6 for **conducive, progressively, repel, reduce, contained,** and **except.**)
8. (Check spellings and have students rewrite any missed words.)

Independent Work

1. Complete the rest of the worksheet on your own.
   Be sure to read the instructions carefully.
2. (Check and correct all work.)

━━━━━ **EXERCISE 1** ━━━━━

Homonyms

1. (Write on the board: **plane.**)
   This word is **plane.** What word? (S) *Plane.*
2. This **plane** means: **a thing that flies.**
   What does this **plane** mean? (S) *A thing that flies.*
3. And how is it spelled? Get ready. (S)
   (Erase the board.)
4. Everybody, spell the **plane** that means: **a thing that flies.** Get ready. (S)
5. Everybody, spell the **plain** that means: **ordinary.** Get ready. (S)
6. (Repeat steps 4 and 5 until firm. Give individual turns.)

━━━━━ **EXERCISE 2** ━━━━━

Affix Introduction

1. (Write on the board: **transport, transact, transfuse,** and **transform.**)
   Each of these words has a morphograph **trans** at the beginning.
   What morphograph? (S) *trans.*
2. Read these words. (Point to **transport.**)
   What word? (S) *Transport.*
   What is the first morphograph in **transport**? (S) *trans.*
   What is the next morphograph in **transport**? (S) *port.*
3. (Point to **transact.**)
   What word? (S) *Transact.*
   What is the first morphograph in **transact**? (S) *trans.*
   What is the next morphograph in **transact**? (S) *act.*
4. (Point to **transfuse.**)
   What word? (S) *Transfuse.*
   What is the first morphograph in **transfuse**? (S) *trans.*
   What is the next morphograph in **transfuse**? (S) *fuse.*

5. (Point to **transform.**)
   What word? (S) *Transform.*
   What is the first morphograph in **transform**? (S) *trans.*
   What is the next morphograph in **transform**? (S) *form.*
6. (Erase the board.)
   Everybody, spell the word **port.**
   Get ready. (S)
   Now spell the word **transport.**
   Get ready. (S)
7. Everybody, spell the word **act.**
   Get ready. (S)
   Now spell the word **transact.**
   Get ready. (S)
8. Everybody, spell the word **fuse.**
   Get ready. (S)
   Now spell the word **transfuse.**
   Get ready. (S)
9. Everybody, spell the word **form.**
   Get ready. (S)
   Now spell the word **transform.**
   Get ready. (S)
10. (Repeat spelling **transport, transact, transfuse,** and **transform** until firm. Give individual turns.)

━━━━━ **EXERCISE 3** ━━━━━

Word and Spelling Introduction

1. (Write on the board: **verse, danger,** and **chance.**)
   These words are made up of only one morphograph.
2. (Point to **verse.**)
   What word? (S) *Verse.*
   Spell **verse.** Get ready. (S)
   (Repeat this procedure for each word.)
3. (Erase the words.)
   Spell the words again.
   First word: **chance.** Get ready. (S)
   (Repeat until firm.)
4. (Repeat step 3 for **danger** and **verse.**)

5. Find part **A** on your worksheet.
   Get ready to write the words you just spelled.
6. First word: **danger.**
   What word? (S) *Danger.*
   Write **danger.**
   (Repeat for **verse** and **chance.**)
7. You'll find the spelling of the words we're going to check in appendix **I,** section **C.**
8. (Call on a student.)
   Look up the spelling of the word **danger.**
9. (Assign **verse** and **chance** to different students.)
10. Get ready to check part **A.**
    Put an **X** next to any word you missed and write that word correctly.
11. (Call on the student who looked up **danger.**)
    Spell **danger.**
    (Write **danger** on the board.)
12. (Repeat step 11 for **verse** and **chance.**)

EXERCISE 4

Spelling Review

1. I'll spell some words quickly.
   See if you can figure out each word.
2. Listen: **r - e - q - u - e - s - t.**
   Everybody, what word? (S) *Request.*
3. Listen: **t - h - o - u - s - a - n - d - s.**
   What word? (S) *Thousands.*
4. (Repeat step 3 for **uncover, failure, planter, traction, quarts, breathless, heaviest, physical, photograph,** and **spirited.**)
5. Find part **B** on your worksheet.
   Get ready to write some of those words.
6. First word: **uncover.** Write it.
7. Next word: **photograph.** Write it.
8. (Repeat step 7 for **planter, heaviest, physical, failure, thousands,** and **spirited.**)
9. I will spell each word.
   Put an **X** next to any word you missed and write that word correctly.
   (Write each word on the board as you spell it.)

EXERCISE 5

Word Building

Get ready to spell some words that have more than one morphograph.

1. First word: **artistic.**
   What is the first morphograph in **artistic?** (S) *art.*
   What is the next morphograph in **artistic?** (S) *ist.*
   What is the next morphograph in **artistic?** (S) *ic.*
   Spell **artistic.** Get ready. (S)
2. Next word: **transform.**
   What is the first morphograph in **transform?** (S) *trans.*
   What is the next morphograph in **transform?** (S) *form.*
   Spell **transform.** Get ready. (S)
3. (For **quicken, gainfully, rental,** and **displace,** have students identify each morphograph and spell each word.)
4. Find part **C** on your worksheet.
   You are going to write the words you just spelled.
5. First word: **quicken.** Write it.
6. Next word: **gainfully.** Write it.
7. (Repeat step 6 for **artistic, transform, displace,** and **rental.**)
8. (Check spellings and have students rewrite any missed words.)

EXERCISE 6

Independent Work

1. Complete the rest of the worksheet on your own.
   Be sure to read the instructions carefully.
2. (Check and correct all work.)

┌─ **Answer Key** ──────────

Part E

1.	human	5.	namable
2.	safer	6.	straightest
3.	I'll	7.	passive
4.	reserve	8.	lonely

EXERCISE 1

Homonyms

1. Everybody, spell the **plain** that means: **ordinary.** Get ready. (S)
2. Everybody, spell the **plane** that means: **a thing that flies.**
   Get ready. (S)
3. (Repeat steps 1 and 2 until firm. Give individual turns.)

EXERCISE 2

Word and Spelling Introduction

1. (Write on the board: **old, hold, bold, cold,** and **fold.**)
   These words are made up of only one morphograph.
2. (Point to **old.**)
   What word? (S) *Old.*
   Spell **old.** Get ready. (S)
   (Repeat this procedure for each word.)
3. (Erase the words.)
   Spell the words again.
   First word: **cold.** Get ready. (S)
   (Repeat until firm.)
4. (Repeat step 3 for **hold, bold, fold,** and **old.**)
5. Find part **A** on your worksheet.
   Get ready to write the words you just spelled.
6. First word: **bold.**
   What word? (S) *Bold.*
   Write **bold.**
   (Repeat for **old, fold, cold,** and **hold.**)
7. You'll find the spellings of the words we're going to check in appendix **I,** section **C.**
8. (Call on a student.)
   Look up the spelling of the word **bold.**
9. (Assign each of the remaining words to different students.)

10. Get ready to check part **A.**
    Put an **X** next to any word you missed and write that word correctly.
11. (Call on the student who looked up **bold.**)
    Spell **bold.**
    (Write **bold** on the board.)
12. (Repeat step 11 for each remaining word.)

EXERCISE 3

Spelling Review

Find part **B** on your worksheet.

You are going to write some words made up of morphographs you have spelled before.

1. First word: **heavy.**
   What word? (S) *Heavy.*
   Write **heavy.**
2. Next word: **failure.**
   What word? (S) *Failure.*
   Write **failure.**
3. (Repeat step 2 for **planted, cover, happiness, thousands, danger, chiefly, whether,** and **strengthen.**)
4. I'll spell each word.
   Put an **X** next to any word you missed and write that word correctly.
   (Write each word on the board as you spell it.)

EXERCISE 4

Nonword Base

1. (Write on the board: **fer.**)
   Here is a new morphograph that cannot stand alone.
   It is pronounced **fer.**
   What morphograph? (S) *fer.*
2. Everybody, spell **fer.** Get ready. (S)
   (Repeat until firm.)

3. Get ready to spell words that have the morphograph **fer**.
   First word: **refer**.
   What is the first morphograph in **refer**? (S) *re*.
   What is the next morphograph in **refer**? (S) *fer*.
   Spell **refer**. Get ready. (S)
4. Next word: **defer**.
   What is the first morphograph in **defer**? (S) *de*.
   What is the next morphograph in **defer**? (S) *fer*.
   Spell **defer**. Get ready. (S)
5. (Repeat step 4 for **confer, infer, transfer, and prefer.**)

EXERCISE 5

Homonyms

1. (Write on the board: **sew**.)
   This word is **sew**. What word? (S) *Sew*.
2. This **sew** does not mean: **to plant**.
   This **sew** means: **to make clothes**.
   What does this **sew** mean? (S) *To make clothes*.
3. And how is it spelled? Get ready. (S)
4. (Erase the board.)
   Spell **sew** again. Get ready. (S)
5. Remember that word.

EXERCISE 6

Bingo

Find part **C** on your worksheet.

1. We're going to play bingo.
   I'll dictate words for you to write in the boxes.
2. Remember:
   a. A row may go across, or down, or corner to corner.
   b. The first student or students to get four words in a row earn four bonus points.
   c. If you have misspelled any words in your row, that row won't count for bonus points.

3. First word: **verse**.
   Write **verse** in one of the boxes.
4. Next word: **blower**.
   Write **blower** in one of the boxes.
5. (Repeat step 4 for **chance, south, doesn't, grief, curable, spirit, quote, request, physical, restore, state, thought, straight,** and **civilly**.)
6. Now we'll mark the boxes.
7. (Spell each word quickly.)
   First word: **g - r - i - e - f**.
   Mark an **X** in the box containing that word.
8. Next word: **s - t - r - a - i - g - h - t**.
   Mark an **X** in the box containing that word.
9. (Repeat step 8 for as many of the following words as necessary: **south, spirit, restore, civilly, blower, request, verse, quote, chance, physical, curable, thought, doesn't,** and **state**.)
10. (When one or more students get a bingo, stop the game and award bonus points.)

EXERCISE 7

Independent Work

1. Complete the rest of the worksheet on your own.
   Be sure to read the instructions carefully.
2. (Check and correct all work.)

Supplemental Blackline Masters

Supplemental blackline masters 33 and 34 provide additional practice on material covered in Lessons 81 through 85. You may assign any or all of the activities, and you may award bonus points.

Lesson 87

EXERCISE 1

Spelling Review

1. I'll spell some words quickly.
   See if you can figure out each word.
2. Listen: **h - o - l - d.**
   Everybody, what word? (S) *Hold.*
3. Listen: **t - r - a - n - s - p - o - r - t.**
   What word? (S) *Transport.*
4. (Repeat step 3 for **coldly, heroic, realistic, breathless, chances, fried, briefly, reversing, south, lengthen, pausing, spinning, hopping,** and **uncovered.**)
5. Find part **A** on your worksheet.
   Get ready to write some of those words.
6. First word: **breathless.**
   Write it.
7. Next word: **fried.**
   Write it.
8. (Repeat step 7 for **briefly, reversing, lengthen, pausing, spinning,** and **uncovered.**)
9. I will spell each word.
   Put an **X** next to any word you missed and write that word correctly.
   (Write each word on the board as you spell it.)

EXERCISE 2

Sentence Dictation

Find part **B** on your worksheet.

Get ready to write sentences made of words you know.

1. Remember, the first letter of the sentence is capitalized, and you put a period at the end of the sentence.
2. Listen. <u>My</u> niece <u>was</u> filled with grief.
   Everybody, say that sentence.
   Get ready. (S)
   My niece was filled with grief.
   (Repeat until firm.)

3. Write that sentence by number one on your worksheet.
   Remember to spell every word correctly.
   (Repeat the sentence as students write.)
4. Listen. <u>The</u> rich woman has <u>an</u> incurable disease.
   Everybody, say that sentence.
   Get ready. (S)
   The rich woman has an incurable disease.
   (Repeat until firm.)
5. Write that sentence by number two on your worksheet.
   Remember to spell every word correctly.
   (Repeat the sentence as students write.)
6. (Check and correct misspellings. Underlined words—<u>my</u>, <u>was</u>, <u>the</u>, and <u>an</u>—have not been taught. If any of those words are missed, include them in the next Word and Spelling Introduction.)

EXERCISE 3

Word Building

Get ready to spell some words that have more than one morphograph.
These words are made up of morphographs that cannot stand alone.

1. First word: **protection.**
   What is the first morphograph in **protection**? (S) *pro.*
   What is the next morphograph in **protection**? (S) *tect.*
   What is the next morphograph in **protection**? (S) *ion.*
   Spell **protection.** Get ready. (S)
2. Next word: **dispel.**
   What is the first morphograph in **dispel**?
   (S) *dis.*
   What is the next morphograph in **dispel**?
   (S) *pel.*
   Spell **dispel.** Get ready. (S)

3. (For **confer, detain, transgress, defer, produce,** and **contained,** have students identify each morphograph and spell each word.)
4. Find part **C** on your worksheet.
   You are going to write the words you just spelled.
5. First word: **contained.** Write it.
6. Next word: **protection.** Write it.
7. (Repeat step 6 for **produce, trangress, dispel, defer, detain,** and **confer.**)
8. (Check spellings and have students rewrite any missed words.)

EXERCISE 4

En Variation

1. (Write on the board: **show** + **en** = **shown.**)
   Here is a new rule: When a word ends with the letter **w** and you add **en,** drop the **e.**
2. (Point to **show.**)
   The word **show** ends with the letter **w.**
   So we drop the **e** from **en** when we write **shown.**
   (Cross out the **e** in **en.**)
3. Everybody, spell **shown.** Get ready. (S)
4. The word **throw** ends with the letter **w.**
   So tell me how to spell the word **thrown.**
   (Pause.) Get ready. (S)
5. What letter does the word **blow** end with?
   (S) *w.*
   So tell me how to spell the word **blown.**
   (Pause.) Get ready. (S)
6. What letter does the word **grow** end with?
   (S) *w.*
   So tell me how to spell the word **grown.**
   (Pause.) Get ready. (S)
7. Find part **D** on your worksheet.
   Some of the words end with the letter **w.**
   Some don't.
8. Remember, when a word ends with the letter **w** and you add **en,** drop the **e.**
   (Pause.)
9. (Check and correct.)

EXERCISE 5

Independent Work

1. Complete the rest of the worksheet on your own.
   Be sure to read the instructions carefully.
2. (Check and correct all work.)

Word and Spelling Introduction

1. (Write on the board: **bid, get, road, coat, vote,** and **class.**)
   These words are made up of only one morphograph.
2. (Point to **bid.**)
   What word? (S) *Bid.*
   Spell **bid.** Get ready. (S)
   (Repeat this procedure for each word.)
3. (Erase the words.)
   Spell the words again.
   First word: **vote.** Get ready. (S)
   (Repeat until firm.)
4. (Repeat step 3 for **get, road, class, coat,** and **bid.**)
5. Find part **A** on your worksheet.
   Get ready to write the words you just spelled.
6. First word: **road.**
   What word? (S) *Road.*
   Write **road.**
   (Repeat for **bid, class, vote, get,** and **coat.**)
7. You'll find the spellings of the words we're going to check in appendix **I,** section **C.**
8. (Call on a student.)
   Look up the spelling of the word **road.**
9. (Assign each of the remaining words to different students.)
10. Get ready to check part **A.**
    Put an **X** next to any word you missed and write that word correctly.
11. (Call on the student who looked up **road.**)
    Spell **road.**
    (Write **road** on the board.)
12. (Repeat step 11 for each remaining word.)

Spelling Review

1. I'll spell some words quickly.
   Then I'll call on different people to spell each word.
   When I call on you, spell the word quickly.
2. My turn: **w - i - t - h - h - o - l - d.**
   Everybody, what word? (S) *Withhold.*
3. Next word: **i - n - c - u - r - a - b - l - e.**
   What word? (S) *Incurable.*
4. (Repeat step 3 for **thirsty, chiefly, class, artist, heroic, disease, hopped, design, maintain, pieces, spirited, deserve, hurrying,** and **shipping.**)
5. Your turn.
   (Call on a student.)
   Spell **artist.** Go.
6. (Praise students who respond correctly.)
7. (Call on a student.)
   Spell **incurable.** Go.
8. (Repeat step 7 for **chiefly, disease, pieces, shipping, hurrying, maintain, heroic, thirsty, design, deserve, spirited, hopped, class,** and **withhold.**
   A word may be used more than once.)

Homonyms

1. (Write on the board: **sow.**)
   This word is **sow.** What word? (S) *Sow.*
2. This **sow** means: **to plant.**
   What does this **sow** mean? (S) *To plant.*
3. And how is it spelled? Get ready. (S)
   (Erase the board.)
4. Everybody, spell the **sow** that means: **to plant.** Get ready. (S)
5. Everybody, spell the **sew** that means: **to make clothes.** Get ready. (S)
6. (Repeat steps 4 and 5 until firm. Give individual turns.)

EXERCISE 4

Word Building

Get ready to spell some words that have more than one morphograph.

These words are made up of morphographs that cannot stand alone.

1. First word: **infer.**
   What is the first morphograph in **infer**?
   (S) *in.*
   What is the next morphograph in **infer**?
   (S) *fer.*
   Spell **infer.** Get ready. (S)
2. Next word: **reception.**
   What is the first morphograph in
   reception? (S) *re.*
   What is the next morphograph in
   reception? (S) *cept.*
   What is the next morphograph in
   reception? (S) *ion.*
   Spell **reception.** Get ready. (S)
3. (For **regression, induce, refer, injection, except,** and **transfer,** have students identify each morphograph and spell each word.)
4. Find part **B** on your worksheet.
   You are going to write the words you just spelled.
5. First word: **injection.** Write it.
6. Next word: **transfer.** Write it.
7. (Repeat step 6 for **induce, reception, refer, except, infer,** and **regression.**)
8. (Check spellings and have students rewrite any missed words.)

EXERCISE 5

En Variation

Everybody, find part **C** on your worksheet.

1. Some of these words end with the letter **w.** Some don't.
2. When a word ends with the letter **w** and you add **en,** what do you drop? (S) *The e.* (Repeat until firm.)

3. (Call on a student to read the instructions for part **C.**)
   Add the morphographs together.
   Remember to use your rule.
4. You'll do this part on your own.

EXERCISE 6

Independent Work

1. Complete the rest of the worksheet on your own.
   Be sure to read the instructions carefully.
2. (Check and correct all work.)

┌─ **Answer Key** ──────────

Part D
1. quart
2. quotable
3. briefly
4. heaviness
5. breath
6. shown

Lesson 89

EXERCISE 1

Affix Introduction

1. (Write on the board: **forbid, forget,** and **forgive.**)
   Each of these words has a morphograph **for** at the beginning.
   What morphograph? (S) *for.*

2. Read these words. (Point to **forbid.**)
   What word? (S) *Forbid.*
   What is the first morphograph in **forbid**?
   (S) *for.*
   What is the next morphograph in **forbid**?
   (S) *bid.*

3. (Point to **forget.**)
   What word? (S) *Forget.*
   What is the first morphograph in **forget**?
   (S) *for.*
   What is the next morphograph in **forget**?
   (S) *get.*

4. (Point to **forgive.**)
   What word? (S) *Forgive.*
   What is the first morphograph in **forgive**?
   (S) *for.*
   What is the next morphograph in **forgive**?
   (S) *give.*

5. (Erase the board.)
   Everybody, spell the word **bid.**
   Get ready. (S)
   Now spell the word **forbid.** Get ready. (S)

6. Everybody, spell the word **get.**
   Get ready. (S)
   Now spell the word **forget.** Get ready. (S)

7. Everybody, spell the word **give.**
   Get ready. (S)
   Now spell the word **forgive.** Get ready. (S)

8. (Repeat spelling of **forbid, forget,** and **forgive** until firm. Give individual turns.)

EXERCISE 2

Word and Spelling Introduction

1. (Write on the board: **muse, cube, huge, cute,** and **athlete.**)
   These words are made up of only one morphograph.

2. (Point to **muse.**)
   What word? (S) *Muse.*
   Spell **muse.** Get ready. (S)
   (Repeat this procedure for each word.)

3. (Erase the words.)
   Spell the words again.
   First word: **cute.** Get ready. (S)
   (Repeat until firm.)

4. (Repeat step 3 for **cube, huge, muse,** and **athlete.**)

5. Find part **A** on your worksheet.
   Get ready to write the words you just spelled.

6. First word: **huge.**
   What word? (S) *Huge.*
   Write **huge.**
   (Repeat for **muse, athlete, cute,** and **cube.**)

7. You'll find the spellings of the words we're going to check in appendix **I**, section **C.**

8. (Call on a student.)
   Look up the spelling of the word **huge.**

9. (Assign each of the remaining words to different students.)

10. Get ready to check part **A.**
    Put an **X** next to any word you missed and write that word correctly.

11. (Call on the student who looked up **huge.**)
    Spell **huge.**
    (Write **huge** on the board.)

12. (Repeat step 11 for each remaining word.)

Homonyms

1. Everybody, spell the **sew** that means: **to make clothes.** Get ready. (S)
2. Everybody, spell the **sow** that means: **to plant.** Get ready. (S)
3. (Repeat steps 1 and 2 until firm. Give individual turns.)

Spelling Review

Find part **B** on your worksheet.

You are going to write some words made up of morphographs you have spelled before.

1. First word: **reverse.**
   What word? (S) *Reverse.*
   Write **reverse.**
2. Next word: **contain.**
   What word? (S) *Contain.*
   Write **contain.**
3. (Repeat step 2 for **failure, artistic, transfer, weren't, vision,** and **basic.**)
4. I'll spell each word.
   Put an **X** next to any word you missed and write that word correctly.
   (Write each word on the board as you spell it.)

En Variation

Everybody, find part **C** on your worksheet.

1. Some of these words end with the letter **w.** Some don't.
2. When a word ends with the letter **w** and you add **en,** what do you drop? (S) *The e.* (Repeat until firm.)
3. (Call on a student to read the instructions for part **C.**)
   Add the morphographs together.
   Remember to use your rule.
4. You'll do this part on your own.

Independent Work

1. Complete the rest of the worksheet on your own.
   Be sure to read the instructions carefully.
2. (Check and correct all work.)

Lesson 90

EXERCISE 1

Word and Spelling Introduction

1. (Write on the board: **magic, fashion, shake, shed, push,** and **shout.**)
   These words are made up of only one morphograph.
2. (Point to **magic.**)
   What word? (S) *Magic.*
   Spell **magic.** Get ready. (S)
   (Repeat this procedure for each word.)
3. (Erase the words.)
   Spell the words again.
   First word: **shed.** Get ready. (S)
   (Repeat until firm.)
4. (Repeat step 3 for **fashion, shake, shout, push,** and **magic.**)
5. Find part **A** on your worksheet.
   Get ready to write the words you just spelled.
6. First word: **shake.**
   What word? (S) *Shake.*
   Write **shake.**
   (Repeat for **magic, shout, push, fashion,** and **shed.**)
7. You'll find the spellings of the words we're going to check in appendix **I**, section **C.**
8. (Call on a student.)
   Look up the spelling of the word **shake.**
9. (Assign each of the remaining words to different students.)
10. Get ready to check part **A.**
    Put an **X** next to any word you missed and write that word correctly.
11. (Call on the student who looked up **shake.**)
    Spell **shake.**
    (Write **shake** on the board.)
12. (Repeat step 11 for each remaining word.)

EXERCISE 2

Nonword Base

1. (Write on the board: **struct.**)
   Here is a new morphograph that cannot stand alone.
   It is pronounced **struct.**
   What morphograph? (S) *struct.*
2. Everybody, spell **struct.** Get ready. (S)
   (Repeat until firm.)
3. Get ready to spell words that have the morphograph **struct.**
   First word: **destruction.**
   What is the first morphograph in **destruction**? (S) *de.*
   What is the next morphograph in **destruction**? (S) *struct.*
   What is the next morphograph in **destruction**? (S) *ion.*
   Spell **destruction.** Get ready. (S)
4. Next word: **construct.**
   What is the first morphograph in **construct**? (S) *con.*
   What is the next morphograph in **construct**? (S) *struct.*
   Spell **construct.** Get ready. (S)
5. (Repeat step 4 for **instructive, structure, construction,** and **structural.**)

EXERCISE 3

Spelling Review

1. I'll spell some words quickly.
   See if you can figure out each word.
2. Listen: a - t - h - l - e - t - e.
   Everybody, what word? (S) *Athlete.*
3. Listen: c - o - n - f - e - r.
   What word? (S) *Confer.*
4. (Repeat step 3 for **detained, haven't, briefly, pieces, spirited, quart, physics, nastiness, shapely, huge, cutest,** and **boldly.**)

5. Find part **B** on your worksheet.
   Get ready to write some of those words.
6. First word: **haven't.**
   Write it.
7. Next word: **briefly.**
   Write it.
8. (Repeat step 7 for **spirited, physics, huge,** and **boldly.**)
9. I will spell each word.
   Put an **X** next to any word you missed and write that word correctly.
   (Write each word on the board as you spell it.)

EXERCISE 4

Word Building

Get ready to spell some words that have more than one morphograph.

1. First word: **famous.**
   What is the first morphograph in **famous**? (S) *fame.*
   What is the next morphograph in **famous**? (S) *ous.*
   Spell **famous.** Get ready. (S)
2. Next word: **classes.**
   What is the first morphograph in **classes**? (S) *class.*
   What is the next morphograph in **classes**? (S) *es.*
   Spell **classes.** Get ready. (S)
3. (For **harpist** and **classic,** have students identify each morphograph and spell each word.)
4. Find part **C** on your worksheet.
   You are going to write the words you just spelled.
5. First word: **classic.** Write it.
6. Next word: **harpist.** Write it.
7. (Repeat step 6 for **famous** and **classes.**)
8. (Check spellings and have students rewrite any missed words.)

EXERCISE 5

Vowel-Consonant Worksheet

1. Let's go over some of the things you have learned about vowel letters and consonant letters.
2. (Call on a student.)
   When is **y** a vowel letter?
   At the end of a morphograph.
3. (Call on another student.)
   When is **w** a vowel letter?
   At the end of a morphograph.
4. The letter **x** acts like two consonant letters because it has two consonant sounds. Everybody, how many letters does **x** act like? (S) *Two.*
5. Find part **D** on your worksheet.
6. There are some morphographs in part **D.** Some of them are short **CVC** morphographs. Some are not. Short morphographs have four letters or less.
7. Look at number one.
   (Call on a student.)
   Is **ship** a short **CVC** morphograph? *Yes.*
8. **Ship** is a short **CVC** morphograph. Everyone, circle **ship.**
9. Look at number two.
   (Call on a student.)
   Is **tect** a short **CVC** morphograph? *No.*
10. **Tect** is not a short **CVC** morphograph, so don't circle it.
11. You will finish part **D** on your own.

EXERCISE 6

Independent Work

1. Complete the rest of the worksheet on your own.
   Be sure to read the instructions carefully.
2. (Check and correct all work.)

═══════════ **EXERCISE 7** ═══════════

Mastery Test

1. You are going to have a test today. It will help you see how well you are learning to spell.

2. Everybody, take out a sheet of lined paper and draw a line down the middle. Then number the paper from 1 through 20.

3. (Check and correct.)

4. Word 1 is **hold.**
   How much will the basket **hold?**
   What word? (S) *Hold.*
   Write **hold.**

5. Word 2 is **failure.**
   The new show was a **failure.**
   What word? (S) *Failure.*
   Write **failure.**

6. (Repeat step 5 for the remaining words on the list.)

3.	**thousand**	12.	**wonderful**
4.	**happiness**	13.	**danger**
5.	**verse**	14.	**produce**
6.	**chiefly**	15.	**dutiful**
7.	**chance**	16.	**cold**
8.	**neatly**	17.	**transform**
9.	**fold**	18.	**pound**
10.	**protection**	19.	**cloudy**
11.	**shown**	20.	**south**

7. Everybody, exchange papers with your partner. (Pause.)

8. I'll spell each word. If the word is not spelled correctly on the paper you're marking, put an **X** next to it.
   If the word is spelled correctly, don't put any mark next to it.

9. Word 1 is **hold: h - o - l - d.**
   Check it.

10. (Repeat step 9 for each remaining word.)

11. Return your partner's test paper.

12. Now correct any errors you made. If there is an **X** next to a word on your test, write the word correctly in the right column. Raise your hand if your don't know how to spell any words.

13. Turn your paper over when you're finished. I'll come around and check your paper.

14. If you didn't make any mistakes, raise your hand now.

15. Write the number correct at the top of your test.

EXERCISE 1

Rule Discrimination

I'll say words.
Figure out whether the doubling rule, the **y**-to-**i** rule, or no rule applies.

1. The first word begins with **flat**.
   Spell **flat**. Get ready. (S)
   Could a rule apply? (S) *Yes*.
   Which rule? (Call on a student.) *The rule about doubling a letter*.
   Everybody, how do you know the doubling rule could apply? (S)
   Flat is a short cvc word.

2. The word is **flattest**.
   Does the doubling rule apply? (S) *Yes*.
   How do you know? (Call on a student.)
   Est begins with v.
   Spell **flattest**. Get ready. (S)

3. The next word begins with **worry**.
   Spell **worry**. Get ready. (S)
   Could a rule apply? (S) *Yes*.
   Which rule? (Call on a student.) *The rule about changing y to i*.
   Everybody, how do you know the **y**-to-**i** rule could apply? (S)
   Worry ends with a consonant-and-y.

4. The word is **worried**.
   Does the **y**-to-**i** rule apply? (S) *Yes*.
   How do you know? (Call on a student.)
   E-d does not begin with i.
   Spell **worried**. Get ready. (S)

5. The next word begins with **hurry**.
   Spell **hurry**. Get ready. (S)
   Could a rule apply? (S) *Yes*.
   Which rule? (Call on a student.) *The rule about changing y to i*.
   Everybody, how do you know the **y**-to-**i** rule could apply? (S)
   Hurry ends with a consonant-and-y.

6. The word is **hurrying**.
   Does the **y**-to-**i** rule apply? (S) *No*.
   How do you know? (Call on a student.)
   Ing begins with i.
   Spell **hurrying**. Get ready. (S)

7. The next word begins with **length**.
   Spell **length**. Get ready. (S)
   Could a rule apply? (S) *No*.
   Why not? (Call on a student.) *Length does not end with cvc or a consonant-and-y*.

8. The word is **lengthen**.
   Spell **lengthen**. Get ready. (S)

EXERCISE 2

Spelling Review

1. I'll spell some words quickly.
   See if you can figure out each word.

2. Listen: **r - e - v - e - r - s - e**.
   Everybody, what word? (S) *Reverse*.

3. Listen: **c - h - a - n - c - e - s**.
   What word? (S) *Chances*.

4. (Repeat step 3 for **danger, classic, magic, straight, fashionable, realistic, transformed, joyously, construction,** and **injection.**)

5. Find part **A** on your worksheet.
   Get ready to write some of those words.

6. First word: **magic**.
   Write it.

7. Next word: **straight**.
   Write it.

8. (Repeat step 7 for **reverse, realistic, joyously,** and **injection.**)

9. I will spell each word.
   Put an **X** next to any word you missed and write that word correctly.
   (Write each word on the board as you spell it.)

Homonyms

1. Everybody, spell the **tale** that means: **a story.** Get ready. (S)
2. Everybody, spell the **tail** that means: **the end.** Get ready. (S)
3. (Repeat steps 1 and 2 until firm. Give individual turns.)
4. Everybody, spell the **plain** that means: **ordinary.** Get ready. (S)
5. Everybody, spell the **plane** that means: **a thing that flies.** Get ready. (S)
6. (Repeat steps 4 and 5 until firm. Give individual turns.)
7. Everybody, spell the **sow** that means: **to plant.** Get ready. (S)
8. Everybody, spell the **sew** that means: **to make clothes.** Get ready. (S)
9. (Repeat steps 7 and 8 until firm. Give individual turns.)

Proofreading

1. Find part **B** on your worksheet.
2. (Call on a student to read the instructions for part **B**.)
   Underline any word that is misspelled and write it correctly in the right-hand column.
3. You will complete part **B** later.

Study for Spelling Contest

Find appendix **I,** section **C.**

1. During Lesson **92,** we're going to have a spelling contest.
2. Most of the contest words will come from appendix **I,** section **C.**
3. When you've completed your worksheet, study the words.

Note. Students may study in pairs or independently.

Independent Work

1. Complete the rest of the worksheet on your own.
   Be sure to read the instructions carefully.
2. (Check and correct all work.)

Answer Key

Part B
boys, playing, friendly, chance, quick, breath, heavy

Part D

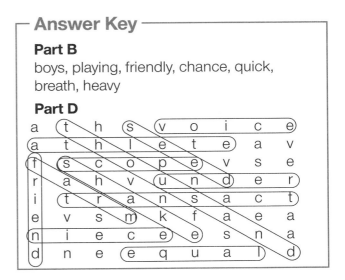

Supplemental Blackline Masters

Supplemental blackline masters 35 and 36 provide additional practice on material covered in Lessons 86 through 90. You may assign any or all of the activities, and you may award bonus points.

============ **EXERCISE 1** ============

Spelling Contest

Note. There is no student worksheet for Lesson 92.

Today we're going to have a spelling contest.

1. We'll make up two teams.
   (Assign students to each team.)
2. (Make a scorebox on the board.)

Team A	Team B

3. Here are the rules for the contest.
   a. I will dictate words to the teams.
   b. Every time a team spells a word correctly, it gets a point.
   c. If a team misses a word, the other team gets to try that word.
   d. The first team to get 30 points wins the spelling contest.
4. (Praise correct spellings and mark them in the scorebox.)

To correct misspellings:
   a. That's not how the word _____ is spelled.
   b. (Call on a member of the other team to spell that word.)

5. (Call on teams alternately to spell words from the following list.
   Words may be used more than once.)

shakiness	instruction	poisonous
forbid	grounded	station
classes	shedding	exception
dangerous	forgiven	usable
reversal	unstructured	snapping
inversion	oldest	remove
transfusion	musical	unequal

cover	transformed	contract
hugeness	underground	signal
pushy	folder	civil
thrown	constructive	misspelled
voters	boldness	mistake
athlete	spirit	wonderful
refer	revise	quietly
known	questionable	designer
chance	physical	author
fashionable	expression	notable
thousands	lengthy	
overcoat	famous	

First team to get 30 points . . . .
    10 bonus points.
If the other team has 27–29 points . . . .
    8 bonus points.
If the other team has 24–26 points . . . .
    5 bonus points.
If the other team has less than 24 points . . . . . .
    0 bonus points.

Crossword Puzzles
The crossword puzzles are made up exclusively of the words presented in the review lessons. Every word in these lessons has been used. For each review lesson, there are two or three sets of puzzles, depending on how many words are in the lesson. A set is made up of two puzzles—an original and an alternate. The alternate uses the same words and clues as the original, but in a different arrangement. This gives you a good deal of flexibility in how you use the puzzles.

The crossword puzzle blackline masters are located at the back of this Teacher Presentation Book.

Lesson 93

EXERCISE 1

Affix Introduction

1. (Write on the board: **obstruct, observe, obtain,** and **object.**)
   Each of these words has a morphograph **ob** at the beginning.
   What morphograph? (S) *ob.*

2. Read these words. (Point to **obstruct.**)
   What word? (S) *Obstruct.*
   What is the first morphograph in **obstruct**? (S) *ob.*
   What is the next morphograph in **obstruct**? (S) *struct.*

3. (Point to **observe.**)
   What word? (S) *Observe.*
   What is the first morphograph in **observe**?
   (S) *ob.*
   What is the next morphograph in **observe**? (S) *serve.*

4. (Point to **obtain.**)
   What word? (S) *Obtain.*
   What is the first morphograph in **obtain**?
   (S) *ob.*
   What is the next morphograph in **obtain**?
   (S) *tain.*

5. (Point to **object.**)
   What word? (S) *Object.*
   What is the first morphograph in **object**?
   (S) *ob.*
   What is the next morphograph in **object**?
   (S) *ject.*

6. (Erase the board.)
   Everybody, spell the morphograph **struct.**
   Get ready. (S)
   Now spell the word **obstruct.** Get ready. (S)

7. Everybody, spell the word **serve.**
   Get ready. (S)
   Now spell the word **observe.** Get ready. (S)

8. Everybody, spell the morphograph **tain.**
   Get ready. (S)
   Now spell the word **obtain.** Get ready. (S)

9. Everybody, spell the morphograph **ject.**
   Get ready. (S)
   Now spell the word **object.** Get ready. (S)

10. (Repeat spelling of **obstruct, observe, obtain,** and **object** until firm. Give individual turns.)

EXERCISE 2

Word and Spelling Introduction

1. (Write on the board: **logic, part, settle, little, ample,** and **middle.**)
   These words are made up of only one morphograph.

2. (Point to **logic.**)
   What word? (S) *Logic.*
   Spell **logic.** Get ready. (S)
   (Repeat this procedure for each word.)

3. (Erase the words.)
   Spell the words again.
   First word: **little.** Get ready. (S)
   (Repeat until firm.)

4. (Repeat step 3 for **part, settle, ample, middle,** and **logic.**)

5. Find part **A** on your worksheet.
   Get ready to write the words you just spelled.

6. First word: **settle.**
   What word? (S) *Settle.*
   Write **settle.**
   (Repeat for **logic, middle, ample, little,** and **part.**)

7. You'll find the spellings of the words we're going to check in appendix **J**, section **C.**

8. (Call on a student.)
   Look up the spelling of the word **settle.**

9. (Assign each of the remaining words to different students.)

10. Get ready to check part **A.**
    Put an **X** next to any word you missed and write that word correctly.

11. (Call on the student who looked up **settle.**)
    Spell **settle.**
    (Write **settle** on the board.)

12. (Repeat step 11 for each remaining word.)

EXERCISE 3

Homonyms

1. (Write on the board: **four.**)
   This word is **four.** What word? (S) *Four.*
2. This **four** does not mean: **in front of.**
   This **four** means: **the number four.**
   What does this **four** mean? (S) *The number four.*
3. And how is it spelled? Get ready. (S)
4. (Erase the board.)
   Spell **four** again. Get ready. (S)
5. Remember that word.

EXERCISE 4

Spelling Review

1. I'll spell some words quickly.
   See if you can figure out each word.
2. Listen: **c - l - a - s - s - y.**
   Everybody, what word? (S) *Classy.*
3. Listen: **f - a - s - h - i - o - n.**
   What word? (S) *Fashion.*
4. (Repeat step 3 for **shout, danger, pushy, request, blown, thousands, chance, athlete, whether, magic, business,** and **failure.**)
5. Find part **B** on your worksheet.
   Get ready to write some of those words.
6. First word: **danger.** Write it.
7. Next word: **fashion.** Write it.
8. (Repeat step 7 for **blown, thousands, athlete, failure, magic,** and **whether.**)
9. I will spell each word.
   Put an **X** next to any word you missed and write that word correctly.
   (Write each word on the board as you spell it.)

EXERCISE 5

Word Building

Get ready to spell some words that have more than one morphograph.
These words are made up of morphographs that cannot stand alone.

1. First word: **destructive.**
   What is the first morphograph in **destructive**? (S) *de.*
   What is the next morphograph in **destructive**? (S) *struct.*
   What is the next morphograph in **destructive**? (S) *ive.*
   Spell **destructive.** Get ready. (S)
2. Next word: **prefer.**
   What is the first morphograph in **prefer**? (S) *pre.*
   What is the next morphograph in **prefer**? (S) *fer.*
   Spell **prefer.** Get ready. (S)
3. (For **devise, instruction, obtain, deceptive, confer,** and **produce,** have students identify each morphograph and spell each word.)
4. Find part **C** on your worksheet.
   You are going to write the words you just spelled.
5. First word: **confer.** Write it.
6. Next word: **produce.** Write it.
7. (Repeat step 6 for **destructive, instruction, prefer, obtain, devise,** and **deceptive.**)
8. (Check spellings and have students rewrite any missed words.)

EXERCISE 6

Independent Work

1. Complete the rest of the worksheet on your own.
   Be sure to read the instructions carefully.
2. (Check and correct all work.)

Answer Key

Part D
unknown, athlete, famous
progressed, photography

EXERCISE 1

Spelling Review

1. I'll spell some words quickly.
   Then I'll call on different people to spell each word.
   When I call on you, spell the word quickly.
2. My turn: **e - x - p - l - a - i - n.**
   Everybody, what word? (S) *Explain.*
3. Next word: **r - e - q - u - e - s - t.**
   What word? (S) *Request.*
4. (Repeat step 3 for **fashionable, unknown, stepping, friendliness, wouldn't, athletic, lengthen, equally, thrown, logic, ample, where, wander, whose, straightest, wonder, poison,** and **resort.**)
5. Your turn.
   (Call on a student.)
   Spell **request.** Go.
6. (Praise students who respond correctly.)
7. (Call on a student.)
   Spell **logic.** Go.
8. (Repeat step 7 for **whose, thrown, friendliness, explain, wouldn't, logic, straightest, fashionable, unknown, stepping, athletic, ample, wonder, lengthen, where, poison, equally, resort,** and **wander.** A word may be used more than once.)

EXERCISE 2

Affix Introduction

1. (Write on the board: **basement, placement, shipment,** and **department.**)
   Each of these words has a morphograph **ment** at the end.
   What morphograph? (S) *ment.*
2. Read these words. (Point to **basement.**)
   What word? (S) *Basement.*
   What is the first morphograph in **basement**? (S) *base.*
   What is the next morphograph in **basement**? (S) *ment.*
3. (Point to **placement.**)
   What word? (S) *Placement.*
   What is the first morphograph in **placement**? (S) *place.*
   What is the next morphograph in **placement**? (S) *ment.*
4. (Point to **shipment.**)
   What word? (S) *Shipment.*
   What is the first morphograph in **shipment**? (S) *ship.*
   What is the next morphograph in **shipment**? (S) *ment.*
5. (Point to **department.**)
   What word? (S) *Department.*
   What is the first morphograph in **department**? (S) *de.*
   What is the next morphograph in **department**? (S) *part.*
   What is the next morphograph in **department**? (S) *ment.*
6. (Erase the board.)
   Everybody, spell the word **base.**
   Get ready. (S)
   Now spell the word **basement.**
   Get ready. (S)
7. Everybody, spell the word **place.**
   Get ready. (S)
   Now spell the word **placement.**
   Get ready. (S)
8. Everybody, spell the word **ship.**
   Get ready. (S)
   Now spell the word **shipment.**
   Get ready. (S)
9. Everybody, spell the word **depart.**
   Get ready. (S)
   Now spell the word **department.**
   Get ready. (S)
10. (Repeat spelling **basement, placement, shipment,** and **department** until firm. Give individual turns.)

EXERCISE 3

Word Building

Get ready to spell some words that have more than one morphograph.

1. First word: **construct.**
   What is the first morphograph in **construct**? (S) *con.*
   What is the next morphograph in **construct**? (S) *struct.*
   Spell **construct.** Get ready. (S)

2. Next word: **obtain.**
   What is the first morphograph in **obtain**?
   (S) *ob.*
   What is the next morphograph in **obtain**?
   (S) *tain.*
   Spell **obtain.** Get ready. (S)

3. (For **forgive, transfer, forget,** and **classical,** have students identify each morphograph and spell each word.)

4. Find part **A** on your worksheet.
   You are going to write the words you just spelled.

5. First word: **forget.** Write it.

6. Next word: **forgive.** Write it.

7. (Repeat step 6 for **construct, classical, obtain,** and **transfer.**)

8. (Check spellings and have students rewrite any missed words.)

EXERCISE 4

Word and Spelling Introduction

1. (Write on the board: **leaf, half, thief, wolf, calf,** and **self.**)
   These words are made up of only one morphograph.

2. (Point to **leaf.**)
   What word? (S) *Leaf.*
   Spell **leaf.** Get ready. (S)
   (Repeat this procedure for each word.)

3. (Erase the words.)
   Spell the words again.
   First word: **thief.** Get ready. (S)
   (Repeat until firm.)

4. (Repeat step 3 for **half, wolf, calf, self,** and **leaf.**)

5. Find part **B** on your worksheet.
   Get ready to write the words you just spelled.

6. First word: **wolf.**
   What word? (S) *Wolf.*
   Write **wolf.**
   (Repeat for **leaf, self, calf, thief,** and **half.**)

7. You'll find the spellings of the words we're going to check in appendix **J,** section **C.**

8. (Call on a student.)
   Look up the spelling of the word **wolf.**

9. (Assign each of the remaining words to different students.)

10. Get ready to check part **B.**
    Put an **X** next to any word you missed and write that word correctly.

11. (Call on the student who looked up **wolf.**)
    Spell **wolf.**
    (Write **wolf** on the board.)

12. (Repeat step 11 for each remaining word.)

EXERCISE 5

Independent Work

1. Complete the rest of the worksheet on your own.
   Be sure to read the instructions carefully.

2. (Check and correct all work.)

Answer Key

Part D	Part E
1. forget	1. misspell
2. destructive	2. respell
3. transfer	3. repel
4. reduce	4. dispel
5. dangerous	

========== EXERCISE 1 ==========

Affix Introduction

Note. Pronounce the morphograph **a** as in the first sound in **alike: uh.**

1. (Write on the board: **alike, ahead, apart,** and **around.**) Each of these words has a morphograph **a** at the beginning. What morphograph? (S) *a.*
2. Read these words. (Point to **alike.**) What word? (S) *Alike.* What is the first morphograph in **alike**? (S) *a.* What is the next morphograph in **alike**? (S) *like.*
3. (Point to **ahead.**) What word? (S) *Ahead.* What is the first morphograph in **ahead**? (S) *a.* What is the next morphograph in **ahead**? (S) *head.*
4. (Point to **apart.**) What word? (S) *Apart.* What is the first morphograph in **apart**? (S) *a.* What is the next morphograph in **apart**? (S) *part.*
5. (Point to **around.**) What word? (S) *Around.* What is the first morphograph in **around**? (S) *a.* What is the next morphograph in **around**? (S) *round.*
6. (Erase the board.) Everybody, spell the word **like.** Get ready. (S) Now spell the word **alike.** Get ready. (S)
7. Everybody, spell the word **head.** Get ready. (S) Now spell the word **ahead.** Get ready. (S)
8. Everybody, spell the word **part.** Get ready. (S) Now spell the word **apart.** Get ready. (S)
9. Everybody, spell the word **round.** Get ready. (S) Now spell the word **around.** Get ready. (S)
10. (Repeat spelling of **alike, ahead, apart,** and **around** until firm. Give individual turns.)

========== EXERCISE 2 ==========

Word and Spelling Introduction

1. (Write on the board: **tend, type, pose, train, faint, wife,** and **loaf.**) These words are made up of only one morphograph.
2. (Point to **tend.**) What word? (S) *Tend.* Spell **tend.** Get ready. (S) (Repeat this procedure for each word.)
3. (Erase the words.) Spell the words again. First word: **train.** Get ready. (S) (Repeat until firm.)
4. (Repeat step 3 for **type, pose, wife, faint, loaf,** and **tend.**)
5. Find part **A** on your worksheet. Get ready to write the words you just spelled.
6. First word: **pose.** What word? (S) *Pose.* Write **pose.** (Repeat for **wife, faint, tend, loaf, train,** and **type.**)
7. You'll find the spellings of the words we're going to check in appendix **J,** section **C.**
8. (Call on a student.) Look up the spelling of the word **pose.**
9. (Assign each of the remaining words to different students.)
10. Get ready to check part **A.** Put an **X** next to any word you missed and write that word correctly.

11. (Call on the student who looked up **pose.**)
    Spell **pose.**
    (Write **pose** on the board.)
12. (Repeat step 11 for each remaining word.)

EXERCISE 3

Homonyms

1. (Write on the board: **son.**)
   This word is **son.** What word? (S) *Son.*
2. This **son** does not mean: **the thing in the sky.**
   This **son** means: **a male child.**
   What does this **son** mean? (S)
   A male child.
3. And how is it spelled? Get ready. (S)
4. (Erase the board.)
   Spell **son** again. Get ready. (S)
5. Remember that word.

EXERCISE 4

Al Insertion

1. Here is a new rule for words that end in **ic.**
   Listen: When the word ends in the letters **ic,** you must add the morphograph **al** before adding **ly.**
2. Listen again: When the word ends in the letters **ic,** you must add the morphograph **al** before adding **ly.**
3. Everybody, tell me when you add **al** before **ly.** (Pause.) Get ready. (S) *When the word ends in the letters ic.*
   (Repeat until firm.)
4. (Write on the board: **logic, magic,** and **physic.**)
   What letters do these words end in? (S) *ic.*
5. (Point to **logic.**)
   So if we write the word **logically,** what morphograph must we add before the **ly**? (S) *al.*
6. (Write +**al** after **logic.**)
   Now we add **ly.**
   (Write +**ly** after **logic** + **al.**)
7. Everybody, spell **logically.** Get ready. (S)
   (Repeat until firm.)

8. (Point to **magic.**)
   What letters does **magic** end in? (S) *ic.*
   So what morphograph would we add before the **ly** in **magically**? (S) *al.*
9. Everybody, spell **magically.** Get ready. (S)
   (Repeat until firm.)
10. (Point to **physic.**)
    What letters does **physic** end in? (S) *ic.*
    So what morphograph would we add before the **ly** in **physically**? (S) *al.*
11. Everybody, spell **physically.** Get ready. (S)
    (Repeat until firm.)

EXERCISE 5

Al Insertion Worksheet

Everybody, find part **B** on your worksheet.

1. You are gong to add **ly** to all the words in part **B.**
   Don't get fooled. Some of those words end in **ic.**
   When the words end in the letters **ic,** you must add the morphograph **al** before adding **ly.**
2. You have two minutes to do the words in part **B.**
3. (At the end of two minutes . . .) Stop.
   I will call on people to spell the words you just wrote.
   Put an **X** next to any word you missed and write that word correctly.
4. (Call on a student.)
   Spell **really.** (Pause for corrections.)
5. (Repeat step 4 for **hopefully, magically, flatly, surely, basically, classically,** and **equally.**)

Oral Spelling Review

You are going to write some words made up of morphographs you have spelled before.

1. First word: **settle.**
   What word? (S) *Settle.*
   Spell **settle.** Get ready. (S)
   (Repeat until firm.)
2. Next word: **depart.**
   What word? (S) *Depart.*
   Spell **depart.** Get ready. (S)
   (Repeat until firm.)
3. (Repeat step 2 for **fashionable, shaking, ample, obstruct, transfer, shedding, studies, middle, muse,** and **spirit.**)

━━━ **EXERCISE 7** ━━━

Independent Work

1. Complete the rest of the worksheet on your own.
   Be sure to read the instructions carefully.
2. (Check and correct all work.)

EXERCISE 1

Nonword Base

1. (Write on the board: **fect.**)
   Here is a new morphograph that cannot stand alone.
   It is pronounced **fect.**
   What morphograph? (S) *fect.*
2. Everybody, spell **fect.** Get ready. (S)
   (Repeat until firm.)
3. Get ready to spell words that have the morphograph **fect.**
   First word: **defective.**
   What is the first morphograph in **defective**? (S) *de.*
   What is the next morphograph in **defective**? (S) *fect.*
   What is the next morphograph in **defective**? (S) *ive.*
   Spell **defective.** Get ready. (S)
4. Next word: **infect.**
   What is the first morphograph in **infect**? (S) *in.*
   What is the next morphograph in **infect**? (S) *fect.*
   Spell **infect.** Get ready. (S)
5. (Repeat step 4 for **confection** and **infection.**)

EXERCISE 2

Affix Introduction

1. (Write on the board: **pertain, perform,** and **perfect.**)
   Each of these words has a morphograph **per** at the beginning.
   What morphograph? (S) *per.*
2. Read these words. (Point to **pertain.**)
   What word? (S) *Pertain.*
   What is the first morphograph in **pertain**? (S) *per.*
   What is the next morphograph in **pertain**? (S) *tain.*

3. (Point to **perform.**)
   What word? (S) *Perform.*
   What is the first morphograph in **perform**? (S) *per.*
   What is the next morphograph in **perform**? (S) *form.*
4. (Point to **perfect.**)
   What word? (S) *Perfect.*
   What is the first morphograph in **perfect**? (S) *per.*
   What is the next morphograph in **perfect**? (S) *fect.*
5. (Erase the board.)
   Everybody, spell the morphograph **tain.** Get ready. (S)
   Now spell the word **pertain.** Get ready. (S)
6. Everybody, spell the word **form.** Get ready. (S)
   Now spell the word **perform.** Get ready. (S)
7. Everybody, spell the morphograph **fect.** Get ready. (S)
   Now spell the word **perfect.** Get ready. (S)
8. (Repeat spelling of **pertain, perform,** and **perfect.**)

EXERCISE 3

Word and Spelling Introduction

Note. Accept **lĭve** or **līve** when students read the word. Use either pronunciation in subsequent exercises.

1. (Write on the board: **reach, speak, reason, court, live,** and **life.**)
   These words are made up of only one morphograph.
2. (Point to **reach.**)
   What word? (S) *Reach.*
   Spell **reach.** Get ready. (S)
   (Repeat this procedure for each word.)

3. (Erase the words.)
   Spell the words again.
   First word: **court.** Get ready. (S)
   (Repeat until firm.)
4. (Repeat step 3 for **speak, reason, life, live,** and **reach.**)
5. Find part **A** on your worksheet.
   Get ready to write the words you just spelled.
6. First word: **reason.**
   What word? (S) *Reason.*
   Write **reason.**
   (Repeat for **reach, court, live, speak,** and **life.**)
7. You'll find the spellings of the words we're going to check in appendix **J,** section **C.**
8. (Call on a student.)
   Look up the spelling of the word **reason.**
9. (Assign each of the remaining words to different students.)
10. Get ready to check part **A.**
    Put an **X** next to any word you missed and write that word correctly.
11. (Call on the student who looked up **reason.**)
    Spell **reason.**
    (Write **reason** on the board.)
12. (Repeat step 11 for each remaining word.)

Homonyms

1. (Write on the board: **fore.**)
   This word is **fore.** What word? (S) *fore.*
2. This **fore** means: **in front of.**
   What does this **fore** mean? (S) *In front of.*
3. And how is it spelled? Get ready. (S)
4. (Erase the board.)
   Everybody, spell the **fore** that means: **in front of.** Get ready. (S)
5. Everybody, spell the **four** that means: **the number four.** Get ready. (S)
6. (Repeat steps 4 and 5 until firm. Give individual turns.)

AI Insertion

1. Here is the rule for words that end in **ic.**
   Listen: When the word ends in the letters **ic,** you must add the morphograph **al** before adding **ly.**
2. Listen again: When the word ends in the letters **ic,** you must add the morphograph **al** before adding **ly.**
3. Everybody, tell me when you add **al** before **ly.** (Pause.) Get ready. (S) *When the word ends in the letters ic.*
4. (Write on the board: **music, athletic,** and **basic.**)
5. (Point to **music.**)
   So if we write the word **musically,** what morphograph must we add before the **ly**? (S) *al.*
6. (Write + **al** after **music.**)
   Now we add **ly.**
   (Write + **ly** after **music** + **al.**)
7. Everybody, spell **musically.** Get ready. (S) (Repeat until firm.)
8. (Point to **athletic.**)
   What letters does **athletic** end in? (S) *ic.*
   So what morphograph would we add before the **ly** in **athletically**? (S) *al.*
9. Everybody, spell **athletically.**
   Get ready. (S)
   (Repeat until firm.)
10. (Point to **basic.**)
    What letters does **basic** end in? (S) *ic.*
    So what morphograph do we add before the **ly** in **basically**? (S) *al.*
11. Everybody, spell **basically.** Get ready. (S) (Repeat until firm.)

AI Insertion Worksheet

Everybody, find part **B** on your worksheet.

1. You are going to add **ly** to all the words in part **B.**
   Don't get fooled. Some of those words end in **ic.**
   When the words end in the letters **ic,** you must add the morphograph **al** before adding **ly.**

2. You have two minutes to do the words in part **B.**

3. (At the end of two minutes . . .) Stop.
   I will call on people to spell the words you just wrote.
   Put an **X** next to any word you missed and write that word correctly.

4. (Call on a student.)
   Spell **cutely.** (Pause for corrections.)

5. (Repeat step 4 for **physically, faintly, heavily, logically, gainfully, quickly,** and **heroically.**)

Independent Work

1. Complete the rest of the worksheet on your own.
   Be sure to read the instructions carefully.

2. (Check and correct all work.)

Answer Key

Part E
2. shed
5. bar
6. bit
7. hop
8. ship
9. fer
11. pel

Supplemental Blackline Masters

Supplemental blackline masters 37 and 38 provide additional practice on material covered in Lessons 91 through 95. You may assign any or all of the activities, and you may award bonus points.

======= **EXERCISE 1** =======

Affix Introduction

1. (Write on the board: **compose,
   compress, compass,** and **complain.**)
   Each of these words has a morphograph
   com at the beginning.
   What morphograph? (S) *com.*

2. Read these words. (Point to **compose.**)
   What word? (S) *Compose.*
   What is the first morphograph in
   compose? (S) *com.*
   What is the next morphograph in
   compose? (S) *pose.*

3. (Point to **compress.**)
   What word? (S) *Compress.*
   What is the first morphograph in
   compress? (S) *com.*
   What is the next morphograph in
   compress? (S) *press.*

4. (Point to **compass.**)
   What word? (S) *Compass.*
   What is the first morphograph in
   compass? (S) *com.*
   What is the next morphograph in
   compass? (S) *pass.*

5. (Point to **complain.**)
   What word? (S) *Complain.*
   What is the first morphograph in
   complain? (S) *com.*
   What is the next morphograph in
   complain? (S) *plain.*

6. (Erase the board.)
   Everybody, spell the word **pose.**
   Get ready. (S)
   Now spell the word **compose.**
   Get ready. (S)

7. Everybody, spell the word **press.**
   Get ready. (S)
   Now spell the word **compress.**
   Get ready. (S)

8. Everybody, spell the word **pass.**
   Get ready. (S)
   Now spell the word **compass.**
   Get ready. (S)

9. Everybody, spell the word **plain.**
   Get ready. (S)
   Now spell the word **complain.**
   Get ready. (S)

10. (Repeat spelling of **compose, compress,
    compass,** and **complain.**)

======= **EXERCISE 2** =======

Word and Spelling Introduction

1. (Write on the board: **choose, loose, soon,
   cool, room,** and **broom.**)
   These words are made up of only one
   morphograph.

2. (Point to **choose.**)
   What word? (S) *Choose.*
   Spell **choose.** Get ready. (S)
   (Repeat this procedure for each word.)

3. (Erase the words.)
   Spell the words again.
   First word: **cool.** Get ready. (S)
   (Repeat until firm.)

4. (Repeat step 3 for **loose, soon, broom,
   room,** and **choose.**)

5. Find part **A** on your worksheet.
   Get ready to write the words you
   just spelled.

6. First word: **soon.**
   What word? (S) *Soon.*
   Write **soon.**
   (Repeat for **choose, broom, cool, room,**
   and **loose.**)

7. You'll find the spellings of the words we're
   going to check in appendix **J,** section **C.**

8. (Call on a student.)
   Look up the spelling of the word **soon.**

9. (Assign each of the remaining words to
   different students.)

10. Get ready to check part **A.**
    Put an **X** next to any word you missed and
    write that word correctly.

11. (Call on the student who looked up **soon.**)
    Spell **soon.**
    (Write **soon** on the board.)

12. (Repeat step 11 for each remaining word.)

Homonyms

1. Everybody, spell the **four** that means: **the number four.** Get ready. (S)
2. Everybody, spell the **fore** that means: **in front of.** Get ready. (S)
3. (Repeat steps 1 and 2 until firm. Give individual turns.)

Al Insertion

1. Everybody, when do you add the morphograph **al** before adding **ly?** (S) *When the word ends in the letters ic.* (Repeat until firm.)
2. Find part **B** on your worksheet. (Call on a student.) Read the instructions for part **B.** *Add the morphographs together. Remember to use the rule about adding al before ly.*
3. You will do part **B** later.

Word Building

Get ready to spell some words that have more than one morphograph.
These words are made up of morphographs that cannot stand alone.

1. First word: **perception.**
   What is the first morphograph in **perception**? (S) *per.*
   What is the next morphograph in **perception**? (S) *cept.*
   What is the next morphograph in **perception**? (S) *ion.*
   Spell **perception.** Get ready. (S)
2. Next word: **structure.**
   What is the first morphograph in **structure**? (S) *struct.*
   What is the next morphograph in **structure**? (S) *ure.*
   Spell **structure.** Get ready. (S)

3. (For **disinfect, receptive, refer, perfect, perfectionist,** and **deduce,** have students identify each morphograph and spell each word.)
4. Find part **C** on your worksheet. You are going to write the words you just spelled.
5. First word: **receptive.** Write it.
6. Next word: **perfectionist.** Write it.
7. (Repeat step 6 for **perception, deduce, structure, perfect, disinfect,** and **refer.**)
8. (Check spellings and have students rewrite any missed words.)

Independent Work

1. Complete the rest of the worksheet on your own. Be sure to read the instructions carefully.
2. (Check and correct all work.)

Word and Spelling Introduction

1. (Write on the board: **govern, cross, speech, sleep, sweet,** and **shelf.**)
    These words are made up of only one morphograph.
2. (Point to **govern.**)
    What word? (S) *Govern.*
    Spell **govern.** Get ready. (S)
    (Repeat this procedure for each word.)
3. (Erase the words.)
    Spell the words again.
    First word: **sleep.** Get ready. (S)
    (Repeat until firm.)
4. (Repeat step 3 for **cross, speech, shelf, sweet,** and **govern.**)
5. Find part **A** on your worksheet.
    Get ready to write the words you just spelled.
6. First word: **speech.**
    What word? (S) *Speech.*
    Write **speech.**
    (Repeat for **govern, shelf, sweet, sleep,** and **cross.**)
7. You'll find the spellings of the words we're going to check in appendix **J,** section **C.**
8. (Call on a student.)
    Look up the spelling of the word **speech.**
9. (Assign each of the remaining words to different students.)
10. Get ready to check part **A.**
    Put an **X** next to any word you missed and write that word correctly.
11. (Call on the student who looked up **speech.**)
    Spell **speech.**
    (Write **speech** on the board.)
12. (Repeat step 11 for each remaining word.)

Homonyms

1. (Write on the board: **sun.**)
    This word is **sun.** What word? (S) *Sun.*
2. This **sun** means: **the thing in the sky.**
    What does this **sun** mean? (S) *The thing in the sky.*
3. And how is it spelled? Get ready. (S)
4. (Erase the board.)
    Everybody, spell the **sun** that means: **the thing in the sky.** Get ready. (S)
5. Everybody, spell the **son** that means: **a male child.** Get ready. (S)
6. (Repeat steps 4 and 5 until firm. Give individual turns.)

Spelling Review

1. I'll spell some words quickly.
    See if you can figure out each word.
2. Listen: **s - e - l - f.**
    Everybody, what word? (S) *Self.*
3. Listen: **c - o - u - r - t - e - d.**
    What word? (S) *Courted.*
4. (Repeat step 3 for **live, reason, choose, typing, middle, athletic, dispel, sooner, propose, coolly, danger, reverse, graphic, container, betting, loaf,** and **poisonous.**)
5. Find part **B** on your worksheet.
    Get ready to write some of those words.
6. First word: **reason.** Write it.
7. Next word: **choose.** Write it.
8. (Repeat step 7 for **athletic, propose, middle, container, poisonous,** and **danger.**)
9. I will spell each word.
    Put an **X** next to any word you missed and write that word correctly.
    (Write each word on the board as you spell it.)

AI Insertion

1. Everybody, when do you add the morphograph **al** before **ly?** (S)
   When the word ends in the letters ic.
   (Repeat until firm.)
2. Find part **C** on your worksheet.
   (Call on a student.)
   Read the instructions for part **C**.
   Add the morphographs together.
   Remember to use the rule about adding al before ly.
3. You will do part **C** later.

Nonword Base

1. (Write on the board: **cur.**)
   Here is a new morphograph that usually does not stand alone.
   It is pronounced **cur.**
   What morphograph? (S) *cur.*
2. Everybody, spell **cur.** Get ready. (S)
   (Repeat until firm.)
3. Get ready to spell some words that have the morphograph **cur.**
   First word: **recur.**
   What is the first morphograph in **recur**?
   (S) *re.*
   What is the next morphograph in **recur**?
   (S) *cur.*
   Spell **recur.** Get ready. (S)
4. Next word: **concur.**
   What is the first morphograph in **concur**?
   (S) *con.*
   What is the next morphograph in **concur**?
   (S) *cur.*
   Spell **concur.** Get ready. (S)
5. (Repeat step 4 for **incur.**)

Sentence Dictation

Find part **D** on your worksheet.
Get ready to write sentences made of words you know.

1. Remember, the first letter of the sentence is capitalized, and you put a period at the end of the sentence.
2. Listen. The magical ship was flying south with the cold wind.
   Everybody, say that sentence. Get ready.
   (S) *The magical ship was flying south with the cold wind.*
3. Write that sentence by number one on your worksheet.
   Remember to spell every word correctly.
   (Repeat the sentence as students write.)
4. Listen. Some furry foxes are playing with a friendly wolf.
   Everybody, say that sentence. Get ready.
   (S) *Some furry foxes are playing with a friendly wolf.*
   (Repeat until firm.)
5. Write that sentence by number two on your worksheet.
   Remember to spell every word correctly.
   (Repeat the sentence as students write.)
6. (Check and correct misspellings.
   Underlined words—the and a—have not been taught. If either of those words is missed, include them in the next Word and Spelling Introduction.)

Independent Work

1. Complete the rest of the worksheet on your own.
   Be sure to read the instructions carefully.
2. (Check and correct all work.)

Answer Key

Part E

1.	equally	3.	chief	5.	reserve
2.	pushiness	4.	vision	6.	thrown

Affix Introduction

Note. Identify **ual** by its letters, **u - a - l.**

1. (Write on the board: **factual, gradual,** and **usual.**)
   Each of these words has a morphograph **ual** at the end.
   What morphograph? (S) *ual.*
2. Read these words. (Point to **factual.**)
   What word? (S) *Factual.*
   What is the first morphograph in **factual**?
   (S) *fact.*
   What is the next morphograph in **factual**?
   (S) *ual.*
3. (Point to **gradual.**)
   What word? (S) *Gradual.*
   What is the first morphograph in **gradual**?
   (S) *grade.*
   What is the next morphograph in **gradual**?
   (S) *ual.*
4. (Point to **usual.**)
   What word? (S) *Usual.*
   What is the first morphograph in **usual**?
   (S) *use.*
   What is the next morphograph in **usual**?
   (S) *ual.*
5. (Erase the board.)
   Everybody, spell the word **fact.**
   Get ready. (S)
   Now spell the word **factual.** Get ready. (S)
6. Everybody, spell the word **grade.**
   Get ready. (S)
   Now spell the word **gradual.** Be careful.
   Get ready. (S)
7. Everybody, spell the word **use.**
   Get ready. (S)
   Now spell the word **usual.** Be careful. Get ready. (S)
8. (Repeat spelling of **factual, gradual,** and **usual** until firm. Give individual turns.)

Word and Spelling Introduction— Fast Cycle

Everybody, find part **A** on your worksheet.

1. (Call on a student.)
   Read the instructions for part **A.**
   Study these words on your own. There will be a test on these words during your next spelling lesson.
2. Study the words in part **A** after you have finished your worksheet.
   Everyone should do well on the test over these words.
   (Students may study individually or in pairs.)

Homonyms

1. Everybody, spell the **son** that means: **a male child.** Get ready. (S)
2. Everybody, spell the **sun** that means: **the thing in the sky.** Get ready. (S)
3. (Repeat steps 1 and 2 until firm. Give individual turns.)

Spelling Review

Find part **B** on your worksheet.

You are going to write some words made up of morphographs you have spelled before.

1. First word: **govern.**
   What word? (S) *Govern.*
   Write **govern.**
2. Next word: **loose.**
   What word? (S) *Loose.*
   Write **loose.**

3. (Repeat step 2 for **roomy, sweetest, woman, instructive, various,** and **exception.**)
4. I'll spell each word.
   Put an **X** next to any word you missed and write that word correctly.
   (Write each word on the board as you spell it.)

Independent Work

1. Complete the rest of the worksheet on your own.
   Be sure to read the instructions carefully.
2. (Check and correct all work.)

Word Building

Get ready to spell some words that have more than one morphograph.
These words are made up of morphographs that cannot stand alone.

1. First word: **obstruction.**
   What is the first morphograph in **obstruction**? (S) *ob.*
   What is the next morphograph in **obstruction**? (S) *struct.*
   What is the next morphograph in **obstruction**? (S) *ion.*
   Spell **obstruction.** Get ready. (S)
2. Next word: **structural.**
   What is the first morphograph in **structural**? (S) *struct.*
   What is the next morphograph in **structural**? (S) *ure.*
   What is the next morphograph in **structural**? (S) *al.*
   Spell **structural.** Be careful. Get ready. (S)
3. (For **perfection, incur, concur, transfer, compel,** and **induce,** have students identify each morphograph and spell each word.)
4. Find part **C** on your worksheet.
   You are going to write the words you just spelled.
5. First word: **structural.** Write it.
6. Next word: **perfection.** Write it.
7. (Repeat step 6 for **obstruction, transfer, induce,** and **incur.**)
8. (Check spellings and have students rewrite any missed words.)

62   LESSON 99

Lesson 100

===== **EXERCISE 1** =====

Affix Introduction

1. (Write on the board: **motherhood, boyhood, likelihood,** and **womanhood.**)
Each of these words has a morphograph **hood** at the end.
What morphograph? (S) *hood.*

2. Read these words. (Point to **motherhood.**)
What word? (S) *Motherhood.*
What is the first morphograph in **motherhood**? (S) *mother.*
What is the next morphograph in **motherhood**? (S) *hood.*

3. (Point to **boyhood.**)
What word? (S) *Boyhood.*
What is the first morphograph in **boyhood**? (S) *boy.*
What is the next morphograph in **boyhood**? (S) *hood.*

4. (Point to **likelihood.**)
What word? (S) *Likelihood.*
What is the first morphograph in **likelihood**? (S) *like.*
What is the next morphograph in **likelihood**? (S) *ly.*
What is the next morphograph in **likelihood**? (S) *hood.*

5. (Point to **womanhood.**)
What word? (S) *Womanhood.*
What is the first morphograph in **womanhood**? (S) *woman.*
What is the next morphograph in **womanhood**? (S) *hood.*

6. (Erase the board.)
Everybody, spell the word **mother.**
Get ready. (S)
Now spell the word **motherhood.**
Get ready. (S)

7. Everybody, spell the word **boy.**
Get ready. (S)
Now spell the word **boyhood.**
Get ready. (S)

8. Everybody, spell the word **likely.**
Get ready. (S)
Now spell the word **likelihood.** Be careful.
Get ready. (S)

9. Everybody, spell the word **woman.**
Get ready. (S)
Now spell the word **womanhood.**
Get ready. (S)

10. (Repeat spelling of **motherhood, boyhood, likelihood,** and **womanhood** until firm. Give individual turns.)

===== **EXERCISE 2** =====

Word and Spelling Introduction

1. (Write on the board: **range, month, long, came, scribe,** and **love.**)
These words are made up of only one morphograph.

2. (Point to **range.**)
What word? (S) *Range.*
Spell **range.** Get ready. (S)
(Repeat this procedure for each word.)

3. (Erase the words.)
Spell the words again.
First word: **came.** Get ready. (S)
(Repeat until firm.)

4. (Repeat step 3 for **month, scribe, love, range,** and **long.**)

5. Find part **A** on your worksheet.
Get ready to write the words you just spelled.

6. First word: **long.**
What word? (S) *Long.*
Write **long.**
(Repeat for **range, love, came, month,** and **scribe.**)

7. You'll find the spellings of the words we're going to check in appendix **J**, section **C.**

8. (Call on a student.)
Look up the spelling of the word **long.**

9. (Assign each of the remaining words to different students.)

10. Get ready to check part **A.**
    Put an **X** next to any word you missed and write that word correctly.
11. (Call on the student who looked up **long.**)
    Spell **long.**
    (Write **long** on the board.)
12. (Repeat step 11 for each remaining word.)

EXERCISE 3

Spelling Review

1. I'll spell some words quickly.
   Then I'll call on different people to spell each word.
   When I call on you, spell the word quickly.
2. My turn: **p - e - r - s - o - n.**
   Everybody, what word? (S) *Person.*
3. Next word: **h - o - l - d - e - r.**
   What word? (S) *Holder.*
4. (Repeat step 3 for **four, choosy, basement, briefly, reason, across, sleepy, cubic, governmental, perfect, courts,** and **wife.**)
5. Your turn.
   (Call on a student.)
   Spell **choosy.** Go.
6. (Praise students who respond correctly.)
7. (Call on a student.)
   Spell **holder.** Go.
8. (Repeat step 7 for **basement, cubic, wife, sleepy, courts, four, across, perfect, briefly, governmental, reason,** and **person.** A word may be used more than once.)

EXERCISE 4

Fast Cycle Test

Everybody, find part **B** on your workseet.

1. You are going to write the words you studied during your last spelling lesson.
2. First word: Write **dim.**
3. Next word: Write **hid.**
4. (Repeat step 3 for **bed, mud, star, grab, rob, blot, bug,** and **leg.**)
5. (Check and correct.)

EXERCISE 5

Word Building

Get ready to spell some words that have more than one morphograph.
These words are made up of morphographs that cannot stand alone.

1. First word: **recur.**
   What is the first morphograph in **recur**? (S) *re.*
   What is the next morphograph in **recur**? (S) *cur.*
   Spell **recur.** Get ready. (S)
2. Next word: **receptive.**
   What is the first morphograph in **receptive**? (S) *re.*
   What is the next morphograph in **receptive**? (S) *cept.*
   What is the next morphograph in **receptive**? (S) *ive.*
   Spell **receptive.** Get ready. (S)
3. (For **compel, confection, rejecting,** and **container,** have students identify each morphograph and spell each word.)
4. Find part **C** on your worksheet.
   You are going to write the words you just spelled.
5. First word: **rejecting.** Write it.
6. Next word: **confection.** Write it.
7. (Repeat step 6 for **recur, container, receptive, deduce, transgression,** and **compel.**)
8. (Check spellings and have students rewrite any missed words.)

EXERCISE 6

Independent Work

1. Complete the rest of the worksheet on your own.
   Be sure to read the instructions carefully.
2. (Check and correct all work.)

Mastery Test

1. You are going to have a test today. It will help you see how well you are learning to spell.

2. Everybody, take out a sheet of lined paper and draw a line down the middle. Then number the paper from 1 through 20.

3. (Check and correct.)

4. Word 1 is **reach.**
   How high can you **reach**?
   What word? (S) *Reach.*
   Write **reach.**

5. Word 2 is **loaf.**
   Please pick up a **loaf** of bread.
   What word? (S) *Loaf.*
   Write **loaf.**

6. (Repeat step 5 for the remaining words on the list.)

3.	**design**	12.	**withhold**
4.	**settle**	13.	**live**
5.	**wife**	14.	**uncivil**
6.	**maintain**	15.	**train**
7.	**reason**	16.	**photograph**
8.	**leaf**	17.	**court**
9.	**quest**	18.	**half**
10.	**pose**	19.	**straight**
11.	**middle**	20.	**faint**

7. Everybody, exchange papers with your partner. (Pause.)

8. I'll spell each word. If the word is not spelled correctly on the paper you're marking, put an **X** next to it.
   If the word is spelled correctly, don't put any mark next to it.

9. Word 1 is **reach: r - e - a - c - h.**
   Check it.

10. (Repeat step 9 for each remaining word.)

11. Return your partner's test paper.

12. Now correct any errors you made. If there is an **X** next to a word on your test, write the word correctly in the right column. Raise your hand if you don't know how to spell any words.

13. Turn your paper over when you're finished. I'll come around and check your paper.

14. If you didn't make any mistakes, raise your hand now.

15. Write the number correct at the top of your test.

EXERCISE 1

Word and Spelling Introduction

1. (Write on the board: **join, oil, spoil, major,** and **test.**)
   These words are made up of only one morphograph.
2. (Point to **join.**)
   What word? (S) *Join.*
   Spell **join.** Get ready. (S)
   (Repeat this procedure for each word.)
3. (Erase the words.)
   Spell the words again.
   First word: **major.** Get ready. (S)
   (Repeat until firm.)
4. (Repeat step 3 for **join, oil, test,** and **spoil.**)
5. Find part **A** on your worksheet.
   Get ready to write the words you just spelled.
6. First word: **spoil.**
   What word? (S) *Spoil.*
   Write **spoil.**
   (Repeat for **join, test, major,** and **oil.**)
7. You'll find the spellings of the words we're going to check in appendix **J,** section **C.**
8. (Call on a student.)
   Look up the spelling of the word **spoil.**
9. (Assign each of the remaining words to different students.)
10. Get ready to check part **A.**
    Put an **X** next to any word you missed and write that word correctly.
11. (Call on the student who looked up **spoil.**)
    Spell **spoil.**
    (Write **spoil** on the board.)
12. (Repeat step 11 for each remaining word.)

EXERCISE 2

Nonword Base

1. (Write on the board: **mit.**)
   Here is a new morphograph that cannot stand alone.
   It is pronounced **mit.**
   What morphograph? (S) *mit.*
2. Everybody, spell **mit.** Get ready. (S)
   (Repeat until firm.)
3. Get ready to spell words that have the morphograph **mit.**
   First word: **permit.**
   What is the first morphograph in **permit**?
   (S) *per.*
   What is the next morphograph in **permit**?
   (S) *mit.*
   Spell **permit.** Get ready. (S)
4. Next word: **transmit.**
   What is the first morphograph in **transmit**?
   (S) *trans.*
   What is the next morphograph in **transmit**? (S) *mit.*
   Spell **transmit.** Get ready. (S)
5. (Repeat step 4 for **commit.**)

EXERCISE 3

Plural Variation

1. Let's say some words that have the sound **vvv** in the plural.
2. My turn: The plural of leaf is (Pause.) **leaves.**
3. The plural of **half** is (Pause.) **halves.**
4. The plural of **thief** is (Pause.) **thieves.**
5. Your turn: What is the plural of **thief**? (S) *Thieves.*

To correct:
a. The plural of **thief** is **thieves.**
b. (Repeat step 5.)

---

6. What is the plural of **half**? (S) *Halves.*
7. What is the plural of **wolf**? (S) *Wolves.*
8. What is the plural of **calf**? (S) *Calves.*
   (Repeat steps 5–8 until firm.)
9. (Write on the board: **leaf, leaves.**)
10. Listen: Some words that end in the sound **fff** have the letters **v - e - s** in the plural. You can always hear the sound **vvv** in the plural.
11. (Point to **leaf.**)
    Everybody, spell the word **leaf.**
    Get ready. (S)
    Say the plural of **leaf.** (S) *Leaves.*
    Yes, you can hear the sound **vvv** in **leaves.**
    Spell **leaves.** Get ready. (S)
12. Everybody, spell the word **half.**
    Get ready. (S)
    Say the plural of **half.** (S) *Halves.*
13. (For **wolf-wolves** and **thief-thieves,** have students spell the singular, say the plural, and spell the plural.)

━━━━━━ **EXERCISE 4** ━━━━━━

Plural Variation Worksheet

Everybody, find part **B** on your worksheet.

1. There are four words that end in the sound **fff.** Write the plural for each word in the last column.
   Remember to say the plural to yourself. Then you will know how to spell it.
2. You have one minute to write the plurals.
3. (At the end of one minute. . .) Stop.
   We are going to check the words you just wrote.
   Put an **X** next to any word you missed and write that word correctly.
4. The first word is **thief.**
   Everybody, what is the plural of **thief**? (S) *Thieves.*

> **To correct:**
> a. The plural of **thief** is **thieves.** (Pause.) Thieves.
> b. (Repeat step 4.)

5. Yes, you can hear the sound **vvv** in **thieves.**
   Everybody, spell **thieves.** Get ready. (S) (Pause for corrections.)
6. (Repeat steps 4 and 5 for **wife-wives, loaf-loaves,** and **wolf-wolves.**)

━━━━━━ **EXERCISE 5** ━━━━━━

Spelling Review

1. I'll spell some words quickly.
   See if you can figure out each word.
2. Listen: **s - u - n - n - y.**
   Everybody, what word? (S) *Sunny.*
3. Listen: **b - r - o - o - m.**
   What word? (S) *Broom.*
4. (Repeat step 3 for **classical, longest, perfectionist, choosing, basically, describe, lovely, month, flattest, government, loosen, sweetly, loneliness,** and **unknown.**)
5. Find part **C** on your worksheet.
   Get ready to write some of those words.
6. First word: **classical.** Write it.
7. Next word: **lovely.** Write it.
8. (Repeat step 7 for **longest, government, loneliness, loosen, basically,** and **describe.**)
9. I will spell each word.
   Put an **X** next to any word you missed and write that word correctly.
   (Write each word on the board as you spell it.)

━━━━━━ **EXERCISE 6** ━━━━━━

Study for Spelling Contest

Find appendix **J,** section **C.**

1. During Lesson 102, we're going to have a spelling contest.
2. Most of the test words will come from appendix **J,** section **C.**
3. When you've completed your worksheet, study the words.

Note. Students may study in pairs or independently.

Independent Work

1. Complete the rest of the worksheet on your own.
   Be sure to read the instructions carefully.
2. (Check and correct all work.)

— **Answer Key** —

Part D

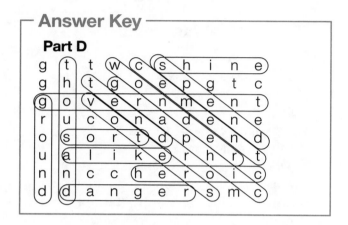

Supplemental Blackline Masters

Supplemental blackline masters 39 and 40 provide additional practice on material covered in Lessons 96 through 100. You may assign any or all of the activities, and you may award bonus points.

Note. There is no student worksheet for Lesson 102.

EXERCISE 1

Spelling Contest

Today we're going to have a spelling contest.

1. We'll make up two teams.
   (Assign students to each team.)
2. (Make a scorebox on the board.)

Team A	Team B

3. Here are the rules for the contest.
   a. I will dictate words to the teams.
   b. Every time a team spells a word correctly, it gets a point.
   c. If a team misses a word, the other team gets to try that word.
   d. The first team to get 30 points wins the spelling contest.
4. (Praise correct spellings and mark them in the scorebox.)

To correct misspellings:
   a. That's not how the word _____ is spelled.
   b. (Call on a member of the other team to spell that word.)

5. (Call on teams alternately to spell words from the following list. Words may be used more than once.)

major	equipment	studies
reach	container	transfer
sweetest	expression	realistic
fashion	spiritual	obtain
actual	middle	swimmer
basically	amusement	lifelessness
recover	poisonous	physical
selfish	compassion	please

performer	spoiled	joined
observe	berries	government
thousand	thief	straight
instructional	around	gradual
across	compose	alike
dangerous	thoughtful	pretend
unreasonable	perfect	
speaker	object	
reinforce	civilly	
statement	forget	

First team to get 30 points . . . .
10 bonus points.
If the other team has 27–29 points . . . .
8 bonus points.
If the other team has 24–26 points . . . .
5 bonus points.
If the other team has less than 24 points . . . . . .
0 bonus points.

Crossword Puzzles
The crossword puzzles are made up exclusively of the words presented in the review lessons. Every word in these lessons has been used. For each review lesson, there are two or three sets of puzzles, depending on how many words are in the lesson. A set is made up of two puzzles— an original and an alternate. The alternate uses the same words and clues as the original, but in a different arrangement. This gives you a good deal of flexibility in how you use the puzzles.

The crossword puzzle blackline masters are located at the back of this Teacher Presentation Book.

Lesson 103

EXERCISE 1

Y Rule Discrimination

I'll say some words. Let's figure out whether the rule about changing **y** to **i** applies to each word.

1. Remember, you change the **y** to **i** in a word when the word ends with a **consonant-and-y,** and the next morphograph begins with anything except **i**.
2. First word: **happiness.**
   Spell the first morphograph in **happiness.** Get ready. (S)
3. Does **happy** end with a **consonant-and-y**? (S) *Yes.*
   So maybe **happiness** follows the **y**-to-**i** rule.
   Does **ness** begin with **i**? (S) *No.*
   So does the **y**-to-**i** rule apply? (S) *Yes.*
   Spell **happiness.** Get ready. (S)
4. Next word: **strengthen.**
   Spell the first morphograph in **strengthen.** Get ready. (S)
5. Does **strength** end with a **consonant-and-y**? (S) *No.*
   So does the **y**-to-**i** rule apply? (S) *No.*
   Why not? (Call on a student.) *Strength does not end with a consonant-and-y.*
   Spell **strengthen.** Get ready. (S)
6. Next word: **carrying.**
   Spell the first morphograph in **carrying.** Get ready. (S)
7. Does **carry** end with a **consonant-and-y**? (S) *Yes.*
   So maybe **carrying** follows the **y**-to-**i** rule.
   Does **ing** begin with **i**? (S) *Yes.*
   So does the **y**-to-**i** rule apply? (S) *No.*
   Why not? (Call on a student.) *Ing begins with i.*
   Spell **carrying.** Get ready. (S)
8. Next word: **joyful.**
   Spell the first morphograph in **joyful.** Get ready. (S)

9. Does **joy** end with a **consonant-and-y**? (S) *No.*
   So does the **y**-to-**i** rule apply? (S) *No.*
   Why not? (Call on a student.) *Joy does not end with a consonant-and-y.*
   Spell **joyful.** Get ready. (S)

EXERCISE 2

Spelling Review

1. I'll spell some words quickly.
   See if you can figure out each word.
2. Listen: **f - r - i - e - n - d - l - y.**
   Everybody, what word? (S) *Friendly.*
3. Listen: **e - q - u -a - l.**
   What word? (S) *Equal.*
4. (Repeat step 3 for **strengthen, quietly, stretch, design, really, misspelling, business, wrong, thoughtful, straight, author, choice,** and **madness.**)
5. Find part **A** on your worksheet.
   Get ready to write some of those words.
6. First word: **quietly.** Write it.
7. Next word: **equal.** Write it.
8. (Repeat step 7 for **friendly, really, choice, wrong, straight,** and **thoughtful.**)
9. I will spell each word.
   Put an **X** next to any word you missed and write that word correctly.
   (Write each word on the board as you spell it.)

EXERCISE 3

Plural Variation

1. Let's say some words that have the sound **vvv** in the plural.
2. Listen: **shelf.** What word? (S) *Shelf.*
   What is the plural of **shelf**? (S) *Shelves.*

To correct:
a. The plural of **shelf** is **shelves.**
b. (Repeat step 2.)

70   LESSON 103

3. **Life.** What word? (S) *Life.*
   What is the plural of **life**? (S) *Lives.*
4. **Loaf.** What word? (S) *Loaf.*
   What is the plural of **loaf**? (S) *Loaves.*
5. **Wife.** What word? (S) *Wife.*
   What is the plural of **wife**? (S) *Wives.*
6. **Thief.** What word? (S) *Thief.*
   What is the plural of **thief**? (S) *Thieves.*
7. Everybody, spell the word **shelf.**
   Get ready. (S)
   Say the plural of **shelf.** (S) *Shelves.*
   Yes, you can hear the sound **vvv** in
   shelves.
   Spell **shelves.** Get ready. (S)
8. Everybody, spell the word **life.**
   Get ready. (S)
   Say the plural of **life.** (S) *Lives.*
   Spell **lives.** Get ready. (S)
9. Everybody, spell the word **loaf.**
   Get ready. (S)
   Say the plural of **loaf.** (S) *Loaves.*
   Spell **loaves.** Get ready. (S)

Plural Variation Worksheet

Everybody, find part **B** on your worksheet.

1. There are four words that end in the sound
   fff. Write the plural for each word in the
   last column.
   Remember to say the plural to yourself.
   Then you will know how to spell it.
2. You have one minute to write the plurals.
3. (At the end of one minute. . .) Stop.
   We are going to check the words you just
   wrote.
   Put an **X** next to any word you missed and
   write that word correctly.
4. The first word is **wolf.**
   Everybody, what is the plural of **wolf?**
   (S) *Wolves.*

To correct:
a. The plural of **wolf** is (Pause.) **wolves.**
b. (Repeat step 4.)

5. Yes, you can hear the sound **vvv** in **wolves.**
   Everybody, spell **wolves.** Get ready. (S)
6. (Repeat steps 4 and 5 for **wife-wives, half-halves,** and **shelf-shelves.**)

Bingo

Find part **C** on your worksheet.

1. We're going to play bingo.
   Quickly write the words in the boxes.
2. Remember:
   a. A row may go across, or down, or
      corner to corner.
   b. The first student or students to get four
      words in a row earn two bonus points.
   c. If you have misspelled any words in
      your row, that row won't count for
      bonus points.
3. (Spell each word quickly.)
4. First word: **r - a - n - g - e.**
   Mark an **X** in the box containing that word.
5. Next word: **d - e - s - c - r - i - b - e.**
   Mark an **X** in the box containing that word.
6. (Repeat step 5 for as many of the following
   words as necessary: **starry, across,
   speechless, reasonable, sleepless,
   infected, pretend, thief, settle, govern,
   request, recover,** and **spirit.**)
7. (When one or more students get a bingo,
   stop the game and award the bonus
   points.)

Independent Work

1. Complete the rest of the worksheet on
   your own.
   Be sure to read the instructions carefully.
2. (Check and correct all work.)

Lesson 104

EXERCISE 1

Sentence Dictation

Find part **A** on your worksheet.
Get ready to write sentences made of words you know.

1. Remember, the first letter of the sentence is capitalized, and you put a period at the end of the sentence.
2. Listen. <u>That</u> woman has <u>a</u> very lovely <u>and</u> musical voice.
   Everybody, say that sentence.
   Get ready. (S)
   That woman has a very lovely and musical voice.
   (Repeat until firm.)
3. Write that sentence by number one on your worksheet.
   Remember to spell every word correctly.
   (Repeat the sentence as students write.)
4. Listen. <u>The</u> author quoted some verses <u>in</u> <u>his</u> speech.
   Everybody, say that sentence.
   Get ready. (S)
   The author quoted some verses in his speech.
   (Repeat until firm.)
5. Write that sentence by number two on your worksheet.
   Remember to spell every word correctly.
   (Repeat the sentence as students write.)
6. (Check and correct misspellings. Underlined words—<u>a</u>, <u>that</u>, <u>the</u>, <u>and</u>, <u>in</u>, and <u>his</u>—have not been taught. If any of those words are missed, include them in the next Word and Spelling Introduction.)

EXERCISE 2

Plural Variation

1. Let's say some words that have the sound **vvv** in the plural.
2. Listen: **calf.** What word? (S) *Calf.*
   What is the plural of **calf**? (S) *Calves.*

> **To correct:**
> a. The plural of **calf** is **calves.**
> b. (Repeat step 2.)

3. **Thief.** What word? (S) *Thief.*
   What is the plural of **thief**? (S) *Thieves.*
4. **Loaf.** What word? (S) *Loaf.*
   What is the plural of **loaf**? (S) *Loaves.*
5. **Wife.** What word? (S) *Wife.*
   What is the plural of **wife**? (S) *Wives.*
6. Everybody, spell the word **calf.**
   Get ready. (S)
   Say the plural of **calf.** (S) *Calves.*
   Yes, you can hear the sound **vvv** in **calves.**
   Spell **calves.** Get ready. (S)
7. Everybody, spell the word **wife.**
   Get ready. (S)
   Say the plural of **wife.** (S) *Wives.*
   Spell **wives.** Get ready. (S)
8. Everybody, spell the word **thief.**
   Get ready. (S)
   Say the plural of **thief.** (S) *Thieves.*
   Spell **thieves.** Get ready. (S)

EXERCISE 3

Plural-Variation Worksheet

Everybody, find part **B** on your worksheet.

1. There are four words that end in the sound **fff.**
   Write the plural for each word in the last column.
   Remember to say the plural to yourself.
   Then you will know how to spell it.
2. You have one minute to write the plurals.

3. (At the end of one minute . . .) Stop.
   We are going to check the words you just wrote.
   Put an **X** next to any word you missed and write that word correctly.
4. The first word is **shelf.**
   Everybody, what is the plural of **shelf**? (S) *Shelves.*

To correct:
a. The plural of **shelf** is (Pause.) **shelves.**
b. (Repeat step 4.)

5. Yes, you can hear the sound **vvv** in **shelves.**
   Everybody, spell **shelves.** Get ready. (S) (Pause for corrections.)
6. (Repeat steps 4 and 5 for **loaf-loaves, calf-calves,** and **thief-thieves.**)

EXERCISE 4

Spelling Review

1. I'll spell some words quickly.
   Then I'll call on different people to spell each word.
   When I call on you, spell the word quickly.
2. My turn: **m - a - j - o - r.**
   Everybody, what word? (S) *Major.*
3. Next word: **r - a - n - g - e.**
   What word? (S) *Range.*
4. (Repeat step 3 for **star, scribe, grab, government, across, speechless, choose, unreasonable, perfect, object, fashionable, recover,** and **reverse.**)
5. Your turn.
   (Call on a student.)
   Spell **scribe.** Go.
6. (Praise students who respond correctly.)
7. (Call on a student.)
   Spell **range.** Go.
8. (Repeat step 7 for **grab, unreasonable, reverse, recover, choose, star, speechless, fashionable, object, perfect, across, government,** and **major.**)

EXERCISE 5

Word Building

Get ready to spell some words that have more than one morphograph.

1. First word: **wondering.**
   What is the first morphograph in **wondering**? (S) *wonder.*
   What is the next morphograph in **wondering**? (S) *ing.*
   Spell **wondering.** Get ready. (S)
2. Next word: **unequally.**
   What is the first morphograph in **unequally**? (S) *un.*
   What is the next morphograph in **unequally**? (S) *equal.*
   What is the next morphograph in **unequally**? (S) *ly.*
   Spell **unequally.** Get ready. (S)
3. (For **designer, informal, variable, preserving, protected, questionable, obstruction,** and **container,** have students identify each morphograph and spell each word.)
4. Find part **C** on your worksheet.
   You are going to write some of the words you just spelled.
5. First word: **designer.** Write it.
6. Next word: **protected.** Write it.
7. (Repeat step 6 for **informal, wondering, container,** and **questionable.**)

EXERCISE 6

Independent Work

1. Complete the rest of the worksheet on your own.
   Be sure to read the instructions carefully.
2. (Check and correct all work.)

Answer Key

Part D

1.	grab	8.	fer
2.	mit	10.	pel
4.	cur	11.	ship
7.	mud	14.	shed

Spelling Review

Find part **A** on your worksheet.

You are going to write some words made up of morphographs you have spelled before.

1. First word: **recover.**
   What word? (S) *Recover.*
   Write **recover.**
2. Next word: **fashion.**
   What word? (S) *Fashion.*
   Write **fashion.**
3. (Repeat step 2 for **shout, middle, major, scribe, govern,** and **loose.**)
4. I'll spell each word.
   Put an **X** next to any word you missed and write that word correctly.
   (Write each word on the board as you spell it.)

Rule Discrimination

I'll say words.
Figure out whether the doubling rule, the **y**-to-**i** rule, or no rule applies.

1. The first word begins with **speech.**
   Spell **speech.** Get ready. (S)
   Could a rule apply? (S) *No.*
   Why not? (Call on a student.)
   Speech does not end with cvc or a consonant-and-y.
2. The word is **speechless.**
   Spell **speechless.** Get ready. (S)
3. The next word begins with **rob.**
   Spell **rob.** Get ready. (S)
   Could a rule apply? (S) *Yes.*
   Which rule? (Call on a student.) *The rule about doubling a letter.*
   Everybody, how do you know the doubling rule could apply? (S)
   Rob is a short cvc word.

4. The word is **robber.**
   Does the doubling rule apply? (S) *Yes.*
   How do you know? (Call on a student.)
   Er begins with v.
   Spell **robber.** Get ready. (S)
5. The next word begins with **carry.**
   Spell **carry.** Get ready. (S)
   Could a rule apply? (S) *Yes.*
   Which rule? (Call on a student.) *The rule about changing y to i.*
   Everybody, how do you know the **y**-to-**i** rule could apply? (S)
   Carry ends with a consonant-and-y.
6. The word is **carrying.**
   Does the **y**-to-**i** rule apply? (S) *No.*
   How do you know? (Call on a student.) *Ing begins with an i.*
   Spell **carrying.** Get ready. (S)
7. The next word begins with **study.**
   Spell **study.** Get ready. (S)
   Could a rule apply? (S) *Yes.*
   Which rule? (Call on a student.) *The rule about changing y to i.*
   Everybody, how do you know the **y**-to-**i** rule could apply? (S)
   Study ends with a consonant-and-y.
8. The word is **studied.**
   Does the **y**-to-**i** rule apply? (S) *Yes.*
   How do you know? (Call on a student.)
   E-d does not begin with i.
   Spell **studied.** Get ready. (S)

Word Building

Get ready to spell some words that have more than one morphograph.

1. First word: **observable.**
   What is the first morphograph in **observable**? (S) *ob.*
   What is the next morphograph in **observable**? (S) *serve.*
   What is the next morphograph in **observable**? (S) *able.*
   Spell **observable.** Get ready. (S)

2. Next word: **unselfish.**
   What is the first morphograph in **unselfish**? (S) *un.*
   What is the next morphograph in **unselfish**? (S) *self.*
   What is the next morphograph in **unselfish**? (S) *ish.*
   Spell **unselfish.** Get ready. (S)
3. (For **perfectionist, factually, compartment, structure, apartment,** and **instruction,** have students identify each morphograph and spell each word.)
4. Find part **B** on your worksheet.
   You are going to write some of the words you just spelled.
5. First word: **factually.** Write it.
6. Next word: **compartment.** Write it.
7. (Repeat step 6 for **unselfish, structure, instruction,** and **apartment.**)
8. (Check spellings and have students rewrite any missed words.)

Al Insertion Worksheet

1. Everybody, when do you add the morphograph **al** before adding **ly**? (S)
   When the word ends in the letters ic.
   (Repeat until firm.)
2. Find part **C** on your worksheet.
   Write the words in the last column.
   Remember to use the rule about adding **al** before adding **ly.**
3. You have two minutes to do the words in part **C.**
4. (At the end of two minutes . . .) Stop.
   I will call on people to spell the words you just wrote.
   Put an **X** next to any word you missed and write that word correctly.
5. (Call on a student.)
   Spell **basically.** (Pause for corrections.)
6. (Repeat step 5 for **imposing, lovely, athletically, critically,** and **faintly.**)

Independent Work

1. Complete the rest of the worksheet on your own.
   Be sure to read the instructions carefully.
2. (Check and correct all work.)

Lesson 106

EXERCISE 1

Homonyms

1. Everybody, spell the **son** that means: **a male child.** Get ready. (S)
2. Everybody, spell the **sun** that means: **the thing in the sky.** Get ready. (S)
3. (Repeat steps 1 and 2 until firm. Give individual turns.)
4. Everybody, spell the **fore** that means: **in the front.** Get ready. (S)
5. Everybody, spell the **four** that means: **the number four.** Get ready. (S)
6. (Repeat steps 4 and 5 until firm. Give individual turns.)

EXERCISE 2

Spelling Review

1. I'll spell some words quickly. See if you can figure out each word.
2. Listen: **m - a - j - o - r.** What word? (S) *Major.*
3. Listen: **c - o - n - t - e - s - t.** What word? (S) *Contest.*
4. (Repeat step 3 for **permit, blotter, speeches, government, broom, reaching, request, cause, grounded,** and **whether.**)
5. Find part **A** on your worksheet. Get ready to write some of those words.
6. First word: **permit.** Write it.
7. Next word: **contest.** Write it.
8. (Repeat step 7 for **government, whether, major, reaching, cause,** and **request.**)
9. I will spell each word. Put an **X** next to any word you missed and write that word correctly.
   (Write each word on the board as you spell it.)

EXERCISE 3

En Variation Worksheet

Everybody, find part **B** on your worksheet.

1. When a word ends with the letter **w** and you add **en,** what do you drop? (S) *The e.* (Repeat until firm.)
2. Remember to say each word to yourself. The way the ending sounds is the way the ending is spelled.
3. You have one and a half minutes to do part **B.**
4. (After one and a half minutes, check and correct.)

EXERCISE 4

Word Building

Get ready to spell some words that have more than one morphograph.

1. First word: **reserve.**
   What is the first morphograph in **reserve**? (S) *re.*
   What is the next morphograph in **reserve**? (S) *serve.*
   Spell **reserve.** Get ready. (S)
2. Next word: **relative.**
   What is the first morphograph in **relative**? (S) *re.*
   What is the next morphograph in **relative**? (S) *late.*
   What is the next morphograph in **relative**? (S) *ive.*
   Spell **relative.** Get ready. (S)
3. (For **famous, proven, contentment, photographic, vision, poisonous, describe,** and **pretended,** have students identify each morphograph and spell each word.)
4. Find part **C** on your worksheet. You are going to write some of the words you just spelled.

5. First word: **vision.** Write it.
6. Next word: **reserve.** Write it.
7. (Repeat step 6 for **famous, relative, describe,** and **poisonous.**)
8. (Check spellings and have students rewrite any missed words.)

EXERCISE 5

Plural Variation

1. Let's say some words that have the sound **vvv** in the plural.
2. Listen: **leaf.** What word? (S) *Leaf.*
   What is the plural of **leaf**? (S) *Leaves.*
3. **Wife.** What word? (S) *Wife.*
   What is the plural of **wife**? (S) *Wives.*
4. **Self.** What word? (S) *Self.*
   What is the plural of **self**? (S) *Selves.*
5. **Loaf.** What word? (S) *Loaf.*
   What is the plural of **loaf**? (S) *Loaves.*
6. **Half.** What word? (S) *Half.*
   What is the plural of **half**? (S) *Halves.*
7. Everybody, spell the word **half.**
   Get ready. (S)
   Say the plural of **half.** (S) *Halves.*
   Yes, you can hear the sound **vvv** in **halves.**
   Spell **halves.** Get ready. (S)
8. Everybody, spell the word **leaf.**
   Get ready. (S)
   Say the plural of **leaf.**
   Get ready. (S) *Leaves.*
   Spell **leaves.** Get ready. (S)
9. Everybody, spell the word **wife.**
   Get ready. (S)
   Say the plural of **wife.** (S) *Wives.*
   Spell **wives.** Get ready. (S)
10. Everybody, spell the word **loaf.**
    Get ready. (S)
    Say the plural of **loaf.** (S) *Loaves.*
    Spell **loaves.** Get ready. (S)

EXERCISE 6

Plural Variation Worksheet

Everybody, find part **D** on your worksheet.

1. (Call on a student.)
   Read the instructions for part **D.**
   Write the plural for each word. Remember to say the plural word to yourself.
2. You will do part **D** on your own.

EXERCISE 7

Independent Work

1. Complete the rest of the worksheet on your own.
   Be sure to read the instructions carefully.
2. (Check and correct all work.)

Supplemental Blackline Masters

Supplemental blackline masters 41 and 42 provide additional practice on material covered in Lessons 101 through 105. You may assign any or all of the activities, and you may award bonus points.

EXERCISE 1

Affix Introduction

1. (Write on the board: **became, beside, belong,** and **behave.**)
   Each of these words has a morphograph **be** at the beginning.
   What morphograph? (S) *be.*

2. Read these words. (Point to **became.**)
   What word? (S) *Became.*
   What is the first morphograph in **became**? (S) *be.*
   What is the next morphograph in **became**? (S) *came.*

3. (Point to **beside.**)
   What word? (S) *Beside.*
   What is the first morphograph in **beside**? (S) *be.*
   What is the next morphograph in **beside**? (S) *side.*

4. (Point to **belong.**)
   What word? (S) *Belong.*
   What is the first morphograph in **belong**? (S) *be.*
   What is the next morphograph in **belong**? (S) *long.*

5. (Point to **behave.**)
   What word? (S) *Behave.*
   What is the first morphograph in **behave**? (S) *be.*
   What is the next morphograph in **behave**? (S) *have.*

6. (Erase the board.)
   Everybody, spell the word **came.**
   Get ready. (S)
   Now spell the word **became.**
   Get ready. (S)

7. Everybody, spell the word **side.**
   Get ready. (S)
   Now spell the word **beside.** Get ready. (S)

8. Everybody, spell the word **long.**
   Get ready. (S)
   Now spell the word **belong.** Get ready. (S)

9. Everybody, spell the word **have.**
   Get ready. (S)
   Now spell the word **behave.** Get ready. (S)

10. (Repeat spelling of **became, beside, belong,** and **behave** until firm. Give individual turns.)

EXERCISE 2

Word and Spelling Introduction

1. (Write on the board: **merge, verge, dress, just, critic,** and **vent.**) These words are made up of only one morphograph.

2. (Point to **merge.**)
   What word? (S) *Merge.*
   Spell **merge.** Get ready. (S)
   (Repeat this procedure for each word.)

3. (Erase the words.)
   Spell the words again.
   First word: **just.** Get ready. (S)
   (Repeat until firm.)

4. (Repeat step 3 for **verge, dress, vent, merge,** and **critic.**)

5. Find part **A** on your worksheet.
   Get ready to write the words you just spelled.

6. First word: **dress.**
   What word? (S) *Dress.*
   Write **dress.**
   (Repeat for **merge, vent, critic, just,** and **verge.**)

7. You'll find the spellings of the words we're going to check in appendix **K,** section **B.**

8. (Call on a student.)
   Look up the spelling of the word **dress.**

9. (Assign each of the remaining words to different students.)

10. Get ready to check part **A.**
    Put an **X** next to any word you missed and write that word correctly.

11. (Call on the student who looked up **dress.**)
    Spell **dress.**
    (Write **dress** on the board.)

12. (Repeat step 11 for each remaining word.)

Word and Spelling Introduction— Fast Cycle

Everybody, find part **B** on your worksheet.

1. (Call on a student.)
    Read the instructions for part **B**.
    Study these words on your own. There will be a test on these words during your next spelling lesson.
2. Study the words in part **B** after you have finished your worksheet.
    Everyone should do well on the test over these words.
    (Students may study individually or in pairs.)

Spelling Review

1. I'll spell some words quickly.
    See if you can figure out each word.
2. Listen: **j - o - i - n.**
    Everybody, what word? (S) *Join.*
3. Listen: **s - p - o - i - l - e - d.**
    What word? (S) *Spoiled.*
4. (Repeat step 3 for **major, ranger, longest, scribe, grabbing, manhood, textual, confection, brother, starring, aren't, structural,** and **halves.**)
5. Find part **C** on your worksheet.
    Get ready to write some of those words.
6. First word: **brother.** Write it.
7. Next word: **spoiled.** Write it.
8. (Repeat step 7 for **major, starring, longest, halves, grabbing,** and **aren't.**)
9. I will spell each word.
    Put an **X** next to any word you missed and write that word correctly.

Word Building

Get ready to spell some words that have more than one morphograph.
These words are made up of morphographs that cannot stand alone.

1. First word: **commit.**
    What is the first morphograph in **commit**?
    (S) *com.*
    What is the next morphograph in **commit**?
    (S) *mit.*
    Spell **commit.** Get ready. (S)
2. Next word: **concur.**
    What is the first morphograph in **concur**?
    (S) *con.*
    What is the next morphograph in **concur**?
    (S) *cur.*
    Spell **concur.** Get ready. (S)
3. (For **confection, structural, transfer, transmit, progressively,** and **detective,** have students identify each morphograph and spell each word.)
4. Find part **D** on your worksheet.
    You are going to write the words you just spelled.
5. First word: **progressively.** Write it.
6. Next word: **transfer.** Write it.
7. (Repeat step 6 for **commit, detective, confection, transmit, concur,** and **structural.**)
8. (Check spellings and have students rewrite any missed words.)

Plural Variation Worksheet

Everybody, find part **E** on your worksheet.

1. (Call on a student.)
    Read the instructions for part **E**.
    Write the plural for each word. Remember to say the plural word to yourself.
2. You will do part **E** on your own.

Independent Work

1. Complete the rest of the worksheet on your own.
    Be sure to read the instructions carefully.
2. (Check and correct all work.)

Affix Introduction

1. (Write on the board: **import, impose, impress,** and **improve.**)
   Each of these words has a morphograph **im** at the beginning.
   What morphograph? (S) *im.*

2. Read these words. (Point to **import.**)
   What word? (S) *Import.*
   What is the first morphograph in **import**?
   (S) *im.*
   What is the next morphograph in **import**?
   (S) *port.*

3. (Point to **impose.**)
   What word? (S) *Impose.*
   What is the first morphograph in **impose**?
   (S) *im.*
   What is the next morphograph in **impose**?
   (S) *pose.*

4. (Point to **impress.**)
   What word? (S) *Impress.*
   What is the first morphograph in **impress**?
   (S) *im.*
   What is the next morphograph in
   impress? (S) *press.*

5. (Point to **improve.**)
   What word? (S) *Improve.*
   What is the first morphograph in **improve**?
   (S) *im.*
   What is the next morphograph in
   improve? (S) *prove.*

6. (Erase the board.)
   Everybody, spell the word **port.**
   Get ready. (S)
   Now spell the word **import.** Get ready. (S)

7. Everybody, spell the word **pose.**
   Get ready. (S)
   Now spell the word **impose.** Get ready. (S)

8. Everybody, spell the word **press.**
   Get ready. (S)
   Now spell the word **impress.**
   Get ready. (S)

9. Everybody, spell the word **prove.**
   Get ready. (S)
   Now spell the word **improve.**
   Get ready. (S)

10. (Repeat spelling of **import, impose, impress,** and **improve** until firm.)

Word and Spelling Introduction

1. (Write on the board: **family, drive, while, double, couple,** and **trouble.**)
   These words are made up of only one morphograph.

2. (Point to **family.**)
   What word? (S) *Family.*
   Spell **family.** Get ready. (S)
   (Repeat this procedure for each word.)

3. (Erase the words.)
   Spell the words again.
   First word: **couple.** Get ready. (S)
   (Repeat until firm.)

4. (Repeat step 3 for **drive, double, while, trouble,** and **family.**)

5. Find part **A** on your worksheet.
   Get ready to write the words you
   just spelled.

6. First word: **double.**
   What word? (S) *Double.*
   Write **double.**
   (Repeat for **family, while, trouble, couple,** and **drive.**)

7. You'll find the spellings of the words we're going to check in appendix **K,** section **B.**

8. (Call on a student.)
   Look up the spelling of the word **double.**

9. (Assign each of the remaining words to different students.)

10. Get ready to check part **A.**
    Put an **X** next to any word you missed and write that word correctly.

11. (Call on the student who looked up **double.**)
    Spell **double.**
    (Write **double** on the board.)
12. (Repeat step 11 for each remaining word.)

Nonword Base

1. (Write on the board: **sist.**)
   Here is a new morphograph that cannot stand alone.
   It is pronounced **sist.**
   What morphograph? (S) *sist.*
2. Everybody, spell **sist.** Get ready. (S)
   (Repeat until firm.)
3. Get ready to spell words that have the morphograph **sist.**
   First word: **persist.**
   What is the first morphograph in **persist**? (S) *per.*
   What is the next morphograph in **persist**? (S) *sist.*
   Spell **persist.** Get ready. (S)
4. Next word: **consist.**
   What is the first morphograph in **consist**? (S) *con.*
   What is the next morphograph in **consist**? (S) *sist.*
   Spell **consist.** Get ready. (S)
5. (Repeat step 4 for **insist** and **resist.**)

Fast-Cycle Test

Everybody, find part **B** on your worksheet.

1. You are going to write the words you studied during your last spelling lesson.
2. First word: write **pig.**
3. Next word: write **net.**
4. (Repeat step 3 for **gun, ton, trip, frog, spot, hit, chin,** and **rat.**)
5. (Check and correct.)

Sentence Dictation

Find part **C** on your worksheet.
Get ready to write sentences made of words you know.

1. Remember, the first letter of the sentence is capitalized, and you put a period at the end of the sentence.
2. Listen. <u>The</u> star <u>of</u> the show is worried about <u>his</u> part.
   Everybody, say that sentence.
   Get ready. (S)
   The star of the show is worried about his part.
   (Repeat until firm.)
3. Write that sentence by number one on your worksheet.
   Remember to spell every word correctly.
   (Repeat the sentence as students write.)
4. Listen. <u>I</u> revised <u>my</u> report <u>on</u> photography.
   Everybody, say that sentence.
   Get ready. (S)
   I revised my report on photography.
   (Repeat until firm.)
5. Write that sentence by number two on your worksheet.
   Remember to spell every word correctly.
   (Repeat the sentence as students write.)
6. (Check and correct misspellings.
   Underlined words—<u>the</u>, <u>of</u>, <u>his</u>, <u>I</u>, <u>my</u>, and <u>on</u>—have not been taught. If any of those words are missed, include them in the next Word and Spelling Introduction.)

Word Building

Get ready to spell some words that have more than one morphograph.
These words are made up of morphographs that cannot stand alone.

1. First word: **transmit.**
   What is the first morphograph in **transmit**? (S) *trans.*

What is the next morphograph in
transmit? (S) *mit.*
Spell **transmit.** Get ready. (S)

2. First word: **incur.**
What is the first morphograph in **incur**?
(S) *in.*
What is the next morphograph in **incur**?
(S) *cur.*
Spell **incur.** Get ready. (S)

3. (For **recur, disinfect, defer, constructive,
reduce,** and **pertaining,** have students
identify each morphograph and spell
each word.)

EXERCISE 7

Independent Work

1. Complete the rest of the worksheet on
your own.
Be sure to read the instructions carefully.

2. (Check and correct all work.)

Affix Introduction

1. (Write on the board: **subtract, subject, submit,** and **subscribe.**)
   Each of these words has a morphograph **sub** at the beginning.
   What morphograph? (S) *sub.*

2. Read these words. (Point to **subtract.**)
   What word? (S) *Subtract.*
   What is the first morphograph in **subtract**?
   (S) *sub.*
   What is the next morphograph in **subtract**? (S) *tract.*

3. (Point to **subject.**)
   What word? (S) *Subject.*
   What is the first morphograph in **subject**?
   (S) *sub.*
   What is the next morphograph in **subject**?
   (S) *ject.*

4. (Point to **submit.**)
   What word? (S) *Submit.*
   What is the first morphograph in **submit**?
   (S) *sub.*
   What is the next morphograph in **submit**?
   (S) *mit.*

5. (Point to **subscribe.**)
   What word? (S) *Subscribe.*
   What is the first morphograph in **subscribe**? (S) *sub.*
   What is the next morphograph in **subscribe**? (S) *scribe.*

6. (Erase the board.)
   Everybody, spell the morphograph **tract.**
   Get ready. (S)
   Now spell the word **subtract.**
   Get ready. (S)

7. Everybody, spell the morphograph **ject.**
   Get ready. (S)
   Now spell the word **subject.** Get ready. (S)

8. Everybody, spell the morphograph **mit.**
   Get ready. (S)
   Now spell the word **submit.** Get ready. (S)

9. Everybody, spell the morphograph **scribe.**
   Get ready. (S)
   Now spell the word **subscribe.**
   Get ready. (S)

10. (Repeat spelling of **subtract, subject, submit,** and **subscribe** until firm. Give individual turns.)

Word and Spelling Introduction

1. (Write on the board: **pretty, shave, knife, strain, puff,** and **gulf.**)
   These words are made up of only one morphograph.

2. (Point to **pretty.**)
   What word? (S) *Pretty.*
   Spell **pretty.** Get ready. (S)
   (Repeat this procedure for each word.)

3. (Erase the words.)
   Spell the words again.
   First word: **strain.** Get ready. (S)
   (Repeat until firm.)

4. (Repeat step 3 for **knife, share, puff, gulf,** and **pretty.**)

5. Find part **A** on your worksheet.
   Get ready to write the words you just spelled.

6. First word: **knife.**
   What word? (S) *Knife.*
   Write **knife.**
   (Repeat for **pretty, gulf, puff, strain,** and **share.**)

7. You'll find the spellings of the words we're going to check in appendix **K,** section **B.**

8. (Call on a student.)
   Look up the spelling of the word **knife.**

9. (Assign each of the remaining words to different students.)

10. Get ready to check part **A.**
    Put an **X** next to any word you missed and write that word correctly.

11. (Call on the student who looked up **knife.**)
    Spell **knife.**
    (Write **knife** on the board.)
12. (Repeat step 11 for each remaining word.)

Nonword Base

1. (Write on the board: **vert.**)
   Here is a new morphograph that cannot stand alone.
   It is pronounced **vert.**
   What morphograph? (S) *vert.*
2. Everybody, spell **vert.** Get ready. (S)
   (Repeat until firm.)
3. Get ready to spell words that have the morphograph **vert.**
   First word: **convert.**
   What is the first morphograph in **convert**?
   (S) *con.*
   What is the next morphograph in **convert**?
   (S) *vert.*
   Spell **convert.** Get ready. (S)
4. Next word: **subvert.**
   What is the first morphograph in **subvert**?
   (S) *sub.*
   What is the next morphograph in **subvert**?
   (S) *vert.*
   Spell **subvert.** Get ready. (S)
5. (Repeat step 4 for **revert** and **invert.**)

EXERCISE 4

Spelling Review

1. I'll spell some words quickly.
   See if you can figure out each word.
2. Listen: **f - a - m - i - l - y.**
   Everybody, what word? (S) *Family.*
3. Listen: **d - r - i - v - e - r.**
   What word? (S) *Driver.*
4. (Repeat step 3 for **while, trouble, couple, converge, hidden, tripping, insist, basically, denied, become, lovely, usual,** and **improve.**)
5. Find part **B** on your worksheet.
   Get ready to write some of those words.

6. First word: **while.**
   Write it.
7. Next word: **usual.**
   Write it.
8. (Repeat step 7 for **family, insist, trouble, improve, become,** and **lovely.**)
9. I will spell each word.
   Put an **X** next to any word you missed and write that word correctly.
   (Write each word on the board as you spell it.)

EXERCISE 5

Word Building

Get ready to spell some words that have more than one morphograph.
These words are made up of morphographs that cannot stand alone.

1. First word: **insisting.**
   What is the first morphograph in **insisting**? (S) *in.*
   What is the next morphograph in **insisting**? (S) *sist.*
   What is the next morphograph in **insisting**? (S) *ing.*
   Spell **insisting.** Get ready. (S)
2. Next word: **persist.**
   What is the first morphograph in **persist**?
   (S) *per.*
   What is the next morphograph in **persist**?
   (S) *sist.*
   Spell **persist.** Get ready. (S)
3. (For **transmit, perfection, structuring,** and **recur,** have students identify each morphograph and spell each word.)
4. Find part **C** on your worksheet.
   You are going to write the words you just spelled.
5. First word: **structuring.** Write it.
6. Next word: **perfection.** Write it.
7. (Repeat step 6 for **recur, insisting, transmit,** and **persist.**)
8. (Check spellings and have students rewrite any missed words.)

Independent Work

1. Complete the rest of the worksheet on your own.
   Be sure to read the instructions carefully.
2. (Check and correct all work.)

┌─ **Answer Key** ──────────────

Part D
1. fashion
2. athlete
3. chiefly
4. concept
5. madness
6. basically

━━━━ **EXERCISE 1** ━━━━

Oral Spelling Review

You are going to spell some words made up of morphographs you have spelled before.

1. First word: **merge.**
   What word? (S) *Merge.*
   Spell **merge.** Get ready. (S)
   (Repeat until firm.)
2. Next word: **critic.**
   What word? (S) *Critic.*
   Spell **critic.** Get ready. (S)
   (Repeat until firm.)
3. (Repeat step 2 for **prevent, major, spoiled, speaker, describe, mouth, sweetly, government, speeches, range, trainer, logical, middle, loosely, lively,** and **reasonable.**)

━━━━ **EXERCISE 2** ━━━━

Rule Discrimination

I'll say words.
Figure out whether the **e** rule, the **y**-to-**i** rule, or no rule applies.

1. The first word begins with **state.**
   Spell **state.** Get ready. (S)
   Could a rule apply? (S) *Yes.*
   Which rule? (Call on a student.) *The rule about dropping an e.*
   Everybody, how do you know the **e** rule could apply? (S)
   State ends with an e.
2. The word is **statement.**
   Does the **e** rule apply? (S) *No.*
   How do you know? (Call on a student.)
   Ment does not begin with a vowel letter.
   Spell **statement.** Get ready. (S)

3. The next word begins with **family.**
   Spell **family.** Get ready. (S)
   Could a rule apply? (S) *Yes.*
   Which rule? (Call on a student.) *The rule about changing y to i.*
   Everybody, how do you know the **y**-to-**i** rule could apply? (S)
   Family ends with a consonant-and-y.
4. The word is **families.**
   Does the **y**-to-**i** rule apply? (S) *Yes.*
   How do you know? (Call on a student.)
   Es does not begin with an i.
   Spell **families.** Get ready. (S)
5. The next word begins with **glory.**
   Spell **glory.** Get ready. (S)
   Could a rule apply? (S) *Yes.*
   Which rule? (Call on a student.) *The rule about changing y to i.*
   Everybody, how do you know the **y**-to-**i** rule could apply? (S)
   Glory ends with a consonant-and-y.
6. The word is **glorious.**
   Does the **y**-to-**i** rule apply? (S) *Yes.*
   How do you know? (Call on a student.)
   Ous does not begin with an i.
   Spell **glorious.** Get ready. (S)
7. The next word is **verse.**
   Spell **verse.** Get ready. (S)
   Could a rule apply? (S) *Yes.*
   Which rule? (Call on a student.) *The rule about dropping an e.*
   Everybody, how do you know the **e** rule could apply? (S)
   Verse ends with an e.
8. The word is **version.**
   Does the **e** rule apply? (S) *Yes.*
   How do you know? (Call on a student.)
   Ion begins with a vowel letter.
   Spell **version.** Get ready. (S)

Word Building

Get ready to spell some words that have more than one morphograph.
These words are made up of morphographs that cannot stand alone.

1. First word: **subsisting.**
   What is the first morphograph in **subsisting**? (S) *sub.*
   What is the next morphograph in **subsisting**? (S) *sist.*
   What is the next morphograph in **subsisting**? (S) *ing.*
   Spell **subsisting.** Get ready. (S)
2. Next word: **transmit.**
   What is the first morphograph in **transmit**?
   (S) *trans.*
   What is the next morphograph in **transmit**? (S) *mit.*
   Spell **transmit.** Get ready. (S)
3. (For **recur, defective, instruction,** and **insisted,** have students identify each morphograph and spell each word.)

Proofreading

Find part **A** on your worksheet.

1. The letter in part **A** has some misspelled words.
   You have studied some of the words.
2. If you can find **12** of the words, you earn **7** worksheet points.
   If you can find more than **12** misspellings, you earn **10** worksheet points.
3. Draw a line through each misspelled word. Write it correctly on a line next to the letter.

Answer Key

Part A

February 2, 2001

Dear Hank,

I got the pet lizard you ~~cent~~ me. Thank you ~~vary~~ much. ~~Woold~~ you believe that the little fellow has begun ~~snaping~~ at people? My aunt was ~~plaing~~ with the lizard last ~~nite~~. Her ~~fase~~ was close to the little thing. All at once, the lizard ~~jumpped~~ up and bit her ~~rite~~ on the nose. ~~Luckyly~~, the bite was not bad. She washed her face with ~~plane~~ water. She ~~did'nt~~ have a mark on her face, so you ~~no~~ the bite ~~realy~~ wasn't bad.

Thanks again for the ~~unusoual~~ pet.

Your ~~frend~~,

Emory

sent	plain
very	didn't
Would	know
snapping	really
playing	unusual
night	friend
face	
jumped	
right	
Luckily	

Mastery Test

1. You are going to have a test today. It will help you see how well you are learning to spell.

2. Everybody, take out a sheet of lined paper and draw a line down the middle. Then number the paper from 1 through 20.

3. (Check and correct.)

4. Word 1 is **shelves.**
   We put new **shelves** in the kitchen.
   What word? (S) *Shelves.*
   Write **shelves.**

5. Word 2 is **recover.**
   We need to **recover** the sofa.
   What word? (S) *Recover.*
   Write **recover.**

6. (Repeat step 5 for the remaining words on the list.)

3. **major**	12. **critic**
4. **factual**	13. **beside**
5. **merge**	14. **contest**
6. **spoil**	15. **verge**
7. **thieves**	16. **join**
8. **became**	17. **loaves**
9. **permit**	18. **just**
10. **boyhood**	19. **govern**
11. **classical**	20. **loneliness**

7. Everybody, exchange papers with your partner. (Pause.)

8. I'll spell each word. If the word is not spelled correctly on the paper you're marking, put an **X** next to it.
   If the word is spelled correctly, don't put any mark next to it.

9. Word 1 is **shelves: s - h - e - l - v - e - s.**
   Check it.

10. (Repeat step 9 for each remaining word.)

11. Return your partner's test paper.

12. Now correct any errors you made. If there is an **X** next to a word on your test, write the word correctly in the right column. Raise your hand if you don't know how to spell any words.

13. Turn your paper over when you're finished. I'll come around and check your paper.

14. If you didn't make any mistakes, raise your hand now.

15. Write the number correct at the top of your test.

EXERCISE 1

Spelling Review

1. I'll spell some words quickly.
   See if you can figure out each word.
2. Listen: **p - r - e - t - t - y.**
   Everybody, what word? (S) *Pretty.*
3. Listen: **k - n - i - f - e.**
   What word? (S) *Knife.*
4. (Repeat step 3 for **strain, puffy, convert, family, couple, impress, subscribe, major, critical, unjust, consists, athlete,** and **uncover.**)
5. Find part **A** on your worksheet.
   Get ready to write some of those words.
6. First word: **family.**
   Write it.
7. Next word: **knife.**
   Write it.
8. (Repeat step 7 for **subscribe, uncover, athlete, major, pretty,** and **critical.**)
9. I will spell each word.
   Put an **X** next to any word you missed and write that word correctly.
   (Write each word on the board as you spell it.)

EXERCISE 2

Word Building

Get ready to spell some words that have more than one morphograph.

1. First word: **improving.**
   What is the first morphograph in **improving**? (S) *im.*
   What is the next morphograph in **improving**? (S) *prove.*
   What is the next morphograph in **improving**? (S) *ing.*
   Spell **improving.** Be careful. Get ready. (S)

2. Next word: **becoming.**
   What is the first morphograph in **becoming**? (S) *be.*
   What is the next morphograph in **becoming**? (S) *come.*
   What is the next morphograph in **becoming**? (S) *ing.*
   Spell **becoming.** Be careful. Get ready. (S)
3. (For **brotherhood, compound, perfect, usual, apart, placement,** and **observe,** have students identify each morphograph and spell each word.)
4. Find part **B** on your worksheet.
   You are going to write the words you just spelled.
5. First word: **brotherhood.** Write it.
6. Next word: **placement.** Write it.
7. (Repeat step 6 for **improving, observe, apart, compound, becoming, usual,** and **perfect.**)
8. (Check spellings and have students rewrite any missed words.)

EXERCISE 3

Bingo

Find part **C** on your worksheet.

1. We're going to play bingo.
   I'll dictate words for you to write in the boxes.
2. Remember:
   a. A row may go across, or down, or corner to corner.
   b. The first student or students to get four words in a row earn four bonus points.
   c. If you have misspelled any words in your row, that row won't count for bonus points.
3. First word: **shave.**
   Write **shave** in one of the boxes.
4. Next word: **knife.**
   Write **knife** in one of the boxes.

5. (Repeat step 4 for **gulf, insist, joining, submerge, dressy, spotted, range, actually, across, shelves, shore, restore, photograph,** and **reduce.**)
6. Now we'll mark the boxes.
7. (Spell each word quickly.)
First word: **d - r - e - s - s - y.**
Mark an **X** in the box containing that word.
8. Next word: **r - e - s - t - o - r - e.**
Mark an **X** in the box containing that word.
9. (Repeat step 8 for as many of the following words as necessary: **reduce, shelves, across, spotted, insist, gulf, actually, photograph, submerge, knife, shave, joining, range,** and **shore.**)
10. (When one or more students get a bingo, stop the game and award the bonus points.)

 **EXERCISE 4**

Independent Work

1. Complete the rest of the worksheet on your own.
Be sure to read the instructions carefully.
2. (Check and correct all work.)

┌─ **Answer Key** ──────────────────
│
│ **Part D**
│ 1. run
│ 3. bar
│ 4. fer
│ 6. mit
│ 8. snap
│ 9. shop
│ 11. cur
│ 12. pel
│
└──────────────────────────────────

Supplemental Blackline Masters

Supplemental blackline masters 43 and 44 provide additional practice on material covered in Lessons 106 through 110. You may assign any or all of the activities, and you may award bonus points.

─────── **EXERCISE 1** ───────

Rule Review

Let's go over some of the spelling rules you have learned.

1. Tell me when you double the final **c** in a short word.
   (Pause 2 seconds.) Get ready. (S)
   When the word ends cvc and the next morphograph begins with v.
2. Tell me when you change the **y** to **i** in a word.
   (Pause 2 seconds.) Get ready. (S)
   When the word ends consonant-and-y, and the next morphograph begins with anything except i.
3. (Repeat steps 1 and 2 until students are firm on both rules.)

─────── **EXERCISE 2** ───────

Plural Variation

1. Some of the words I'll say have the sound **vvv** in the plural.
   Some have the sound **fff** in the plural.
2. Listen: **chief.**
   What word? (S) *Chief.*
   What is the plural of **chief**? (S) *Chiefs.*
3. **Loaf.** What word? (S) *Loaf.*
   What is the plural of **loaf**? (S) *Loaves.*
4. **Gulf.** What word? (S) *Gulf.*
   What is the plural of **gulf**? (S) *Gulfs.*
5. Get ready to spell those words.
6. **Chief.** (Pause.) Spell it. Get ready. (S)
   Say the plural of **chief.** (S) *Chiefs.*
   Spell **chiefs.** Get ready. (S)
   Yes, it is spelled just like it sounds.
7. **Loaf.** (Pause.) Spell it. Get ready. (S)
   Say the plural of **loaf.** (S) *Loaves.*
   Spell **loaves.** Get ready. (S)
8. **Gulf.** (Pause.) Spell it. Get ready. (S)
   Say the plural of **gulf.** (S) *Gulfs.*
   Spell **gulfs.** Get ready. (S)

─────── **EXERCISE 3** ───────

Plural-Variation Worksheet

Everybody, find part **A** on your worksheet.

1. Some of these words have the sound **fff** in the plural.
   Some have the sound **vvv** in the plural.
   Write the plural for each word.
2. You have one and a half minutes to write the plurals.
3. (At the end of one and a half minutes . . .)
   Stop. We are going to check the words you just wrote.
   Put an **X** next to any word you missed and write that word correctly.
4. The first word is **chief.**
   Everybody, what is the plural of **chief**?
   (S) *Chiefs.*
5. Yes, you can hear the sound **fff** in chiefs.
   Everybody, spell **chiefs.** Get ready. (S)
   (Pause for corrections.)
6. (Repeat steps 4 and 5 for **thief-thieves, gulf-gulfs,** and **wolf-wolves.**)

─────── **EXERCISE 4** ───────

Affix Introduction

1. (Write on the board: **eject, emit, emerge, and event.**)
   Each of these words has a morphograph **e** at the beginning.
   What morphograph? (S) *e.*
2. Read these words. (Point to **eject.**)
   What word? (S) *Eject.*
   What is the first morphograph in **eject**?
   (S) *e.*
   What is the next morphograph in **eject**?
   (S) *ject.*

3. (Point to **emit**.)
   What word? (S) *Emit.*
   What is the first morphograph in **emit**?
   (S) *e.*
   What is the next morphograph in **emit**?
   (S) *mit.*
4. (Point to **emerge**.)
   What word? (S) *Emerge.*
   What is the first morphograph in **emerge**?
   (S) *e.*
   What is the next morphograph in **emerge**?
   (S) *merge.*
5. (Point to **event**.)
   What word? (S) *Event.*
   What is the first morphograph in **event**?
   (S) *e.*
   What is the next morphograph in **event**?
   (S) *vent.*
6. (Erase the board.)
   Everybody, spell the morphograph **ject.**
   Get ready. (S)
   Now spell the word **eject.** Get ready. (S)
7. Everybody, spell the morphograph **mit.**
   Get ready. (S)
   Now spell the word **emit.** Get ready. (S)
8. Everybody, spell the morphograph **merge.**
   Get ready. (S)
   Now spell the word **emerge.** Get ready. (S)
9. Everybody, spell the word **vent.**
   Get ready. (S)
   Now spell the word **event.** Get ready. (S)
10. (Repeat spelling of **eject, emerge,** and
    event until firm. Give individual turns.)

EXERCISE 5

Word Building

Get ready to spell some words that have more
than one morphograph.

1. First word: **subhuman.**
   What is the first morphograph in
   subhuman? (S) *sub.*
   What is the next morphograph in
   subhuman? (S) *human.*
   Spell **subhuman.** Get ready. (S)

2. Next word: **impress.**
   What is the first morphograph in **impress**?
   (S) *im.*
   What is the next morphograph in
   impress? (S) *press.*
   Spell **impress.** Get ready. (S)
3. (For **boyhood, actual, compel, pertain,
   aside, department,** and **observe,** have
   students identify each morphograph and
   spell each word.)
4. Find part **B** on your worksheet.
   You are going to write the words you
   just spelled.
5. First word: **compel.** Write it.
6. Next word: **aside.** Write it.
7. (Repeat step 6 for **subhuman, observe,
   impress, department, boyhood, pertain,**
   and **actual.**)

EXERCISE 6

Independent Work

1. Complete the rest of the worksheet on
   your own.
   Be sure to read the instructions carefully.
2. (Check and correct all work.)

┌─ **Answer Key** ─────────────────────

Part C		Part D	
2.	mit	1.	before
3.	chin	2.	classically
4.	cur	3.	subtract
7.	fer	4.	knives
9.	pel	5.	choose
10.	trip	6.	defect

Word and Spelling Introduction

1. (Write on the board: **body, wise, puzzle, table,** and **solve.**)
   These words are made up of only one morphograph.
2. (Point to **body.**)
   What word? (S) *Body.*
   Spell **body.** Get ready. (S)
   (Repeat this procedure for each word.)
3. (Erase the words.)
   Spell the words again.
   First word: **table.** Get ready. (S)
   (Repeat until firm.)
4. (Repeat step 3 for **wise, puzzle, solve,** and **body.**)
5. Find part **A** on your worksheet.
   Get ready to write the words you just spelled.
6. First word: **puzzle.**
   What word? (S) *Puzzle.*
   Write **puzzle.**
   (Repeat for **body, table, solve,** and **wise.**)
7. You'll find the spellings of the words we're going to check in appendix **L,** section **C.**
8. (Call on a student.)
   Look up the spelling of the word **puzzle.**
9. (Assign each of the remaining words to different students.)
10. Get ready to check part **A.**
    Put an **X** next to any word you missed and write that word correctly.
11. (Call on the student who looked up **puzzle.**)
    Spell **puzzle.**
    (Write **puzzle** on the board.)
12. (Repeat step 11 for each remaining word.)

Homonyms

1. (Write on the board: **week.**)
   This word is **week.** What word? (S) *Week.*
2. This **week** does not mean: **not strong.**
   This **week** means: **seven days.**
   What does this **week** mean?
   (S) *Seven days.*
3. And how is it spelled? Get ready. (S)
4. (Erase the board.)
   Spell **week** again. Get ready. (S)
5. Remember that word.

Word and Spelling Introduction— Fast Cycle

Everybody, find part **B** on your worksheet.

1. (Call on a student.)
   Read the instructions for part **B.**
   Study these words on your own. There will be a test on these words during your next spelling lesson.
2. Study the words in part **B** after you have finished your worksheet.
   Everyone should do well on the test over these words.
   (Students may study individually or in pairs.)

Spelling Review

1. I'll spell some words quickly.
   See if you can figure out each word.
2. Listen: **s - t - r - e - n - g - t - h - e - n.**
   Everybody, what word? (S) *Strengthen.*
3. Listen: **c - r - i - t - i - c - a - l.**
   What word? (S) *Critical.*
4. (Repeat step 3 for **insist, instruction, double, family, pretty, major, subscribe, impression, usually,** and **belong.**)

5. Find part **C** on your worksheet.
   Get ready to write some of those words.
6. First word: **instruction.** Write it.
7. Next word: **family.** Write it.
8. (Repeat step 7 for **major, strengthen, usually,** and **pretty.**)
9. I will spell each word.
   Put an **X** next to any word you missed and write that word correctly.
   (Write each word on the board as you spell it.)

━━━━━━━━━ **EXERCISE 5** ━━━━━━━━━

Doubling Rule

1. (Write on the board: **perform, recur, spot, transfer, debug, rob,** and **concur.**)
2. Everybody, when do you double the final **C** in short words? (S)
   When the word ends cvc and the next morphograph begins with v.
3. You are going to use that rule for some new words.
   Listen: When the word ends in a short **CVC** morphograph, use the doubling rule.
   Listen again: When the word ends in a short **CVC** morphograph, use the doubling rule.
4. Everybody, tell me the new rule. (Pause.)
   Get ready. (S)
   When the word ends in a short cvc morphograph, use the doubling rule.
   (Repeat until firm.)
5. (Point to **recur.**)
6. **Recur** ends in a short **CVC** morphograph, so you double when you spell **recurring.**
   Everybody, spell **recurring.** Get ready. (S)
7. (Point to **rob.**)
   This word ends in a short **CVC** morphograph. Tell me what that morphograph is. (Pause.) Get ready. (S) *rob.*

> **To correct:**
> The entire word **rob** is a short **CVC** morphograph.

8. **Rob** ends in a **CVC** morphograph, so you double when you spell **robbing.**
   Everybody, spell **robbing.** Get ready. (S)
9. (Point to **perform.**)
   Tell me, does this word end in a short **CVC** morphograph? (S) *No.*
   So do you double when you spell **performing**? (S) *No.*
   Everybody, spell **performing.** Get ready. (S)
10. (Point to **spot.**)
    Tell me, does this word end in a short **CVC** morphograph? (S) *Yes.*
    Tell me what the morphograph is. (Pause.) Get ready. (S) *spot.*

> **To correct:**
> The entire word **spot** is a short **CVC** morphograph.

11. So do you double when you spell **spotting**? (S) *Yes.*
    Everybody, spell **spotting.** Get ready. (S)
12. (Point to **transfer.**)
    Tell me, does this word end in a short **CVC** morphograph? (S) *Yes.*
    Tell me what that morphograph is. (Pause.) Get ready. (S) *fer.*
13. So do you double when you spell **transferring**? (S) *Yes.*
    Everybody, spell **transferring.** Get ready. (S)
14. (Point to **debug.**)
    Tell me, does this word end in a short **CVC** morphograph? (S) *Yes.*
    Tell me what that morphograph is. (Pause.) Get ready. (S) *bug.*
15. So do you double when you spell **debugging**? (S) *Yes.*
    Everybody, spell **debugging.** Get ready. (S)
16. (Point to **concur.**)
    Tell me, does this word end in a short **CVC** morphograph? (S) *Yes.*
    Tell me what that morphograph is. (Pause.) Get ready. (S) *cur.*
17. So do you double when you spell **concurring**? (S) *Yes.*
    Everybody, spell **concurring.** Get ready. (S)

Independent Work

1. Complete the rest of the worksheet on your own.
   Be sure to read the instructions carefully.
2. (Check and correct all work.)

━━━━━ **EXERCISE 1** ━━━━━

Affix Introduction

1. (Write on the board: **admit, advise, adverb,** and **adjust.**)
   Each of these words has a morphograph **ad** at the beginning.
   What morphograph? (S) *ad.*
2. Read these words. (Point to **admit.**)
   What word? (S) *Admit.*
   What is the first morphograph in **admit**?
   (S) *ad.*
   What is the next morphograph in **admit**?
   (S) *mit.*
3. (Point to **advise.**)
   What word? (S) *Advise.*
   What is the first morphograph in **advise**?
   (S) *ad.*
   What is the next morphograph in **advise**?
   (S) *vise.*
4. (Point to **adverb.**)
   What word? (S) *Adverb.*
   What is the first morphograph in **adverb**?
   (S) *ad.*
   What is the next morphograph in **adverb**?
   (S) *verb.*
5. (Point to **adjust.**)
   What word? (S) *Adjust.*
   What is the first morphograph in **adjust**?
   (S) *ad.*
   What is the next morphograph in **adjust**?
   (S) *just.*
6. (Erase the board.)
   Everybody, spell the morphograph **mit.**
   Get ready. (S)
   Now spell the word **admit.** Get ready. (S)
7. Everybody, spell the word **vise.**
   Get ready. (S)
   Now spell the word **advise.** Get ready. (S)
8. Everybody, spell the word **verb.**
   Get ready. (S)
   Now spell the word **adverb.** Get ready. (S)
9. Everybody, spell the word **just.**
   Get ready. (S)
   Now spell the word **adjust.** Get ready. (S)
10. (Repeat spelling of **admit, advise, adverb,** and **adjust** until firm. Give individual turns.)

━━━━━ **EXERCISE 2** ━━━━━

Word and Spelling Introduction

1. (Write on the board: **ply, build, lake,** and **script.**)
   These words are made up of only one morphograph.
2. (Point to **ply.**)
   What word? (S) *ply.*
   Spell **ply.** Get ready. (S)
   (Repeat this procedure for each word.)
3. (Erase the board.)
   Spell the words again.
   First word: **script.** Get ready. (S)
   (Repeat until firm.)
4. (Repeat step 3 for **build, ply,** and **lake.**)
5. Find part **A** on your worksheet.
   Get ready to write the words you just spelled.
6. First word: **build.**
   What word? (S) *Build.*
   Write **build.**
   (Repeat for **ply, script,** and **lake.**)
7. You'll find the spellings of the words we're going to check in appendix **L,** section **C.**
8. (Call on a student.)
   Look up the spelling of the word **build.**
9. (Assign each of the remaining words to different students.)
10. Get ready to check part **A.**
    Put an **X** next to any word you missed and write that word correctly.
11. (Call on the student who looked up **build.**)
    Spell **build.**
    (Write **build** on the board.)
12. (Repeat step 11 for each remaining word.)

EXERCISE 3

Fast-Cycle Test

Everybody, find part **B** on your worksheet.

1. You are going to write the words you studied during Lesson 113.
2. First word: Write **red.**
3. Next word: Write **cut.**
4. (Repeat step 3 for **gum, top, bud, pan, car, gas,** and **hog.**)
5. (Check and correct.)

EXERCISE 4

Nonword Base

1. (Write on the board: **ceive.**)
   Here is a new morphograph that cannot stand alone.
   It is pronounced **ceive.**
   What morphograph? (S) *ceive.*
2. Everybody, spell **ceive.** Get ready. (S)
   (Repeat until firm.)
3. Get ready to spell words that have the morphograph **ceive.**
   First word: **receive.**
   What is the first morphograph in **receive**?
   (S) *re.*
   What is the next morphograph in **receive**?
   (S) *ceive.*
   Spell **receive.** Get ready. (S)
4. Next word: **conceive.**
   What is the first morphograph in **conceive**? (S) *con.*
   What is the next morphograph in **conceive**? (S) *ceive.*
   Spell **conceive.** Get ready. (S)
5. (Repeat step 4 for **deceive** and **perceive.**)

EXERCISE 5

Plural Variation

1. Some of the words I'll say have the sound **vvv** in the plural.
   Some have the sound **fff** in the plural.
2. Listen: **loaf.**
   What word? (S) *Loaf.*
   What is the plural of **loaf**? (S) *Loaves.*

3. **Gulf.** What word? (S) *Gulf.*
   What is the plural of **gulf**? (S) *Gulfs.*
4. **Puff.** What word? (S) *Puff.*
   What is the plural of **puff**? (S) *Puffs.*
5. Get ready to spell some words.
6. **Loaf.** (Pause.) Spell it. Get ready. (S)
   Say the plural of **loaf.** (S) *Loaves.*
   Spell **loaves.** Get ready. (S)
   Yes, it is spelled just like it sounds.
7. **Gulf.** (Pause.) Spell it. Get ready. (S)
   Say the plural of **gulf.** (S) *Gulfs.*
   Spell **gulfs.** Get ready. (S)
8. **Puff.** (Pause.) Spell it. Get ready. (S)
   Say the plural of **puff.** (S) *Puffs.*
   Spell **puffs.** Get ready. (S)

EXERCISE 6

Plural-Variation Worksheet

Everybody, find part **C** on your worksheet.

1. Some of these words have the sound **fff** in the plural.
   Some have the sound **vvv** in the plural.
   Write the plural for each word.
2. You have one and a half minutes to write the plurals.
3. (At the end of one and a half minutes. . .)
   Stop. We are going to check the words you just wrote.
   Put an **X** next to any word you missed and write that word correctly.
4. The first word is **puff.**
   Everybody, what is the plural of **puff**?
   (S) *Puffs.*
5. Yes, you can hear the sound **fff** in **puffs.**
   Everybody, spell **puffs.** Get ready. (S)
   (Pause for corrections.)
6. (Repeat steps 4 and 5 for **self-selves, half-halves,** and **chief-chiefs.**)

LESSON 114   **97**

Doubling Rule

1. (Write on the board: **transmit, red, strain,** and **spot.**)

2. Remember when you use the doubling rule.
   Everybody, tell me when you use the doubling rule. (Pause.) Get ready. (S) *When the word ends in a short cvc morphograph.*
   (Repeat until firm.)

3. (Point to **transmit.**)
   Tell me, does this word end in a short **CVC** morphograph? (S) *Yes.*
   Tell me what that morphograph is. (Pause.) Get ready. (S) *mit.*

4. So do you double when you spell **transmitter**? (S) *Yes.*
   Everybody, spell **transmitter.**
   Get ready. (S)

5. (Point to **red.**)
   Tell me, does this word end in a short **CVC** morphograph? (S) *Yes.*
   Tell me what that morphograph is. (Pause.) Get ready. (S) *red.*

6. So do you double when you spell **redder**? (S) *Yes.*
   Everybody, spell **redder.** Get ready. (S)

7. (Point to **strain.**)
   Tell me, does this word end in a short **CVC** morphograph? (S) *No.*
   So do you double when you spell **strainer**? (S) *No.*

8. (Point to **spot.**)
   Tell me, does this word end in a short **CVC** morphograph? (S) *Yes.*
   Tell me what that morphograph is. (Pause.) Get ready. (S) *Spot.*

9. So do you double when you spell **spotter**? (S) *Yes.*
   Everybody, spell **spotter.** Get ready. (S)

Independent Work

1. Complete the rest of the worksheet on your own.
   Be sure to read the instructions carefully.

2. (Check and correct all work.)

Lesson 115

EXERCISE 1

Word and Spelling Introduction

1. (Write on the board: **bought, fought, ought, brought,** and **day.**)
    These words are made up of only one morphograph.
2. (Point to **bought.**)
    What word? (S) *Bought.*
    Spell **bought.** Get ready. (S)
    (Repeat this procedure for each word.)
3. (Erase the words.)
    Spell the words again.
    First word: **ought.** Get ready. (S)
    (Repeat until firm.)
4. (Repeat step 3 for **fought, brought, day,** and **bought.**)
5. Find part **A** on your worksheet.
    Get ready to write the words you just spelled.
6. First word: **fought.**
    What word? (S) *Fought.*
    Write **fought.**
    (Repeat for **bought, brought, day,** and **ought.**)
7. You'll find the spellings of the words we're going to check in appendix **L,** section **C.**
8. (Call on a student.)
    Look up the spelling of the word **fought.**
9. (Assign each of the remaining words to different students.)
10. Get ready to check part **A.**
    Put an **X** next to any word you missed and write that word correctly.
11. (Call on the student who looked up **fought.**)
    Spell **fought.**
    (Write **fought** on the board.)
12. (Repeat step 11 for each remaining word.)

EXERCISE 2

Homonyms

1. (Write on the board: **weak.**)
    This word is **weak.** What word? (S) *Weak.*
2. This **weak** means: **not strong.**
    What does this **weak** mean? (S) *Not strong.*
3. And how is it spelled? Get ready. (S)
4. Everybody, spell the **weak** that means: **not strong.** Get ready. (S)
5. Everybody, spell the **week** that means: **seven days.** Get ready. (S)
6. (Repeat steps 4 and 5 until firm. Give individual turns.)

EXERCISE 3

Plural Variation

1. Get ready to spell some words.
2. **Life.** (Pause.) Spell it. Get ready. (S)
    Say the plural of **life.** (S) *Lives.*
    Spell **lives.** Get ready. (S)
3. **Book.** (Pause.) Spell it. Get ready. (S)
    Say the plural of **book.** (S) *Books.*
    Spell **books.** Get ready. (S)
4. **Wife.** (Pause.) Spell it. Get ready. (S)
    Say the plural of **wife.** (S) *Wives.*
    Spell **wives.** Get ready. (S)
5. **Puff.** (Pause.) Spell it. Get ready. (S)
    Say the plural of **puff.** (S) *Puffs.*
    Spell **puffs.** Get ready. (S)

EXERCISE 4

Spelling Review

1. I'll spell some words quickly.
    See if you can figure out each word.
2. Listen: **t - h - o - u - g - h - t.**
    Everybody, what word. (S) *Thought.*
3. Listen: **c - u - r - a - b - l - e.**
    What word? (S) *Curable.*

4. (Repeat step 3 for **cutting, script, builder, puzzle, solve, strain, major, stretch, recover,** and **fashion.**)
5. Find part **B** on your worksheet.
   Get ready to write some of those words.
6. First word: **solve.** Write it.
7. Next word: **recover.** Write it.
8. (Repeat step 7 for **puzzle, fashion, thought,** and **stretch.**)
9. I will spell each word.
   Put an **X** next to any word you missed and write that word correctly.
   (Write each word on the board as you spell it.)

Word Building

Get ready to spell some words that have more than one morphograph.
These words are made up of morphographs that cannot stand alone.

1. First word: **receive.**
   What is the first morphograph in **receive**? (S) *re.*
   What is the next morphograph in **receive**? (S) *ceive.*
   Spell **receive.** Get ready. (S)
2. Next word: **subvert.**
   What is the first morphograph in **subvert**? (S) *sub.*
   What is the next morphograph in **subvert**? (S) *vert.*
   Spell **subvert.** Get ready. (S)
3. (For **vertical, permit, obtain, improvise, disinfect,** and **deceive,** have students identify each morphograph and spell each word.)
4. Find part **C** on your worksheet.
   You are going to write the words you just spelled.
5. First word: **permit.** Write it.
6. Next word: **deceive.** Write it.
7. (Repeat step 6 for **receive, disinfect, subvert, improvise, vertical,** and **obtain.**)
8. (Check spellings and have students rewrite any missed word.)

Doubling Rule

1. (Write on the board: **snap, ship, incur, reform, permit,** and **propel.**)
2. Remember when you use the doubling rule.
   Everybody, tell me when you use the doubling rule. (Pause.)
   Get ready. (S) *When the word ends in a short cvc morphograph.*
   (Repeat until firm.)
3. (Point to **snap.**)
   Tell me, does this word end in a short **CVC** morphograph? (S) *Yes.*
   Tell me what that morphograph is. (Pause.)
   Get ready. (S) *Snap.*
4. So do you double when you spell **snapped**? (S) *Yes.*
   Everybody, spell **snapped.** Get ready. (S)
5. (Point to **ship.**)
   Tell me, does this word end in a short **CVC** morphograph? (S) *Yes.*
   Tell me what that morphograph is. (Pause.)
   Get ready. (S) *Ship.*
6. So do you double when you spell **shipped**? (S) *Yes.*
   Everybody, spell **shipped.** Get ready. (S)
7. (Point to **incur.**)
   Tell me, does this word end in a short **CVC** morphograph? (S) *Yes.*
   Tell me what that morphograph is. (Pause.)
   Get ready. (S) *cur.*
8. So do you double when you spell **incurred**? (S) *Yes.*
   Everybody, spell **incurred.** Get ready. (S)
9. (Point to **reform.**)
   Tell me, does this word end in a short **CVC** morphograph? (S) *No.*
   So do you double when you spell **reformed**? (S) *No.*
10. (Point to **permit.**)
    Tell me, does this word end in a short **CVC** morphograph? (S) *Yes.*
    Tell me what that morphograph is. (Pause.)
    Get ready. (S) *mit.*
11. So do you double when you spell **permitted**? (S) *Yes.*
    Everybody, spell **permitted.** Get ready. (S)

12. (Point to **propel.**)
Tell me, does this word end in a short **CVC** morphograph? (S) *Yes.*
Tell me what that morphograph is. (Pause.)
Get ready. (S) *pel.*
13. So do you double when you spell **propeller**? (S) *Yes.*
Everybody, spell **propeller.** Get ready. (S)

━━━━━━━━ **EXERCISE 7** ━━━━━━━━

Independent Work

1. Complete the rest of the worksheet on your own.
Be sure to read the instructions carefully.
2. (Check and correct all work.)

┌─ **Answer Key** ─────────────────
│
│ **Part D**
│ 1. leaves
│ 2. calves
│ 3. chiefs
│ 4. lives
│ 5. thieves
│ 6. safes
│
└────────────────────────────

Lesson 116

====== EXERCISE 1 ======

Affix Introduction

1. Write on the board: **courtship, friendship,** and **hardship.**)
   Each of these words has a morphograph **ship** at the end.
   What morphograph? (S) *ship*.

2. Read these words. (Point to **courtship.**)
   What word? (S) *Courtship*.
   What is the first morphograph in **courtship**? (S) *court*.
   What is the next morphograph in **courtship**? (S) *ship*.

3. (Point to **friendship.**)
   What word? (S) *Friendship*.
   What is the first morphograph in **friendship**? (S) *friend*.
   What is the next morphograph in **friendship**? (S) *ship*.

4. (Point to **hardship.**)
   What word? (S) *Hardship*.
   What is the first morphograph in **hardship**? (S) *hard*.
   What is the next morphograph in **hardship**? (S) *ship*.

5. (Erase the board.)
   Everybody, spell the word **court**.
   Get ready. (S)
   Now spell the word **courtship**.
   Get ready. (S)

6. Everybody, spell the word **friend**.
   Get ready. (S)
   Now spell the word **friendship**.
   Get ready. (S)

7. Everybody, spell the word **hard**.
   Get ready. (S)
   Now spell the word **hardship**.
   Get ready. (S)

8. (Repeat spelling of **courtship, friendship,** and **hardship** until firm.
   Give individual turns.)

====== EXERCISE 2 ======

Word and Spelling Introduction

1. (Write on the board: **add, sect,** and **stance.**)
   These words are made up of only one morphograph.

2. (Point to **add.**)
   What word? (S) *Add*.
   Spell **add**. Get ready. (S)
   (Repeat this procedure for each word.)

3. (Erase the words.)
   Spell the words again.
   First word: **stance.** Get ready. (S)
   (Repeat until firm.)

4. (Repeat step 3 for **sect** and **add.**)

5. Find part **A** on your worksheet.
   Get ready to write the words you just spelled.

6. First word: **sect.**
   What word? (S) *Sect*.
   Write **sect.**
   (Repeat for **add** and **stance.**)

7. You'll find the spelling of the words we're going to check in appendix **L,** section **C.**

8. (Call on a student.)
   Look up the spelling of the word **sect.**

9. (Assign each of the remaining words to different students.)

10. Get ready to check part **A.**
    Put an **X** next to any word you missed and write that word correctly.

11. (Call on the student who looked up **sect.**)
    Spell **sect.**
    (Write **sect** on the board.)

12. (Repeat step 11 for each remaining word.)

LESSON 116

EXERCISE 3

Homonyms

1. Everybody, spell the **week** that means: **seven days.** Get ready. (S)
2. Everybody, spell the **weak** that means: **not strong.** Get ready. (S)
3. (Repeat steps 1 and 2 until firm. Give individual turns.)

EXERCISE 4

Doubling Rule

1. (Write on the board: **concur, trip, adjust, gum, refer,** and **court.**)
2. Remember when you use the doubling rule.
   Everybody, tell me when you use the doubling rule. (Pause.)
   Get ready. (S) *When the word ends in a short cvc morphograph.*
   (Repeat until firm.)
3. (Point to **concur.**)
   Tell me, does this word end in a short **CVC** morphograph? (S) *Yes.*
   Tell me what that morphograph is. (Pause.)
   Get ready. (S) *cur.*
4. So do you double when you spell **concurred**? (S) *Yes.*
   Everybody, spell **concurred.** Get ready. (S)
5. (Point to **trip.**)
   Tell me, does this word end in a short **CVC** morphograph? (S) *Yes.*
   Tell me what that morphograph is. (Pause.)
   Get ready. (S) *trip.*
6. So do you double when you spell **tripped**? (S) *Yes.*
   Everybody, spell **tripped.** Get ready. (S)
7. (Point to **adjust.**)
   Tell me, does this word end in a short **CVC** morphograph? (S) *No.*
   So do you double when you spell **adjusted**? (S) *No.*
8. (Point to **gum.**)
   Tell me, does this word end in a short **CVC** morphograph? (S) *Yes.*
   Tell me what that morphograph is. (Pause.)
   Get ready. (S) *gum.*
9. So do you double when you spell **gummed**? (S) *Yes.*
   Everybody, spell **gummed.** Get ready. (S)
10. (Point to **refer.**)
    Tell me, does this word end in a short **CVC** morphograph? (S) *Yes.*
    Tell me what that morphograph is. (Pause.)
    Get ready. (S) *fer.*
11. So do you double when you spell **referred**? (S) *Yes.*
    Everybody, spell **referred.** Get ready. (S)
12. (Point to **court.**)
    Tell me, does this word end in a short **CVC** morphograph? (S) *No.*
    So do you double when you spell **courted**? (S) *No.*

EXERCISE 5

Nonword Base

1. (Write on the board: **sume.**)
   Here is a new morphograph that cannot stand alone.
   It is pronounced **sume** or **zume.**
   What morphograph? (S) *sume.*
2. Everybody, spell **sume.** Get ready. (S)
   (Repeat until firm.)
3. Get ready to spell words that have the morphograph **sume.**
   First word: **resume.**
   What is the first morphograph in **resume**? (S) *re.*
   What is the next morphograph in **resume**? (S) *sume.*
   Spell **resume.** Get ready. (S)
4. Next word: **consumer.**
   What is the first morphograph in **consumer**? (S) *con.*
   What is the next morphograph in **consumer**? (S) *sume.*
   What is the next morphograph in **consumer**? (S) *er.*
   Spell **consumer.** Be careful. Get ready. (S)
5. Next word: **presume.**
   What is the first morphograph in **presume**? (S) *pre.*
   What is the next morphograph in **presume**? (S) *sume.*
   Spell **presume.** Get ready. (S)

Plural Variation

1. Get ready to spell some words.
2. **Wife.** (Pause.) Spell it. Get ready. (S)
   Say the plural of **wife.** (S) *Wives.*
   Spell **wives.** Get ready. (S)
3. **Graph.** (Pause.) Spell it. Get ready. (S)
   Say the plural of **graph.** (S) *Graphs.*
   Spell **graphs.** Get ready. (S)
4. **Half.** (Pause.) Spell it. Get ready. (S)
   Say the plural of **half.** (S) *Halves.*
   Spell **halves.** Get ready. (S)
5. **Shelf.** (Pause.) Spell it. Get ready. (S)
   Say the plural of **shelf.** (S) *Shelves.*
   Spell **shelves.** Get ready. (S)
6. **Knife.** (Pause.) Spell it. Get ready. (S)
   Say the plural of **knife.** (S) *Knives.*
   Spell **knives.** Get ready. (S)
7. **Chief.** (Pause.) Spell it. Get ready. (S)
   Say the plural of **chief.** (S) *Chiefs.*
   Spell **chiefs.** Get ready. (S)

Proofreading Letters

Find part **B** on your worksheet.

1. The letter in part **B** has misspelled words. You have studied some of the words.
2. If you can find at least 10 of the misspelled words, you get zero errors for part **B**. 9 words equal 1 error, 8 words equal 2 errors, and so on.
3. Draw a line through each misspelled word. Write it correctly on a line next to the letter.

Supplemental Blackline Masters

Supplemental blackline masters 45 and 46 provide additional practice on material covered in Lessons 111 through 115. You may assign any or all of the activities, and you may award bonus points.

Answer Key

Part B

January 14, 2001

Dear Customer:

Are you ~~spinding~~ more time than you need to on nasty household jobs? I'm ~~righting~~ to ~~infrom~~ you that we are now ~~produsing~~ the most ~~usefull~~ home appliance ever made. The new E-Z Home Unit can do ~~thousans~~ of jobs in your home. It changes the sheets on your family beds. It replaces bad ~~fuzes~~ and ~~protecs~~ your house from burglars. It will water any plants that you have growing in your house. It also ~~washs~~ windows, serves your dinner, and cures bad ~~breth~~. It comes packed in ~~reuseable~~ cardboard boxes. The E-Z Home Unit can ~~easyly~~ be put together using ~~helpfull~~ ~~instrucshuns~~ that come with each order.

Please send us your order today.

Sincerely,

I.M. Selling

spending	reusable
writing	easily
inform	helpful
producing	instructions
useful	
thousands	
fuses	
protects	
washes	
breath	

Lesson 117

EXERCISE 1

Affix Introduction

1. (Write on the board: **support, suppose, and supply.**)
   Each of these words has a morphograph **sup** at the beginning.
   What morphograph? (S) *sup.*
2. Read these words. (Point to **support.**)
   What word? (S) *Support.*
   What is the first morphograph in **support**? (S) *sup.*
   What is the next morphograph in **support**? (S) *port.*
3. (Point to **suppose.**)
   What word? (S) *Suppose.*
   What is the first morphograph in **suppose**? (S) *sup.*
   What is the next morphograph in **suppose**? (S) *pose.*
4. (Point to **supply.**)
   What word? (S) *Supply.*
   What is the first morphograph in **supply**? (S) *sup.*
   What is the next morphograph in **supply**? (S) *ply.*
5. (Erase the board.)
   Everybody, spell the word **port.**
   Get ready. (S)
   Now spell the word **support.**
   Get ready. (S)
6. Everybody, spell the word **pose.**
   Get ready. (S)
   Now spell the word **suppose.**
   Get ready. (S)
7. Everybody, spell the word **ply.**
   Get ready. (S)
   Now spell the word **supply.** Get ready. (S)
8. (Repeat spelling of **suppose, support, and supply** until firm.
   Give individual turns.)

EXERCISE 2

Word and Spelling Introduction

1. (Write on the board: **view, science, circle, and watch.**)
   These words are made up of only one morphograph.
2. (Point to **view.**)
   What word? (S) *View.*
   Spell **view.** Get ready. (S)
   (Repeat this procedure for each word.)
3. (Erase the words.)
   Spell the words again.
   First word: **watch.** Get ready. (S)
   (Repeat until firm.)
4. (Repeat step 3 for **science, circle,** and **view.**)
5. Find part **A** on your worksheet.
   Get ready to write the words you just spelled.
6. First word: **circle.**
   What word? (S) *Circle.*
   Write **circle.**
   (Repeat for **view, watch,** and **science.**)
7. You'll find the spellings of the words we're going to check in appendix **L,** section **C.**
8. (Call on a student.)
   Look up the spelling of the word **circle.**
9. (Assign each of the remaining words to different students.)
10. Get ready to check part **A.**
    Put an **X** next to any word you missed and write that word correctly.
11. (Call on the student who looked up **circle.**)
    Spell **circle.**
    (Write **circle** on the board.)
12. (Repeat step 11 for each remaining word.)

LESSON 117   105

Oral Spelling Review

You are going to spell some words made up of morphographs you have spelled before.

1. First word: **poison.**
   What word? (S) *Poison.*
   Spell **poison.** Get ready. (S)
   (Repeat until firm.)
2. Next word: **berries.**
   What word? (S) *Berries.*
   Spell **berries.** Get ready. (S)
   (Repeat until firm.)
3. (Repeat step 2 for **recover, statement, breathless, friendliness, danger,** and **admit.**)

Doubling Rule

1. (Write on the board: **transmit, red, strain,** and **rob.**)
2. Remember when you use the doubling rule.
   Everybody, tell me when you use the doubling rule. (Pause.) Get ready. (S)
   When the word ends in a short cvc morphograph.
   (Repeat until firm.)
3. (Point to **transmit.**)
   Tell me, does this word end in a short **CVC** morphograph? (S) *Yes.*
   Tell me what that morphograph is. (Pause.) Get ready. (S) *mit.*
4. So do you double when you spell **transmitter**? (S) *Yes.*
   Everybody, spell **transmitter.** Get ready. (S)
5. (Point to **red.**)
   Tell me, does this word end in a short **CVC** morphograph? (S) *Yes.*
   Tell me what that morphograph is. (Pause.) Get ready. (S) *red.*
6. So do you double when you spell **redder**? (S) *Yes.*
   Everybody, spell **redder.** Get ready. (S)

7. (Point to **strain.**)
   Tell me, does this word end in a short **CVC** morphograph? (S) *No.*
   So do you double when you spell **strainer**? (S) *No.*
8. (Point to **rob.**)
   Tell me, does this word end in a short **CVC** morphograph? (S) *Yes.*
   Tell me what that morphograph is. (Pause.) Get ready. (S) *rob.*
9. So do you double when you spell **robber**? (S) *Yes.*
   Everybody, spell **robber.** Get ready. (S)

Word Building

Get ready to spell some words that have more than one morphograph.
These words are made up of morphographs that cannot stand alone.

1. First word: **resume.**
   What is the first morphograph in **resume**? (S) *re.*
   What is the next morphograph in **resume**? (S) *sume.*
   Spell **resume.** Get ready. (S)
2. Next word: **deceive.**
   What is the first morphograph in **deceive**? (S) *de.*
   What is the next morphograph in **deceive**? (S) *ceive.*
   Spell **deceive.** Get ready. (S)
3. (For **propel, converted, insisting,** and **recur,** have students identify each morphograph and spell each word.)
4. Find part **B** on your worksheet.
   You are going to write the words you just spelled.
5. First word: **converted.** Write it.
6. Next word: **deceive.** Write it.
7. (Repeat step 6 for **resume, insisting, recur,** and **propel.**)
8. (Check spellings and have students rewrite any missed word.)

Morphograph Analysis

Everybody, find part **C** on your worksheet.

1. Each word in part **C** has a morphograph that you have not been taught.
   Here is how to find those morphographs. You identify all the morphographs in the word that you know. The part that is left over is the new morphograph.

2. The first word is **relentless.**
   What is the first morphograph you know in that word? (S) *re.*
   Underline it.

3. What is the next morphograph you know in that word? (S) *less.*
   Underline it.

> **To correct:**
> a. You have not been taught the morphograph **lent.**
> b. What is the morphograph after **lent**? (S) *less.*
> c. That is the next morphograph you know.

4. What is the morphograph in **relentless** that you have **not** been taught? (S) *lent.*

5. Write the three morphographs in **relentless** with a plus sign between each one.

6. Everybody, spell the new morphograph in **relentless.** Get ready. (S)
   (Repeat spelling of **lent** until firm.)

7. Do the next word on your own. Underline the morphographs that you know. Then write the morphographs in **incomplete** with a plus sign between each one.

8. (Pause while students write the morphographs in **incomplete.**)
   Everybody, what is the new morphograph in **incomplete**? (S) *plete.*
   Spell **plete.** Get ready. (S)
   (Repeat spelling of **plete** until firm.)

9. Do the next word on your own. Underline the morphographs that you know.
   Then write the morphographs in **surround** with a plus sign between each one.

10. (Pause.)
    Everybody, what is the new morphograph in surround? (S) *sur.*
    Spell **sur.** Get ready. (S)
    (Repeat spelling of **sur** until firm.)

11. (Repeat steps 9 and 10 for **explore.**)

Independent Work

1. Complete the rest of the worksheet on your own.
   Be sure to read the instructions carefully.

2. (Check and correct all work.)

Answer Key

Part D
spotted, magical, puzzle
thief, compounded, losing

========

EXERCISE 1

O-R Ending

1. (Write on the board: **actor** and **helper.**)
2. In words like **actor,** the ending is spelled **o-r.**
   In words like **helper,** the ending is spelled **e-r.**
3. Here is a rule for spelling many words that end with the morphograph **o-r.**
4. Use **o-r** if a form of the word ends **i-o-n.**
5. Listen again: Use **o-r** if a form of the word ends **i-o-n.**
6. When do you spell the ending **o-r**? (S) *If a form of the word ends i-o-n.* (Repeat until firm.)
7. Listen to this word: **instruct.**
   What word? (S) *Instruct.*
   Tell me if there is a form of the word that ends **i-o-n.** (Pause.)
   Get ready. (S) *Yes.*
   What word is that? (S) *Instruction.*
8. So how do we spell the last morphograph in **instructor**? (S) *o-r.*
9. Listen to this word: **compose.**
   What word? (S) *Compose.*
   Tell me if there is a form of the word that ends **i-o-n.** (Pause.)
   Get ready. (S) *No.*
   There is no word '**compose-shun.**'
10. So how do we spell the last morphograph in **compose**? (S) *e-r.*
11. Listen to this word: **perform.**
    What word? (S) *Perform.*
    Tell me if there is a form of the word that ends **i-o-n.** (Pause.)
    Get ready. (S) *No.*
    There is no word '**perform-shun.**'
12. So how do we spell the last morphograph in **performer**? (S) *e-r.*

13. Listen to this word: **protect.**
    What word? (S) *Protect.*
    Tell me if there is a form of the word that ends **i-o-n.** (Pause.)
    Get ready. (S) *Yes.*
    What word is that? (S) *Protection.*
14. So how do we spell the last morphograph in **protector**? (S) *o-r.*

========

EXERCISE 2

O-R Ending Worksheet

Everybody, find part **A** on your worksheet.

1. There are words in column one.
   For some of these words there is a form that ends **i-o-n.**
   For others, there is no **i-o-n** form.
2. If there is an **i-o-n** form of the word, write that form in the second column.
   If there is no **i-o-n** form, leave the second column blank.
   In the last column, write the word with the morphograph **o-r** or **e-r.**
3. When do you spell the ending **o-r**? (S) *If a form of the word ends i-o-n.* (Repeat until firm.)
4. Word one is **fact.**
   Is there an **i-o-n** form of that word? (S) *Yes.*
   Write it in the second column.
5. There is an **i-o-n** form of **fact.**
   So how do we spell the last morphograph in **fact**? (S) *o-r.*
   Write **factor** in the last column.
6. Word two is **design.**
   Is there an **i-o-n** form of that word? (S) *No.*
   Leave the second column blank and write **designer** in the last column.
7. Do the rest of the words on your own.
8. (Check and correct.)

Spelling Review

1. I'll spell some words quickly.
   Then I'll call on different people to spell each word.
   When I call on you, spell the word quickly.
2. My turn: **s - c - r - i - p - t - u - r - e.**
   Everybody, what word? (S) *Scripture.*
3. Next word: **s - u - r - r - o - u - n - d.**
   What word? (S) *Surround.*
4. (Repeat step 3 for **deplore, circle, statement, science, athletically, watches, review, spotted, stance, reply, doubling, family,** and **friendliness.**)
5. Your turn.
   (Call on a student.)
   Spell **family.** Go.
6. (Praise students who respond correctly.)
7. (Call on a student.)
   Spell **surround.** Go.
8. (Repeat step 7 for **statement, spotted, friendliness, review, circle, deplore, watches, doubling, reply, athletically, stance, science,** and **scripture.** A word may be used more than once.)

Doubling Rule

1. (Write on the board: **rob, repel, subvert, outfit, cut,** and **derail.**)
2. Remember when you use the doubling rule.
   Everybody, tell me when you use the doubling rule. (Pause.) Get ready. (S) *When the word ends in a short cvc morphograph.*
   (Repeat until firm.)
3. (Point to **rob.**)
   Tell me, does this word end in a short **CVC** morphograph? (S) *Yes.*
   Tell me what that morphograph is. (Pause.) Get ready. (S) *rob.*
4. So do you double when you spell **robbing**? (S) *Yes.*
   Everybody, spell **robbing.** Get ready. (S)

5. (Point to **repel.**)
   Tell me, does this word end in a short **CVC** morphograph? (S) *Yes.*
   Tell me what that morphograph is. (Pause.) Get ready. (S) *pel.*
6. So do you double when you spell **repelling**? (S) *Yes.*
   Everybody, spell **repelling.** Get ready. (S)
7. (Point to **subvert.**)
   Tell me, does this word end in a short **CVC** morphograph? (S) *No.*
   So do you double when you spell **subverting**? (S) *No.*
8. (Point to **outfit.**)
   Tell me, does this word end in a short **CVC** morphograph? (S) *Yes.*
   Tell me what that morphograph is. (Pause.) Get ready. (S) *fit.*
9. So do you double when you spell **outfitting**? (S) *Yes.*
   Everybody, spell **outfitting.** Get ready. (S)
10. (Point to **cut.**)
    Tell me, does this word end in a short **CVC** morphograph? (S) *Yes.*
    Tell me what that morphograph is. (Pause.) Get ready. (S) *cut.*
11. So do you double when you spell **cutting**? (S) *Yes.*
    Everybody, spell **cutting.** Get ready. (S)
12. (Point to **derail.**)
    Tell me, does this word end in a short **CVC** morphograph? (S) *No.*
    So do you double when you spell **derailing**? (S) *No.*

Nonword Base

1. (Write on the board: **mote.**)
   Here is a morphograph that does not stand alone.
   It is pronounced **mote.**
   What morphograph? (S) *mote.*
2. Everybody, spell **mote.** Get ready. (S)
   (Repeat until firm.)

3. Get ready to spell words that have the morphograph **mote.**
   First word: **demote.**
   What is the first morphograph in **demote**? (S) *de.*
   What is the next morphograph in **demote**? (S) *mote.*
   Spell **demote.** Get ready. (S)
4. Next word: **promote.**
   What is the first morphograph in **promote**? (S) *pro.*
   What is the next morphograph in **promote**? (S) *mote.*
   Spell **promote.** Get ready. (S)
5. (Repeat step 4 for **motive** and **promotion.**)

EXERCISE 6

Word Building

Get ready to spell some words that have more than one morphograph.
These words are made up of morphographs that cannot stand alone.

1. First word: **consumer.**
   What is the first morphograph in **consumer**? (S) *con.*
   What is the next morphograph in **consumer**? (S) *sume.*
   What is the next morphograph in **consumer**? (S) *er.*
   Spell **consumer.** Get ready. (S)
2. Next word: **perceiving.**
   What is the first morphograph in **perceiving**? (S) *per.*
   What is the next morphograph in **perceiving**? (S) *ceive.*
   What is the next morphograph in **perceiving**? (S) *ing.*
   Spell **perceiving.** Get ready. (S)
3. (For **obtain, compel, disinfect,** and **explore,** have students identify each morphograph and spell each word.)
4. Find part **B** on your worksheet.
   You are going to write the words you just spelled.
5. First word: **compel.** Write it.
6. Next word: **explore.** Write it.

7. (Repeat step 6 for **consumer, disinfect, obtain,** and **perceiving.**)
8. (Check spellings and have students rewrite any missed words.)

EXERCISE 7

Independent Work

1. Complete the rest of the worksheet on your own.
   Be sure to read the instructions carefully.
2. (Check and correct all work.)

┌─ **Answer Key** ─

Part C		**Part D**	
1.	snap	1.	civil
2.	fer	2.	pitiful
4.	ship	3.	reason
5.	pel	4.	basically
8.	cur		

Lesson 119

EXERCISE 1

Affix Introduction

1. (Write on the board: **attest, attract,** and **attain.**)
   Each of these words has a morphograph **at** at the beginning.
   What morphograph? (S) *at.*

2. Read these words. (Point to **attest.**)
   What word? (S) *Attest.*
   What is the first morphograph in **attest**?
   (S) *at.*
   What is the next morphograph in **attest**?
   (S) *test.*

3. (Point to **attract.**)
   What word? (S) *Attract.*
   What is the first morphograph in **attract**?
   (S) *at.*
   What is the next morphograph in **attract**?
   (S) *tract.*

4. (Point to **attain.**)
   What word? (S) *Attain.*
   What is the first morphograph in **attain**?
   (S) *at.*
   What is the next morphograph in **attain**?
   (S) *tain.*

5. (Erase the board.)
   Everybody, spell the word **test.**
   Get ready. (S)
   Now spell the word **attest.** Get ready. (S)

6. Everybody, spell the word **tract.**
   Get ready. (S)
   Now spell the word **attract.** Get ready. (S)

7. Everybody, spell the morphograph **tain.**
   Get ready. (S)
   Now spell the word **attain.** Get ready. (S)

8. (Repeat spelling of **attest, attract,** and **attain** until firm. Give individual turns.)

EXERCISE 2

Word and Spelling Introduction

1. (Write on the board: **speed, screen,** and **freeze.**)
   These words are made up of only one morphograph.

2. (Point to **speed.**)
   What word? (S) *Speed.*
   Spell **speed.** Get ready. (S)
   (Repeat this procedure for each word.)

3. (Erase the words.)
   Spell the words again.
   First word: **freeze.** Get ready. (S)
   (Repeat until firm.)

4. (Repeat step 3 for **screen** and **speed.**)

5. Find part **A** on your worksheet.
   Get ready to write the words you just spelled.

6. First word: **screen.**
   What word? (S) *Screen.*
   Write **screen.**
   (Repeat for **freeze** and **speed.**)

7. You'll find the spellings of the words we're going to check in appendix **L,** section **C.**

8. (Call on a student.)
   Look up the spelling of the word **screen.**

9. (Assign each of the remaining words to different students.)

10. Get ready to check part **A.**
    Put an **X** next to any word you missed and write that word correctly.

11. (Call on the student who looked up **screen.**)
    Spell **screen.**
    (Write **screen** on the board.)

12. (Repeat step 11 for each remaining word.)

O-R Ending

1. (Write on the board: **factor** and **farmer**.)
2. In words like **factor**, the ending is spelled **o-r**.
   In words like **farmer**, the ending is spelled **e-r**.
3. Here is a rule for spelling many words that end with the morphograph **o-r**.
4. Use **o-r** if a form of the word ends **i-o-n**.
5. Listen again: Use **o-r** if a form of the word ends **i-o-n**.
6. When do you spell the ending **o-r**? (S)
   If a form of the word ends i-o-n.
   (Repeat until firm.)
7. Listen to this word: **react**.
   What word? (S) *React.*
   Tell me if there is a form of the word that ends **i-o-n**. (Pause.)
   Get ready. (S) *Yes.*
   What word is that? (S) *Reaction.*
8. So how do we spell the last morphograph in **reactor**? (S) *o-r.*
9. Listen to this word: **retain**.
   What word? (S) *retain.*
   Tell me if there is a form of the word that ends **i-o-n**. (Pause.)
   Get ready. (S) *No.*
   There is no word **'retain-shun.'**
10. So how do we spell the last morphograph in **retainer**? (S) *e-r.*
11. Listen to this word: **tract**.
    What word? (S) *tract.*
    Tell me if there is a form of the word that ends **i-o-n**. (Pause.)
    Get ready. (S) *Yes.*
    What word is that? (S) *Traction.*
12. So how do we spell the last morphograph in **tractor**? (S) *o-r.*
13. Listen to this word: **detect**.
    What word? (S) *Detect.*
    Tell me if there is a form of the word that ends **i-o-n**. (Pause.)
    Get ready. (S) *Yes.*
    What word is that? (S) *Detection.*
14. So how do we spell the last morphograph in **detector**? (S) *o-r.*

O-R Ending Worksheet

Everybody, find part **B** on your worksheet.

1. There are words in column one.
   For some of these words there is a form that ends **i-o-n**.
   For others, there is no **i-o-n** form.
2. If there is an **i-o-n** form of the word, write that form in the second column.
   If there is no **i-o-n** form, leave the second column blank.
   In the last column, write the word with the morphograph **o-r** or **e-r**.
3. When do you spell the ending **o-r**? (S)
   If a form of the word ends i-o-n.
   (Repeat until firm.)
4. Word one is **transgress**.
   Is there an **i-o-n** form of that word? (S) *Yes.*
   Write it in the second column.
5. There is an **i-o-n** form of **transgress**.
   So how do we spell the last morphograph in **transgressor**? (S) *o-r.*
   Write **transgressor** in the last column.
6. Word two is **plant**.
   Is there an **i-o-n** form of that word? (S) *No.*
   Leave the second column blank and write **planter** in the last column.
7. Do the rest of the words on your own.
8. (Check and correct.)

Nonword Base

1. (Write on the board: **dict**.)
   Here is a new morphograph that cannot stand alone.
   It is pronounced **dict**.
   What morphograph? (S) *dict.*
2. Everybody, spell **dict**. Get ready. (S)
   (Repeat until firm.)
3. Get ready to spell words that have the morphograph **dict**.
   First word: **predict**.
   What is the first morphograph in **predict**?
   (S) *pre.*

What is the next morphograph in **predict**?
(S) *dict.*
Spell **predict.** Get ready. (S)
4. Next word: **diction.**
    What is the first morphograph in **diction**?
    (S) *dict.*
    What is the next morphograph in **diction**?
    (S) *i-o-n.*
    Spell **diction.** Get ready. (S)
5. (Repeat step 4 for **addictive.**)

Independent Work

1. Complete the rest of the worksheet on
    your own.
    Be sure to read the instructions carefully.
2. (Check and correct all work.)

EXERCISE 6

Doubling Rule

Everybody, find part **C** on your worksheet.

Some of these words end in short **CVC**
morphographs.
Some end in short morphographs that are
not **CVC.**

1. Listen: Underline the morphograph that
    each word ends with.
    If these is only one morphograph in the
    word, underline that morphograph.
2. Write the words in the last column.
    Remember, the underlined morphograph
    tells you if you will double.
    (Pause while students write the words.)
3. Everybody, look at the first word.
    What morphograph does **rerun** end with?
    (S) *run.*
    (Repeat for **infer, hit, disarm, commit,
    ship, detect,** and **snap.**)
4. (Check and correct spellings.)
5. Everybody, turn your worksheet over and
    get ready to spell some words from the last
    column without looking.
6. Word one: **disarmed.** (Pause.)
    Spell **disarmed.** Get ready. (S)
7. (Repeat step 6 for **inferred, rerunning,**
    and **detective.**)
8. (Repeat each word until firm. Give
    individual turns.)

Lesson 120

━━━━━ **EXERCISE 1** ━━━━━

Affix Introduction

1. (Write on the board: **diverge, diverse, divert,** and **divide.**)
   Each of these words has a morphograph **d-i** at the beginning.
   What morphograph? (S) *d-i.*
2. Read these words. (Point to **diverge.**)
   What word? (S) *Diverge.*
   What is the first morphograph in **diverge**? (S) *d-i.*
   What is the next morphograph in **diverge**? (S) *verge.*
3. (Point to **diverse.**)
   What word? (S) *Diverse.*
   What is the first morphograph in **diverse**? (S) *d-i.*
   What is the next morphograph in **diverse**? (S) *verse.*
4. (Point to **divert.**)
   What word? (S) *Divert.*
   What is the first morphograph in **divert**? (S) *d-i.*
   What is the next morphograph in **divert**? (S) *vert.*
5. (Point to **divide.**)
   What word? (S) *Divide.*
   What is the first morphograph in **divide**? (S) *d-i.*
   What is the next morphograph in **divide**? (S) *vide.*
6. (Erase the board.)
   Everybody, spell the word **verge.**
   Get ready. (S)
   Now spell the word **diverge.** Get ready. (S)
7. Everybody, spell the word **verse.**
   Get ready. (S)
   Now spell the word **diverse.** Get ready. (S)
8. Everybody, spell the morphograph **vert.**
   Get ready. (S)
   Now spell the word **divert.** Get ready. (S)
9. Everybody, spell the morphograph **vide.**
   Get ready. (S)
   Now spell the word **divide.** Get ready. (S)

10. (Repeat spelling of **diverge, diverse, divert,** and **divide** until firm. Give individual turns.)

━━━━━ **EXERCISE 2** ━━━━━

O-R Ending Worksheet

Everybody, find part **A** on your worksheet.

1. There are words in column one.
   For some of these words there is a form that ends **i-o-n.**
   For others, there is no **i-o-n** form.
2. If there is an **i-o-n** form of the word, write that form in the second column.
   If there is no **i-o-n** form, leave the second column blank.
   In the last column, write the word with the morphograph **o-r** or **e-r.**
3. When do you spell the ending **o-r**? (S) *If a form of the word ends i-o-n.*
   (Repeat until firm.)
4. Do the words on your own.
5. (Check and correct.)

━━━━━ **EXERCISE 3** ━━━━━

Spelling Review

1. I'll spell some words quickly.
   Then I'll call on different people to spell each word.
   When I call on you, spell the word quickly.
2. My turn: **r - e - v - i - e - w.**
   Everybody, what word? (S) *Review.*
3. Next word: **s - u - r - f - a - c - e.**
   What word? (S) *Surface.*
4. (Repeat step 3 for **explore, asleep, science, predict, freeze, instance, photography, invention, screen,** and **section.**)
5. Your turn.
   (Call on a student.)
   Spell **freeze.** Go.
6. (Praise students who respond correctly.)

7. (Call on a student.)
   Spell **surface**. Go.
8. (Repeat step 7 for **science, photography, review, predict, invention, explore, asleep, screen, instance,** and **section**. A word may be used more than once.)

EXERCISE 4

Doubling Rule Worksheet

Everybody, find part **B** on your worksheet.

1. (Call on a student.)
   Read the instructions for part **B**.
   Underline the morphograph that each word ends with. Then add the next morphograph.
2. Remember, the underlined morphograph tells you if you will double.
3. (Call on a student.)
   When do you use the doubling rule?
   When the word ends in a short cvc morphograph.
4. You will do part **B** later in the lesson.

EXERCISE 5

Nonword Base

Note. Pronounce **cise** as **sise**.

1. (Write on the board: **cise**.)
   Here is a new morphograph that cannot stand alone.
   It is usually pronounced **cise**.
   What morphograph? (S) *cise*.
2. Everybody, spell **cise**. Get ready. (S)
   (Repeat until firm.)
3. Get ready to spell words that have the morphograph **cise**.
   First word: **concise**.
   What is the first morphograph in **concise**? (S) *con*.
   What is the next morphograph in **concise**? (S) *cise*.
   Spell **concise**. Get ready. (S)

4. Next word: **decisive**.
   What is the first morphograph in **decisive**? (S) *de*.
   What is the next morphograph in **decisive**? (S) *cise*.
   What is the next morphograph in **decisive**? (S) *ive*.
   Spell **decisive**. Get ready. (S)
5. (Repeat step 4 for **precise** and **incision**.)

EXERCISE 6

Morphograph Analysis

Everybody, find part **C** on your worksheet.

1. Each word in part **C** has a morphograph that you have not been taught.
   Here is how to find those morphographs.
   You identify all the morphographs in the word that you know.
   The part that is left over is the new morphograph.
2. The first word is **profess**.
   What is the first morphograph you know in that word? (S) *pro*.
   Underline it.
3. What is the morphograph in **profess** that you have **not** been taught? (S) *fess*.
4. Write the two morphographs in **profess** with a plus sign between each one.
5. Everybody, spell the new morphograph in **profess**. Get ready. (S)
   (Repeat spelling of **fess** until firm.)
6. Do the next word on your own. Underline the morphographs that you know.
   Then write the morphographs in **proceed** with a plus sign between each one.
7. (Pause while students write the morphographs in **proceed**.)
   Everybody, what is the new morphograph in **proceed**? (S) *ceed*.
   Spell **ceed**. Get ready. (S)
   (Repeat spelling of **ceed** until firm.)

Independent Work

1. Complete the rest of the worksheet on your own.
   Be sure to read the instructions carefully.
2. (Check and correct all work.)

Answer Key

Part D
impressed, author
adventurers, hoped, found

Mastery Test

1. You are going to have a test today. It will help you see how well you are learning to spell.
2. Everybody, take out a sheet of lined paper and draw a line down the middle. Then number the paper from 1 through 20.
3. (Check and correct.)
4. Word 1 is **science.**
   My favorite class is **science.**
   What word? (S) *Science.*
   Write **science.**
5. Word 2 is **basement.**
   The pool table is in the **basement.**
   What word? (S) *Basement.*
   Write **basement.**
6. (Repeat step 5 for the remaining words on the list.)

3.	**graphics**	12.	**shipped**
4.	**furious**	13.	**knives**
5.	**bought**	14.	**fashion**
6.	**breathless**	15.	**watch**
7.	**athlete**	16.	**huge**
8.	**friendship**	17.	**vertical**
9.	**subtract**	18.	**transmitter**
10.	**circle**	19.	**construction**
11.	**disinfect**	20.	**fought**

7. Everybody, exchange papers with your partner. (Pause.)
8. I'll spell each word. If the word is not spelled correctly on the paper you're marking, put an **X** next to it.
   If the word is spelled correctly, don't put any mark next to it.
9. Word 1 is **science: s-c-i-e-n-c-e.**
   Check it.
10. (Repeat step 9 for each remaining word.)
11. Return your partner's test paper.
12. Now correct any errors you made. If there is an **X** next to a word on your test, write the word correctly in the right column. Raise your hand if you don't know how to spell any words.
13. Turn your paper over when you're finished. I'll come around and check your paper.
14. If you didn't make any mistakes, raise your hand now.
15. Write the number correct at the top of your test.

Homonyms

1. (Write on the board: **marry.**)
   This word is **marry.** What word? (S) *Marry.*
2. This **marry** does not mean: **happy.**
   This **marry** means: **to become husband and wife.**
   What does this **marry** mean? (S) *To become husband and wife.*
3. And how is it spelled? Get ready. (S)
4. (Erase the board.)
   Spell **marry** again. Get ready. (S)
5. Remember that word.

Word and Spelling Introduction

1. (Write on the board: **point, ready, beauty, over,** and **value.**)
   These words are made up of only one morphograph.
2. (Point to **point.**)
   What word? (S) *Point.*
   Spell **point.** Get ready. (S)
   (Repeat this procedure for each word.)
3. (Erase the words.)
   Spell the words again.
   First word: **beauty.** Get ready. (S)
   (Repeat until firm.)
4. (Repeat step 3 for **ready, value, over,** and **point.**)
5. Find part **A** on your worksheet.
   Get ready to write the words you just spelled.
6. First word: **over.**
   What word? (S) *Over.*
   Write **over.**
   (Repeat for **beauty, point, value,** and **ready.**)
7. You'll find the spellings of the words we're going to check in appendix **L,** section **C.**
8. (Call on a student.)
   Look up the spelling of the word **over.**

9. (Assign each of the remaining words to different students.)
10. Get ready to check part **A.**
    Put an **X** next to any word you missed and write that word correctly.
11. (Call on the student who looked up **over.**)
    Spell **over.**
    (Write **over** on the board.)
12. (Repeat step 11 for each remaining word.)

O-R Ending Worksheet

Everybody, find part **B** on your worksheet.

1. There are words in column one.
   For some of these words there is a form that ends **i-o-n.**
   For others, there is no **i-o-n** form.
2. If there is an **i-o-n** form of the word, write that form in the second column.
   If there is no **i-o-n** form, leave the second column blank.
   In the last column, write the word with the morphograph **o-r** or **e-r.**
3. When do you spell the ending **o-r**? (S) *If a form of the word ends in i-o-n.*
4. Do the words on your own.
5. (Check and correct.)

Spelling Review

1. I'll spell some words quickly.
   See if you can figure out each word.
2. Listen: **c - o - n - t - r - a - c - t.**
   Everybody, what word? (S) *Contract.*
3. Listen: **s - c - i - e - n - c - e.**
   What word? (S) *Science.*
4. (Repeat step 3 for **equally, furious, unbeaten, incurable, civilly, preview, inhuman, government, pleasure,** and **strengthen.**)

5. Find part **C** on your worksheet.
   Get ready to write some of those words.
6. First word: **preview.**
   Write it.
7. Next word: **equally.**
   Write it.
8. (Repeat step 7 for **science, furious, strengthen, government, incurable,** and **contract.**)
9. I will spell each word.
   Put an **X** next to any word you missed and write that word correctly.
   (Write each word on the board as you spell it.)

EXERCISE 5

Doubling Rule Worksheet

Everybody, find part **D** on your worksheet.

1. (Call on a student.)
   Read the instructions for part **D.**
   Underline the morphograph that each word ends with. Then add the next morphograph.
2. Remember, the underlined morphograph tells you if you will double.
3. (Call on a student.)
   When do you use the doubling rule?
   When the word ends in a short cvc morphograph.
4. You will do part **D** later in the lesson.

EXERCISE 6

Word Building

Get ready to spell some words that have more than one morphograph.
These words are made up of morphographs that cannot stand alone.

1. First word: **precise.**
   What is the first morphograph in **precise**?
   (S) *pre.*
   What is the next morphograph in **precise**?
   (S) *cise.*
   Spell **precise.** Get ready. (S)

2. Next word: **prediction.**
   What is the first morphograph in **prediction**? (S) *pre.*
   What is the next morphograph in **prediction**? (S) *dict.*
   What is the next morphograph in **prediction**? (S) *i-o-n.*
   Spell **prediction.** Get ready. (S)
3. (For **remote, decisive, converted,** and **infection,** have students identify each morphograph and spell each word.)
4. Find part **E** on your worksheet.
   You are going to write the words you just spelled.
5. First word: **remote.** Write it.
6. Next word: **infection.** Write it.
7. (Repeat step 6 for **precise, converted, prediction,** and **decisive.**)
8. (Check spellings and have students rewrite any missed words.)

EXERCISE 7

Independent Work

1. Complete the rest of the worksheet on your own.
   Be sure to read the instructions carefully.
2. (Check and correct all work.)

Supplemental Blackline Masters

Supplemental blackline masters 47 and 48 provide additional practice on material covered in Lessons 116 through 120. You may assign any or all of the activities, and you may award bonus points.

Lesson 122

EXERCISE 1

Affix Introduction

1. (Write on the board: **dictate, evaluate,** and **designate.**)
   Each of these words has a morphograph **ate** at the end.
   What morphograph? (S) *ate.*

2. Read these words. (Point to **dictate.**)
   What word? (S) *Dictate.*
   What is the first morphograph in **dictate**? (S) *dict.*
   What is the next morphograph in **dictate**? (S) *ate.*

3. (Point to **evaluate.**)
   What word? (S) *Evaluate.*
   What is the first morphograph in **evaluate**? (S) *e.*
   What is the next morphograph in **evaluate**? (S) *value.*
   What is the next morphograph in **evaluate**? (S) *ate.*

4. (Point to **designate.**)
   What word? (S) *Designate.*
   What is the first morphograph in **designate**? (S) *de.*
   What is the next morphograph in **designate**? (S) *sign.*
   What is the next morphograph in **designate**? (S) *ate.*

5. (Erase the board.)
   Everybody, spell the morphograph **dict.**
   Get ready. (S)
   Now spell the word **dictate.** Get ready. (S)

6. Everybody, spell the word **value.**
   Get ready. (S)
   Now spell the word **evaluate.**
   Be careful. Get ready. (S)

7. Everybody, spell the word **design.**
   Get ready. (S)
   Now spell the word **designate.**
   Get ready. (S)

8. (Repeat spelling of **dictate, evaluate,** and **designate** until firm. Give individual turns.)

EXERCISE 2

Word and Spelling Introduction— Fast Cycle

Everybody, find part **A** on your worksheet.

1. (Call on a student.)
   Read the instructions for part **A.**
   Study these words on your own. There will be a test on these words during Lesson 124.

2. Study the words in part **A** after you have finished your worksheet.
   Everyone should do well on the test over these words.
   (Students may study individually or in pairs.)

EXERCISE 3

Spelling Review

Find part **B** on your worksheet.

You are going to write some words made up of morphographs you have spelled before.

1. First word: **realistically.**
   What word? (S) *Realistically.*
   Write **realistically.**

2. Next word: **destructive.**
   What word? (S) *Destructive.*
   Write **destructive.**

3. (Repeat step 2 for **poisonous, statement, pointless, value, submerge,** and **friendship.**)

4. I'll spell each word.
   Put an **X** next to any word you missed and write that word correctly.
   (Write each word on the board as you spell it.)

O-R Ending Worksheet

1. (Call on a student.)
   Read the instructions for part **C**.
   If there is an i-o-n form of the word, write it in the second column.
   If there is no i-o-n form, leave the second column blank.
   In the last column, write the word with the morphograph o-r or e-r.
2. When do you spell the ending **o-r**? (S)
   If a form of the word ends i-o-n.
   (Repeat until firm.)
3. You will do part **C** later in the lesson.

EXERCISE 5

Study for Spelling Test

Find appendix **L**, section **C**.

1. During Lesson 123, we're going to have a spelling test.
2. Most of the test words will come from appendix **L**, section **C**.
3. When you've completed your worksheet, study the words.

Note. Students may study in pairs or independently.

EXERCISE 6

Independent Work

1. Complete the rest of the worksheet on your own.
   Be sure to read the instructions carefully.
2. (Check and correct all work.)

====== EXERCISE 1 ======

Spelling Test

Note. There is no student worksheet for Lesson 123.

1. Everyone, take out a sheet of paper for the spelling test.
2. I'll dictate 50 words.
   Some of them you haven't spelled before.
   But you have spelled all the morphographs.
   If you get 45 words or more correct, you earn 12 worksheet points.
3. Word one: **value.**
   What word? (S) *Value.*
   Write **value.**
4. Word two: **review.**
   What word? (S) *Review.*
   Write **review.**
5. (Repeat step 4 for the following list of words.)

3. depression	21. sweet	39. completely	45. recover
4. graphic	22. subscription	40. reply	46. preview
5. circle	23. prediction	41. unsupported	47. breathless
6. friendship	24. receive	42. thousand	48. adventure
7. perform	25. divide	43. physically	49. poisonous
8. weakness	26. unusual	44. adverb	50. photograph
9. actor	27. instance		
10. reason	28. halves		
11. discover	29. science		
12. incomplete	30. support		
13. puzzle	31. surface		
14. section	32. instruction		
15. equally	33. expression		
16. thieves	34. beauty		
17. professional	35. athlete		
18. object	36. authorship		
19. attend	37. consume		
20. container	38. motion		

6. I'll spell each word. Put an **X** next to any word you missed and write that word correctly.
   (Write each word on the board as you spell it.)
7. (Award points: 45–50 . . . . 12 points
   43–44 . . . . 10 points
   41–42 . . . . 7 points
   39–40 . . . . 5 points
   37–38 . . . . 3 points)

Crossword Puzzles

The crossword puzzles are made up exclusively of the words presented in the review lessons. Every word in these lessons has been used. For each review lesson, there are two or three sets of puzzles, depending on how many words are in the lesson. A set is made up of two puzzles—an original and an alternate. The alternate uses the same words and clues as the original, but in a different arrangement. This gives you a good deal of flexibility in how you use the puzzles.

The crossword puzzle blackline masters are located at the back of this Teacher Presentation Book.

━━━━━ **EXERCISE 1** ━━━━━

Affix Introduction

1. (Write on the board: **partial, racial, adverbial,** and **facial.**)
   Each of these words has a morphograph **ial** at the end.
   What morphograph? (S) *ial.*
2. Read these words. (Point to **partial.**)
   What word? (S) *Partial.*
   What is the first morphograph in **partial**?
   (S) *part.*
   What is the next morphograph in **partial**?
   (S) *ial.*
3. (Point to **racial.**)
   What word? (S) *Racial.*
   What is the first morphograph in **racial**?
   (S) *race.*
   What is the next morphograph in **racial**?
   (S) *ial.*
4. (Point to **adverbial.**)
   What word? (S) *Adverbial.*
   What is the first morphograph in **adverbial**? (S) *ad.*
   What is the next morphograph in **adverbial**? (S) *verb.*
   What is the next morphograph in **adverbial**? (S) *ial.*
5. (Point to **facial.**)
   What word? (S) *Facial.*
   What is the first morphograph in **facial**?
   (S) *face.*
   What is the next morphograph in **facial**?
   (S) *ial.*
6. (Erase the board.)
   Everybody, spell the word **part.**
   Get ready. (S)
   Now spell the word **partial.** Get ready. (S)
7. Everybody, spell the word **race.**
   Get ready. (S)
   Now spell the word **racial.** Get ready. (S)
8. Everybody, spell the word **adverb.**
   Get ready. (S)
   Now spell the word **adverbial.**
   Get ready. (S)
9. Everybody, spell the word **face.**
   Get ready. (S)
   Now spell the word **facial.** Get ready. (S)

━━━━━ **EXERCISE 2** ━━━━━

Homonyms

1. (Write on the board: **merry.**)
   This word is **merry.** What word? (S) *Merry.*
2. This **merry** means: **happy.**
   What does this **merry** mean? (S) *Happy.*
3. And how is it spelled? Get ready. (S)
   (Erase the board.)
4. Everybody, spell the **merry** that means: **happy.** Get ready. (S)
5. Everybody, spell the **marry** that means: **to become husband and wife.**
   Get ready. (S)
6. (Repeat steps 4 and 5 until firm.
   Give individual turns.)

━━━━━ **EXERCISE 3** ━━━━━

Word and Spelling Introduction

1. (Write on the board: **spire, sane,** and **post.**)
   These words are made up of only one morphograph.
2. (Point to **spire.**)
   What word? (S) *Spire.*
   Spell **spire.** Get ready. (S)
   (Repeat this procedure for each word.)
3. (Erase the words.)
   Spell the words again.
   First word: **post.** Get ready. (S)
   (Repeat until firm.)
4. (Repeat step 3 for **sane** and **spire.**)
5. Find part **A** on your worksheet.
   Get ready to write the words you just spelled.
6. First word: **sane.**
   What word? (S) *Sane.*
   Write **sane.**
   (Repeat for **spire** and **post.**)

7. You'll find the spellings of the words we're going to check in appendix **M,** section **B.**
8. (Call on a student.)
   Look up the spelling of the word **sane.**
9. (Assign each of the remaining words to different students.)
10. Get ready to check part **A.**
    Put an **X** next to any word you missed and write that word correctly.
11. (Call on the student who looked up **sane.**)
    Spell **sane.**
    (Write **sane** on the board.)
12. (Repeat step 11 for each remaining word.)

Fast-Cycle Test

Everybody, find part **B** on your worksheet.

1. You are going to write the words you studied during Lesson 122.
2. First word: Write **pop.**
3. Next word: Write **sit.**
4. (Repeat step 3 for **cap, dig, set, tip, up, stir, fog,** and **bat.**)
5. (Check and correct.)

Oral Spelling Review

You are going to spell some words made up of morphographs you have spelled before.

1. First word: **beauty.**
   What word? (S) *Beauty.*
   Spell **beauty.** Get ready. (S)
   (Repeat until firm.)
2. Next word: **poison.**
   What word? (S) *Poison.*
   Spell **poison.** Get ready. (S)
   (Repeat until firm.)
3. (Repeat step 2 for **produce, likelihood, action, quietest, stretcher, friendliness, author, strengthen, hopefully,** and **athlete.**)

Morphograph Analysis

Everybody, find part **C** on your worksheet.

1. Each word in part **C** has a morphograph that you have not been taught.
   Here is how to identify those morphographs.
   You identify all the morphographs in the word that you know.
   The part that is left over is the new morphograph.
2. The first word is **dismiss.**
   What is the first morphograph you know in that word? (S) *dis.*
   Underline it.
3. What is the morphograph in **dismiss** that you have **not** been taught? (S) *miss.*
4. Write the two morphographs in **dismiss** with a plus sign between them.
5. Everybody, spell the new morphograph in **dismiss.** Get ready. (S)
   (Repeat spelling of **miss** until firm.)
6. Do the next word on your own. Underline the morphographs that you know.
   Then write the morphographs in **record** with a plus sign between each one.
7. (Pause while the students write the morphographs in **record.**)
   Everybody, what is the new morphograph in **record**? (S) *cord.*
   Spell **cord.** Get ready. (S)
   (Repeat spelling of **cord** until firm.)
8. Do the next word on your own. Underline the morphograph that you know.
   Then write the morphographs in **appointment** with a plus sign between each one.
9. (Pause.) Everybody, what is the new morphograph in **appointment**? (S) *ap.*
   Spell **ap.** Get ready. (S)
   (Repeat spelling of **ap** until firm.)

Independent Work

1. Complete the rest of the worksheet on your own.
   Be sure to read the instructions carefully.

2. (Check and correct all work.)

Homonyms

1. Everybody, spell the **marry** that means: **to become husband and wife.** Get ready. (S)
2. Everybody, spell the **merry** that means: **happy.** Get ready. (S)
3. (Repeat steps 1 and 2 until firm. Give individual turns.)

Affix Introduction

1. (Write on the board: **accept, account, acclaim, accent,** and **accord.**)
   Each of these words has a morphograph **ac** at the beginning.
   What morphograph? (S) *ac.*
2. Read these words. (Point to **accept.**)
   What word? (S) *Accept.*
   What is the first morphograph in **accept**?
   (S) *ac.*
   What is the next morphograph in **accept**?
   (S) *cept.*
3. (Point to **account.**)
   What word? (S) *Account.*
   What is the first morphograph in **account**?
   (S) *ac.*
   What is the next morphograph in **account**? (S) *count.*
4. (Point to **acclaim.**)
   What word? (S) *Acclaim.*
   What is the first morphograph in **acclaim**?
   (S) *ac.*
   What is the next morphograph in **acclaim**?
   (S) *claim.*
5. (Point to **accent.**)
   What word? (S) *Accent.*
   What is the first morphograph in **accent**?
   (S) *ac.*
   What is the next morphograph in **accent**?
   (S) *cent.*
6. (Point to **accord.**)
   What word? (S) *Accord.*
   What is the first morphograph in **accord**?
   (S) *ac.*
   What is the next morphograph in **accord**?
   (S) *cord.*
7. (Erase the board.)
   Everybody, spell the morphograph **cept.**
   Get ready. (S)
   Now spell the word **accept.** Get ready. (S)
8. Everybody, spell the word **count.**
   Get ready. (S)
   Now spell the word **account.**
   Get ready. (S)
9. Everybody, spell the word **claim.**
   Get ready. (S)
   Now spell the word **acclaim.** Get ready. (S)
10. Everybody, spell the word **cord.**
    Get ready. (S)
    Now spell the word **accord.** Get ready. (S)
11. (Repeat spelling of **accept, account, acclaim, accent,** and **accord** until firm. Give individual turns.)

Word and Spelling Introduction

1. (Write on the board: **tour, dense,** and **simple.**)
   These words are made up of only one morphograph.
2. (Point to **tour.**)
   What word? (S) *Tour.*
   Spell **tour.** Get ready. (S)
   (Repeat this procedure for each word.)
3. (Erase the words.)
   Spell the words again.
   First word: **dense.** Get ready. (S)
   (Repeat until firm.)
4. (Repeat step 3 for **simple** and **tour.**)
5. Find part **A** on your worksheet.
   Get ready to write the words you just spelled.

6. First word: **simple.**
What word? (S) *Simple.*
Write **simple.**
(Repeat for **dense** and **tour.**)

7. You'll find the spellings of the words we're going to check in appendix **M**, section **B.**

8. (Call on a student.)
Look up the spelling of the word **simple.**

9. (Assign each of the remaining words to different students.)

10. Get ready to check part **A.**
Put an **X** next to any word you missed and write that word correctly.

11. (Call on the student who looked up **simple.**)
Spell **simple.**
(Write **simple** on the board.)

12. (Repeat step 11 for each remaining word.)

EXERCISE 4

Doubling Rule

1. (Write on the board: **water, freshen, poison,** and **motor.** Point to **water.**)
What is the first morphograph in **water**? (S) *water.*

2. Does **water** end in a short **CVC** morphograph? (S) *No.*

> **To correct:**
> a. Water ends in the morphograph
>   **w - a - t - e - r.**
> b. That is not a **short** cvc morphograph.
> c. (Repeat step 2.)

3. Everybody, spell **watering.** Get ready. (S)

4. (Point to **freshen.**)
What is the first morphograph in **freshen**? (S) *fresh.*
What is the next morphograph in **freshen**? (S) *en.*

5. Does **freshen** end in a short **CVC** morphograph? (S) *No.*
Right. **En** is not a **CVC** morphograph.

6. Everybody, spell **freshening.**
Get ready. (S)

7. (Point to **poison.**)
What is the first morphograph in **poison**? (S) *poison.*

8. Does **poison** end in a short **CVC** morphograph? (S) *No.*

9. Everybody, spell **poisonous.** Get ready. (S)

10. (Point to **motor.**)
What is the first morphograph in **motor**? (S) *motor.*

11. Does **motor** end in a short **CVC** morphograph? (S) *No.*

12. Everybody, spell **motoring.** Get ready. (S)

13. (Repeat spelling of **watering, freshening, poisonous,** and **motoring** until all students are firm.)

EXERCISE 5

Word Building

Find part **B** on your worksheet.

Get ready to write some words that have more than one morphograph.

1. First word: **evaluate.**
What is the first morphograph in **evaluate**? (S) *e.*
What is the next morphograph in **evaluate**? (S) *value.*
What is the next morphograph in **evaluate**? (S) *ate.*
Write **evaluate.**

2. Next word: **partial.**
What is the first morphograph in **partial**? (S) *part.*
What is the next morphograph in **partial**? (S) *ial.*
Write **partial.**

3. (For **dictate, attraction, suppose, adjustment, impression, belonging, artistic,** and **pleasure,** have students identify each morphograph and write each word.)

4. (Check and have students rewrite any missed words.)

Proofreading Letters

Find part **C** on your worksheet.

1. The letter in part **C** has misspelled words. You have studied some of these words.

2. If you can find at least 13 of the misspelled words, you get zero errors for part **C.**
   12 words equal 1 error, 11 words equal 2 errors, and so on.

3. Draw a line through each misspelled word. Write it correctly on a line next to the letter.

Answer Key

Part C

November 19, 2001

Dear Mr. Swiss,

We were glad to ~~recieve~~ your ~~subscripshun~~ to the Clock-of-the-Month Club. Your ~~furst~~ clock ~~owt~~ to arrive within a ~~weak~~. Each month, you will receive a new clock with a ~~beautyful~~, original ~~dezign~~. In the past, we have ~~sent~~ ~~thouzunds~~ of clocks that double as ~~plantters~~, ships, ~~wolfs~~, eyedroppers, and many other ~~objecs~~.

If you like the Clock-of-the-Month, keep it. We will bill you. If you ~~do'nt~~ like it, send it back in the original ~~packege~~ within ~~fore~~ days.

Thank you for ~~choozing~~ the Clock-of-the-Month Club.

receive	
subscription	
first	
ought	
week	
beautiful	
design	
sent	
thousands	
planters	
wolves	
objects	
don't	
package	
four	
choosing	

Homonyms

1. (Write on the board: **their.**)
   This word is **their.** What word? (S) *Their.*
2. This **their** does not mean: **in that place.**
   This **their** means: **they own it.**
   What does **their** mean? (S) *They own it.*
3. And how is it spelled? Get ready. (S)
4. (Erase the board.)
   Spell **their** again. Get ready. (S)
5. Remember that word.

Affix Introduction

Note. Pronounced **ite** as in **bite.**

1. Write on the board: **graphite, definite,**
   and **composite.**)
   Each of these words has a morphograph
   ite at the end.
2. Read these words. (Point to **graphite.**)
   What word? (S) *Graphite.*
   What is the first morphograph in **graphite**?
   (S) *graph.*
   What is the next morphograph in
   graphite? (S) *ite.*
3. (Point to **definite.**)
   What word? (S) *Definite.*
   What is the first morphograph in **definite**?
   (S) *de.*
   What is the next morphograph in **definite**?
   (S) *fine.*
   What is the next morphograph in **definite**?
   (S) *ite.*

4. (Point to **composite.**)
   What word? (S) *Composite.*
   What is the first morphograph in
   composite? (S) *com.*
   What is the next morphograph in
   composite? (S) *pose.*
   What is the next morphograph in
   composite? (S) *ite.*
5. (Erase the board.)
   Everybody, spell the word **graph.**
   Get ready. (S)
   Now spell the word **graphite.**
   Get ready. (S)
6. Everybody, spell the word **define.**
   Get ready. (S)
   Now spell the word **definite.** Be careful.
   Get ready. (S)
7. Everybody, spell the word **compose.**
   Get ready. (S)
   Now spell the word **composite.** Be
   careful. Get ready. (S)
8. (Repeat spelling of **graphite, definite,** and
   composite until firm. Give individual
   turns.)

Spelling Review

1. I'll spell some words quickly.
   See if you can figure out each word.
2. Listen: **t - o - u - r - i - s - t.**
   Everybody, what word? (S) *Tourist.*
3. Listen: **d - e - n - s - e - l - y.**
   What word? (S) *Densely.*
4. (Repeat step 3 for **simple, athletic,
   grown, dictation, record, accept,
   except, dismiss, divide,** and **thoughtful.**)
5. Find part **A** on your worksheet.
   Get ready to write some of those words.
6. First word: **dismiss.**
   Write it.
7. Next word: **tourist.**
   Write it.
8. (Repeat step 7 for **thoughtful, athletic,
   simple,** and **divide.**)

9. I will spell each word.
   Put an **X** next to any word you missed and write that word correctly.
   (Write each word on the board as you spell it.)

Doubling Rule

1. (Write on the board: **magic, straighten, critic,** and **wandering.**)
   What is the first morphograph in **magic**? (S) *magic.*
2. Does **magic** end in a short **CVC** morphograph? (S) *No.*

To correct:
a. **Magic** ends in the morphograph **m-a-g-i-c.**
b. That is not a **short CVC** morphograph.
c. (Repeat step 2.)

---

3. Everybody, spell **magical.** Get ready. (S)
4. (Point to **straighten.**)
   What is the first morphograph in **straighten**? (S) *straight.*
   What is the next morphograph in **straighten**? (S) *en.*
5. Does **straighten** end in a short **CVC** morphograph? (S) *No.*
   Right. **En** is not a **CVC** morphograph.
6. Everybody, spell **straightened.** Get ready. (S)
7. (Point to **critic.**)
   What is the first morphograph in **critic**? (S) *critic.*
8. Does critic end in a short **CVC** morphograph? (S) *No.*
9. Everybody, spell **critical.** Get ready. (S)
10. (Point to **wandering.**)
    What is the first morphograph in **wandering**? (S) *wander.*
11. Does **wander** end in a short **CVC** morphograph? (S) *No.*
12. Everybody, spell **wandering.** Get ready. (S)
13. (Repeat spelling of **magical, straightened, critical,** and **wandering** until firm.)

Nonword Base

1. (Write on the board: **cess.**)
   Here is a new morphograph that cannot stand alone.
   It is usually pronounced **cess.**
   What morphograph? (S) *cess.*
2. Everybody, spell **cess.** Get ready. (S)
   (Repeat until firm.)
3. Get ready to spell words that have the morphograph **cess.**
   First word: **process.**
   What is the first morphograph in **process**? (S) *pro.*
   What is the next morphograph in **process**? (S) *cess.*
   Spell **process.** Get ready. (S)
4. Next word: **recession.**
   What is the first morphograph in **recession**? (S) *re.*
   What is the next morphograph in **recession**? (S) *cess.*
   What is the next morphograph in **recession**? (S) *i-o-n.*
5. (Repeat step 4 for **excessive** and **access.**)

Morphograph Analysis

Note. Pronounce **ian** (step 7) by its letter names: **i - a - n.**

Everybody, find part **B** on your worksheet.

1. Each word in part **B** has a morphograph that you have **not** been taught.
   Here is how to find those morphographs.
   You identify all the morphographs in the word that you know.
   The part that is left over is the new morphograph.
2. The first word is **concern.**
   What is the first morphograph you know in that word? (S) *con.*
   Underline it.
3. What is the morphograph in **concern** that you have **not** been taught? (S) *cern.*

4. Write the two morphographs in **concern** with a plus sign between each one.

5. Everybody, spell the new morphograph in **concern.** Get ready. (S)
   (Repeat spelling of **cern** until firm.)

6. Do the next word on your own. Underline the morphographs that you know.
   Then write the morphographs in **magician** with a plus sign between each one.

7. (Pause while students write the morphographs in **magician.**)
   Everybody, what is the new morphograph in **magician**? (S) *i - a - n.*
   Yes, **i - a - n.**

8. Do the next word on your own. Underline the morphographs that you know.
   Then write the morphographs in **direct** with a plus sign between each one.

9. (Pause.)
   Everybody, what is the new morphograph in **direct**? (S) *rect.*
   Spell **rect.** Get ready. (S)
   (Repeat spelling of **rect** until firm.)

 **EXERCISE 7**

Independent Work

1. Complete the rest of the worksheet on your own.
   Be sure to read the instructions carefully.

2. (Check and correct all work.)

┌─ **Answer Key** ───────────

Part C
  1. stir
  4. mit
  5. cur
  8. fer
 11. pel
 12. spin
 15. trap

Supplemental Blackline Masters

Supplemental blackline masters 49 and 50 provide additional practice on material covered in Lessons 121 through 125. You may assign any or all of the activities, and you may award bonus points.

Affix Introduction

1. Write on the board: **introduce** and **introvert.**)
   Each of these words has a morphograph **intro** at the beginning.
   What morphograph? (S) *intro.*

2. Read these words. (Point to **introduce.**)
   What word? (S) *Introduce.*
   What is the first morphograph in **introduce**? (S) *intro.*
   What is the next morphograph in **introduce**? (S) *duce.*

3. (Point to **introvert.**)
   What word? (S) *Introvert.*
   What is the first morphograph in **introvert**? (S) *intro.*
   What is the next morphograph in **introvert**? (S) *vert.*

4. (Erase the board.)
   Everybody, spell the morphograph **duce.** Get ready. (S)
   Now spell the word **introduce.** Get ready. (S)

5. Spell the morphograph **vert.** Get ready. (S)
   Now spell the word **introvert.** Get ready. (S)

6. (Repeat spelling of **introduce** and **introvert** until firm. Give individual turns.)

Doubling Rule Worksheet

Everybody, find part **A** on your worksheet.

Some of these words end in short **CVC** morphographs. Some end in short morphographs that are not **CVC.** Some end in long morphographs.

1. Listen: Underline the morphograph that each word ends with. If there is only one morphograph in the word, underline that morphograph.

2. Write the words in the last column. (Pause while students write the words.)

3. Everybody, look at the first word. What morphograph does **water** end with? (S) *water.*
   (Repeat for **mother, permit, critic, contain, major,** and **cap.**)

4. I will spell each word.
   Put an **X** next to any word you missed and write that word correctly.
   (Write each word on the board as you spell it.)

5. Everybody, turn your worksheet over and get ready to spell some words from the last column without looking.

6. Word one: **watered.** (Pause.)
   Spell **watered.** Get ready. (S)

7. (Repeat step 6 for **motherly, capped,** and **permitting.**)

Oral Spelling Review

You are going to spell some words made up of morphographs you have spelled before.

1. First word: **exceed.**
   What word? (S) *Exceed.*
   Spell **exceed.** Get ready. (S)
   (Repeat until firm.)

2. Next word: **example.**
   What word? (S) *Example.*
   Spell **example.** Get ready. (S)
   (Repeat until firm.)

3. (Repeat step 2 for **designate, professor, pleasure, detour, brought,** and **sciences.**)

Proofreading Letters

Find part **B** on your worksheet.

1. The letter in part **B** has misspelled words.
   You have studied some of the words.

2. If you can find at least 16 of the misspelled
   words, you get zero errors for part **B.**
   15 words equal 1 error, 14 words equal 2
   errors, and so on.

3. Draw a line through each misspelled word.
   Write it correctly on a line next to the letter.

Answer Key

Part B

June 30, 2001

Dear Sandy,

I ~~realy~~ like to ~~recieve~~ your letters. You always ~~right~~
about ~~wonderrful~~ ~~advenchures~~. I had not ~~knowen~~
that there are ~~poisonus~~ snakes at the lake. I'll
bet you were ~~vary~~ happy to return home.

I have been ~~studing~~ insects for a ~~sciense~~ project.
Most people don't like insects, but I think many of
them are ~~actualy~~ ~~bueatiful~~. I have been keeping
~~abowt~~ a ~~thousend~~ of them in my bedroom.

As your ~~firend~~, I must tell you about one
~~weekness~~ in your letters. Your ~~speling~~ is ~~pityful~~. I
can barely read ~~haf~~ the words. I hope you will try
to make fewer ~~mistakes~~ in your next letter.

Yours sincerely,

Pat

really	about
receive	thousand
write	friend
wonderful	weakness
adventures	spelling
known	pitiful
poisonous	half
very	mistakes
studying	
science	
actually	
beautiful	

Lesson 128

EXERCISE 1

Affix Introduction

1. (Write on the board: **intersect, interact,** and **intercept.**)
   Each of these words has a morphograph **inter** at the beginning.
   What morphograph? (S) *inter.*

2. Read these words. (Point to **intersect.**)
   What word? (S) *Intersect.*
   What is the first morphograph in **intersect**? (S) *inter.*
   What is the next morphograph in **intersect**? (S) *sect.*

3. (Point to **interact.**)
   What word? (S) *Interact.*
   What is the first morphograph in **interact**? (S) *inter.*
   What is the next morphograph in **interact**? (S) *act.*

4. (Point to **intercept.**)
   What word? (S) *Intercept.*
   What is the first morphograph in **intercept**? (S) *inter.*
   What is the next morphograph in **intercept**? (S) *cept.*

5. (Erase the board.)
   Everybody, spell the word **sect.**
   Get ready. (S)
   Now spell the word **intersect.**
   Get ready. (S)

6. Everybody, spell the word **act.**
   Get ready. (S)
   Now spell the word **interact.** Get ready. (S)

7. Everybody, spell the morphograph **cept.**
   Get ready. (S)
   Now spell the word **intercept.**
   Get ready. (S)

8. (Repeat spelling of **intersect, interact,** and **intercept** until firm.
   Give individual turns.)

EXERCISE 2

Word and Spelling Introduction

1. (Write on the board: **tense, super, mend,** and **cave.**)
   These words are made up of only one morphograph.

2. (Point to **tense.**)
   What word? (S) *Tense.*
   Spell **tense.** Get ready. (S)
   (Repeat this procedure for each word.)

3. (Erase the words.)
   Spell the words again.
   First word: **cave.** Get ready. (S)
   (Repeat until firm.)

4. (Repeat step 3 for **super, mend,** and **tense.**)

5. Find part **A** on your worksheet.
   Get ready to write the words you just spelled.

6. First word: **mend.**
   What word? (S) *Mend.*
   Write **mend.**
   (Repeat for **cave, super,** and **tense.**)

7. You'll find the spellings of the words we're going to check in appendix **M,** section **B.**

8. (Call on a student.)
   Look up the spelling of the word **mend.**

9. (Assign each of the remaining words to different students.)

10. Get ready to check part **A.**
    Put an **X** next to any word you missed and write that word correctly.

11. (Call on the student who looked up **mend.**)
    Spell **mend.**
    (Write **mend** on the board.)

12. (Repeat step 11 for each remaining word.)

EXERCISE 3

Doubling Rule Worksheet

Everybody, find part **B** on your worksheet.

Some of these words end in short **CVC** morphographs.

Some end in short morphographs that are not **CVC**.

Some end in long morphographs.

1. Listen: Underline the morphograph that each word ends with.
   If there is only one morphograph in the word, underline that morphograph.

2. Write the words in the last column.
   (Pause while students write the words.)

3. Everybody, look at the first word.
   What morphograph does **infer** end with? (S) *fer.*
   (Repeat for **unstop, uncover, recur, spirit,** and **stir.**)

4. I will spell each word.
   Put an **X** next to any word you missed and write that word correctly.
   (Write each word on the board as you spell it.)

5. Everybody, turn your worksheet over and get ready to spell some words from the last column without looking.

6. Word one: **unstoppable.** (Pause.)
   Spell **unstoppable.** Get ready. (S)

7. (Repeat step 6 for **uncovered, spiritual,** and **recurred.**)

8. (Repeat each word until firm. Give individual turns.)

EXERCISE 4

Spelling Review

1. I'll spell some words quickly.
   Then I'll call on different people to spell each word.
   When I call on you, spell the word quickly.

2. My turn: **t - o - u - r - i - n - g.**
   Everybody, what word? (S) *Touring.*

3. Next word: **g - r - a - p - h - i - t - e.**
   What word? (S) *Graphite.*

4. (Repeat step 3 for **freezer, dictator, family, planning, halves, proceed, design, major, predict, concerning, direct, physically,** and **reason.**)

5. Your turn.
   (Call on a student.)
   Spell **design.** Go.

6. (Praise students who respond correctly.)

7. (Call on a student.)
   Spell **dictator.** Go.

8. (Repeat step 7 for **family, major, reason, physically, freezer, proceed, direct, concerning, halves, graphite, touring, planning,** and **predict.** A word may be used more than once.)

EXERCISE 5

Independent Work

1. Complete the rest of the worksheet on your own.
   Be sure to read the instructions carefully.

2. (Check and correct all work.)

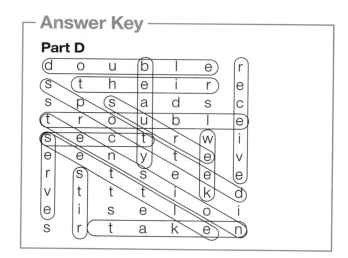

Answer Key

Part D

Lesson 129

EXERCISE 1

Affix Introduction

Note. Refer to the morphograph **ice** by its letter names, **i-c-e.**

1. (Write on the board: **justice, service,** and **notice.**)
   Each of these words has a morphograph **i-c-e** at the end.
   What morphograph? (S) *i-c-e.*

2. Read these words. (Point to **justice.**)
   What word? (S) *Justice.*
   What is the first morphograph in **justice**? (S) *just.*
   What is the next morphograph in **justice**? (S) *i-c-e.*

3. (Point to **service.**)
   What word? (S) *Service.*
   What is the first morphograph in **service**? (S) *serve.*
   What is the next morphograph in **service**? (S) *i-c-e.*

4. (Point to **notice.**)
   What word? (S) *Notice.*
   What is the first morphograph in **notice**? (S) *note.*
   What is the next morphograph in **notice**? (S) *i-c-e.*

5. (Erase the board.)
   Everybody, spell the word **just.**
   Get ready. (S)
   Now spell the word **justice.** Get ready. (S)

6. Everybody, spell the word **serve.**
   Get ready. (S)
   Now spell the word **service.** Be careful.
   Get ready. (S)

7. Everybody, spell the word **note.**
   Get ready. (S)
   Now spell the word **notice.** Be careful.
   Get ready. (S)

8. (Repeat spelling of **justice, service,** and **notice** until firm. Give individual turns.)

EXERCISE 2

Homonyms

1. (Write on the board: **there.**)
   This word is **there.** What word? (S) *There.*

2. This **there** means: **in that place.**
   What does this **there** mean? (S) *In that place.*

3. And how is it spelled? Get ready. (S)
   (Erase the board.)

4. Everybody, spell the **there** that means:
   In that place.
   Get ready. (S)

5. Everybody, spell the **their** that means:
   They own it.
   Get ready. (S)

6. (Repeat steps 4 and 5 until firm. Give individual turns.)

EXERCISE 3

Doubling Rule Worksheet

Everybody, find part **A** on your worksheet.

Some of these words end in short **CVC** morphographs. Some end in short morphographs that are not **CVC**. Some end in long morphographs.

1. Listen: Underline the morphograph that each word ends with.
   If there is only one morphograph in the word, underline that morphograph.

2. Write the words in the last column.
   (Pause while students write the words.)

3. Everybody, look at the first word.
   What morphograph does **expel** end with? (S) *pel.*
   (Repeat for **poison, project, combat, wonder,** and **dig.**)

4. I will spell each word.
   Put an **X** next to any word you missed and write that word correctly.
   (Write each word on the board as you spell it.)

5. Everybody, turn your worksheet over and get ready to spell some words from the last column without looking.
6. Word one: **projection.** (Pause.)
   Spell **projection.** Get ready. (S)
7. (Repeat step 6 for **expelling, combatted, and digger.**)
8. (Repeat each word until firm. Give individual turns.)

EXERCISE 4

Spelling Review

1. I'll spell some words quickly.
   See if you can figure out each word.
2. Listen: **b - e - a - u - t - y.**
   Everybody, what word? (S) *Beauty.*
3. Listen: **c - o - m - p - l - y.**
   What word? (S) *Comply.*
4. (Repeat step 3 for **tension, super, stopper, mending, caves, intercept, graphite, readiness, majority, accent, evaluate, compose,** and **insanely.**)
5. Find part **B** on your worksheet.
   Get ready to write some of those words.
6. First word: **stopper.**
   Write it.
7. Next word: **comply.**
   Write it.
8. (Repeat step 7 for **readiness, intercept, caves, beauty, evaluate,** and **majority.**)
9. I will spell each word.
   Put an **X** next to any word you missed and write that word correctly.
   (Write each word on the board as you spell it.)

EXERCISE 5

Independent Work

1. Complete the rest of the worksheet on your own.
   Be sure to read the instructions carefully.
2. (Check and correct all work.)

---- **EXERCISE 1** ----

Word and Spelling Introduction

1. (Write on the board: **scarce, ideal, grave,** and **duct.**)
   These words are made up of only one morphograph.

2. (Point to **scarce.**)
   What word? (S) *Scarce.*
   Spell **scarce.** Get ready. (S)
   (Repeat this procedure for each word.)

3. (Erase the words.)
   Spell the words again.
   First word: **grave.** Get ready. (S)
   (Repeat until firm.)

4. (Repeat step 3 for **ideal, duct,** and **scarce.**)

5. Find part **A** on your worksheet.
   Get ready to write the words you just spelled.

6. First word: **duct.**
   What word? (S) *Duct.*
   Write **duct.**
   (Repeat for **ideal, scarce,** and **grave.**)

7. You'll find the spellings of the words we're going to check in appendix **M,** section **B.**

8. (Call on a student.)
   Look up the spelling of the word **duct.**

9. (Assign each of the remaining words to different students.)

10. Get ready to check part **A.**
    Put an **X** next to any word you missed and write the word correctly.

11. (Call on the student who looked up **duct.**)
    Spell **duct.**
    (Write **duct** on the board.)

12. (Repeat step 11 for each remaining word.)

---- **EXERCISE 2** ----

Nonword Base

1. (Write on the board: **stant.**)
   Here is a new morphograph that cannot stand alone.
   It is pronounced **stant.**
   What morphograph? (S) *stant.*

2. Everybody, spell **stant.** Get ready. (S)
   (Repeat until firm.)

3. Get ready to spell words that have the morphograph **stant.**
   First word: **constant.**
   What is the first morphograph in **constant**? (S) *con.*
   What is the next morphograph in **constant**? (S) *stant.*
   Spell **constant.** Get ready. (S)

4. Next word: **instant.**
   What is the first morphograph in **instant**? (S) *in.*
   What is the next morphograph in **instant**? (S) *stant.*
   Spell **instant.** Get ready. (S)

5. (Repeat step 4 for **distant** and **substantial.**)

---- **EXERCISE 3** ----

Word Building

Find part **B** on your worksheet.

Get ready to write some words that have more than one morphograph.

Some of these words follow the rule you have learned about doubling the final **C** in short words.

1. Word one: Write **author** in the first column.
   (Check.)
   Write **e-d** in the second column. (Check.)
   Now write **authored** in the last column.
   (Check.)

2. (Repeat step 1 for **recap** + **ing, infer** + **ed,** and **perform** + **er.**)

3. (Check work and have students rewrite any misspellings.)

4. Everybody, turn your worksheet over and get ready to spell the words from the last column without looking.

5. Word one: **recapping.** (Pause.)
Spell **recapping.** Get ready. (S)

6. (Repeat step 5 for **performer, inferred,** and **authored.**)

7. (Repeat each word until firm. Give individual turns.)

EXERCISE 4

Spelling Review

Find part **C** on your worksheet.

You are going to write some words made up of morphographs you have spelled before.

1. First word: **matching.**
What word? (S) *Matching.*
Write **matching.**

2. Next word: **friendliness.**
What word? (S) *Friendliness.*
Write **friendliness.**

3. (Repeat step 2 for **strengthen, carried, weren't, thoughtful, recover,** and **beautiful.**)

4. I'll spell each word.
Put an **X** next to any word you missed and write that word correctly.
(Write each word on the board as you spell it.)

EXERCISE 5

Morphograph Analysis

Everybody, find part **D** on your worksheet.

1. The first word is **preparing.**
What word? (S) *Preparing.*
Tell me the new morphograph in **preparing.** (Pause.)
Get ready. (S) *pare.* Yes, **pare.**

2. (Write on the board: **par, pare,** and **preparing.**)
We have to figure out which of these spellings of **pare** is correct.

3. Here is how we do that.
(Point to the second **r** in **preparing.**)
We see if the **r** is doubled in **preparing.**
Is it? (S) *No.*

4. So can the morphograph **pare** end in **CVC**? (S) *No.*
So which spelling of **pare** is correct?
(S) *p - a - r - e.*
Tell me how to spell **prepare.** (Pause.)
Get ready. (S)
(Repeat spelling **prepare** until firm.)

5. The next word is **controlled.**
What word? (S) *Controlled.*
Tell me the new morphograph in **controlled.** (Pause.)
Get ready. (S) *trol.* Yes, **trol.**

6. (Write on the board: **trol, trole,** and **controlled.**)
We have to figure out which of these spellings of **trol** is correct.

7. Here is how we do that.
(Point to **l** in **controlled.**)
We see if the **l** is doubled in **controlled.**
Is it? (S) *Yes.*

8. So can the morphograph **trol** end in **CVC**? (S) *Yes.*
So which spelling of **trol** is correct?
(S) *t - r - o - l.*
Tell me how to spell **control.** (Pause.)
Get ready. (S)
(Repeat spelling of **control** until firm.)

9. Fill in the blanks to show the morphographs in each word.
Remember to write the morphographs with plus signs between them. (Pause.)

10. (Check and correct.)

EXERCISE 6

Independent Work

1. Complete the rest of the worksheet on your own.
Be sure to read the instructions carefully.

2. (Check and correct all work.)

Mastery Test

1. You are going to have a test today. It will help you see how well you are learning to spell.
2. Everybody, take out a sheet of lined paper and draw a line down the middle. Then number the paper from 1 through 20.
3. (Check and correct.)
4. Word 1 is **perform.**
   Our band will **perform** on Thursday.
   What word? (S) *Perform.*
   Write **perform.**
5. Word 2 is **infection.**
   A cold is an **infection.**
   What word? (S) *Infection.*
   Write **infection.**
6. (Repeat step 5 for the remaining words on the list.)

3.	**texture**	12.	**poisonous**
4.	**tourist**	13.	**definite**
5.	**beauty**	14.	**concern**
6.	**account**	15.	**freshen**
7.	**sweet**	16.	**throw**
8.	**statement**	17.	**simple**
9.	**evaluate**	18.	**dangerous**
10.	**process**	19.	**magical**
11.	**critic**	20.	**hurries**

7. Everybody, exchange papers with your partner. (Pause.)
8. I'll spell each word. If the word is not spelled correctly on the paper you're marking, put an **X** next to it. If the word is spelled correctly, don't put any mark next to it.
9. Word 1 is **perform: p-e-r-f-o-r-m.**
   Check it.
10. (Repeat step 9 for each remaining word.)
11. Return your partner's test paper.
12. Now correct any errors you made. If there is an **X** next to a word on your test, write the word correctly in the right column. Raise your hand if you don't know how to spell any words.
13. Turn your paper over when you're finished. I'll come around and check your paper.
14. If you didn't make any mistakes, raise your hand now.
15. Write the number correct at the top of your test.

Affix Introduction

1. (Write on the board: **realism, criticism,** and **tourism.**)
   Each of these words has a morphograph **ism** at the end.
   What morphograph? (S) *ism.*

2. Read these words. (Point to **realism.**)
   What word? (S) *Realism.*
   What is the first morphograph in **realism**? (S) *real.*
   What is the next morphograph in **realism**? (S) *ism.*

3. (Point to **criticism.**)
   What word? (S) *Criticism.*
   What is the first morphograph in **criticism**? (S) *critic.*
   What is the next morphograph in **criticism**? (S) *ism.*

4. (Point to **tourism.**)
   What word? (S) *Tourism.*
   What is the first morphograph in **tourism**? (S) *tour.*
   What is the next morphograph in **tourism**? (S) *ism.*

5. Everybody, spell the word **real.**
   Get ready. (S)
   Now spell the word **realism.** Get ready. (S)

6. Everybody, spell the word **critic.**
   Get ready. (S)
   Now spell the word **criticism.**
   Get ready. (S)

7. Everybody, spell the word **tour.**
   Get ready. (S)
   Now spell the word **tourism.** Get ready. (S)

Word and Spelling Introduction

1. (Write on the board: **date, medic, after,** and **break.**)
   These words are made up of only one morphograph.

2. (Point to **date.**)
   What word? (S) *Date.*
   Spell **date.** Get ready. (S)
   (Repeat this procedure for each word.)

3. (Erase the words.)
   Spell the words again.
   First word: **after.** Get ready. (S)
   (Repeat until firm.)

4. (Repeat step 3 for **medic, date,** and **break.**)

5. Find part **A** on your worksheet.
   Get ready to write the words you just spelled.

6. First word: **medic.**
   What word? (S) *Medic.*
   Write **medic.**
   (Repeat for **break, after,** and **date.**)

7. You'll find the spellings of the words we're going to check in appendix **M,** section **B.**

8. (Call on a student.)
   Look up the spelling of the word **medic.**

9. (Assign each of the remaining words to different students.)

10. Get ready to check part **A.**
    Put an **X** next to any word you missed and write that word correctly.

11. (Call on the student who looked up **medic.**)
    Spell **medic.**
    (Write **medic** on the board.)

12. (Repeat step 11 for each remaining word.)

Nonword Base

1. (Write on the board: **mise**.)
   Here is a new morphograph that cannot stand alone. It is usually pronounced **miss** or **mize**.
   What morphograph? (S) *mise*.
2. Everybody, spell **mise**. Get ready. (S)
   (Repeat until firm.)
3. Get ready to spell words that have the morphograph **mise**.
   First word: **demise**.
   What is the first morphograph in **demise**?
   (S) *de*.
   What is the next morphograph in **demise**?
   (S) *mise*.
   Spell **demise**. Get ready. (S)
4. Next word: **promise**.
   What is the first morphograph in **promise**?
   (S) *pro*.
   What is the next morphograph in **promise**? (S) *mise*.
   Spell **promise**. Get ready. (S)
5. (Repeat step 4 for **compromise** and **premise**.)

Morphograph Analysis

Everybody, find part **B** on your worksheet.

1. Each word in part **B** has a morphograph that you have not been taught.
   Here is how to find those morphographs.
   You identify all the morphographs in the word that you know.
   The part that is left over is the new morphograph.
2. The first word is **elect**.
   What is the first morphograph you know in that word? (S) *e*.
   Underline it.
3. What is the morphograph in **elect** that you have **not** been taught? (S) *lect*.
4. Write the two morphographs in **elect** with

a plus sign between each one.

5. Everybody, spell the new morphograph in **elect**. Get ready. (S)
   (Repeat spelling of **lect** until firm.)
6. Do the next word on your own. Underline the morphographs that you know.
   Then write the morphographs in **perturb** with a plus sign between each one.
7. (Pause while students write the morphographs in **perturb**.)
   Everybody, what is the new morphograph in **perturb**? (S) *turb*.
   Spell **turb**. Get ready. (S)

   (Repeat spelling of **turb** until firm.)

Word Building

Find part **C** on your worksheet.

Get ready to write some words that have more than one morphograph.
Some of these words follow the rule you have learned about doubling final **C** in short words.

1. Word one: write **control** in the first column. (Check.)
   Write **er** in the second column. (Check.)
   Now write **controller** in the last column. (Check.)
2. (Repeat step 1 for **repel** + **ing**, **pack** + **age**, and **critic** + **al**.)
3. (Check work and have students rewrite any misspellings.)
4. Everybody, turn your worksheet over and get ready to spell the words from the last column without looking.
5. Word one: **repelling**. (Pause.)
   Spell **repelling**. Get ready. (S)
6. (Repeat step 5 for **critical, controller,** and **package**.)
7. (Repeat each word until firm. Give individual turns.)

Independent Work

1. Complete the rest of the worksheet on your own.
   Be sure to read the instructions carefully.
2. (Check and correct all work.)

┌─ **Answer Key** ─────────────────

Part E
1. magical
2. science
3. fanciest
4. thoughtfulness
5. proclaim
6. building

└──────────────────────────────

Supplemental Blackline Masters

Supplemental blackline masters 51 and 52 provide additional practice on material covered in Lessons 126 through 130. You may assign any or all of the activities, and you may award bonus points.

Lesson 132

EXERCISE 1

Affix Introduction

Some words end in the letters **i - s - e.**
Some words end in the letters **i - z - e.**

1. Here is the rule. **I - s - e** is not a morphograph.
   I - z - e is a morphograph.

2. The morphograph **ize** often means: **To make more of something.**
   Humanize means to make more human.
   Formalize means to make more formal.
   Civilize means to make more civil.

3. (Write on the board: **humanize, formalize, and civilize.**)
   Each of these words has a morphograph **ize** at the end.
   What morphograph? (S) *ize.*

4. Read these words. (Point to **humanize.**)
   What word? (S) *Humanize.*
   What is the first morphograph in **humanize**? (S) *human.*
   What is the next morphograph in **humanize**? (S) *ize.*

5. (Point to **formalize.**)
   What word? (S) *Formalize.*
   What is the first morphograph in **formalize**? (S) *form.*
   What is the next morphograph in **formalize**? (S) *a-l.*
   What is the next morphograph in **formalize**? (S) *ize.*

6. (Point to **civilize.**)
   What word? (S) *Civilize.*
   What is the first morphograph in **civilize**? (S) *civil.*
   What is the next morphograph in **civilize**? (S) *ize.*

7. (Erase the board.)
   Everybody, spell the word **human.**
   Get ready. (S)
   Now spell the word **humanize.**
   Get ready. (S)

8. Everybody, spell the word **formal.**
   Get ready. (S)
   Now spell the word **formalize.**
   Get ready. (S)

9. Everybody, spell the word **civil.**
   Get ready. (S)
   Now spell the word **civilize.** Get ready. (S)

10. (Repeat spelling of **humanize, formalize, and civilize** until firm. Give individual turns.)

EXERCISE 2

Nonword Base

1. (Write on the board: **clude.**)
   Here is a new morphograph that cannot stand alone.
   It is pronounced **clude.**
   What morphograph? (S) *clude.*

2. Everybody, spell **clude.** Get ready. (S)
   (Repeat until firm.)

3. Get ready to spell some words that have the morphograph **clude.**
   First word: **include.**
   What is the first morphograph in **include**? (S) *in.*
   What is the next morphograph in **include**? (S) *clude.*
   Spell **include.** Get ready. (S)

4. Next word: **excluded.**
   What is the first morphograph in **excluded**? (S) *ex.*
   What is the next morphograph in **excluded**? (S) *clude.*
   What is the next morphograph in **excluded**? (S) *e-d.*
   Spell **excluded.** Get ready. (S)

5. (Repeat step 4 for **concluding.**)

Spelling Review

1. I'll spell some words quickly.
   See if you can figure out each word.

2. Listen: **p - r - o - t - e - c - t - o - r.**
   Everybody, what word? (S) *Protector*.

3. Listen: **s - c - a - r - c - e.**
   What word? (S) *Scarce*.

4. (Repeat step 3 for **idealism, conduct, surface, realism, scripture, recess, precisely, medical, dictation, confession, introvert, reduce,** and **after**.)

5. Find part **A** on your worksheet.
   Get ready to write some of those words.

6. First word: **surface.**
   Write it.

7. Next word: **medical.**
   Write it.

8. (Repeat step 7 for **conduct, scarce, reduce, after, recess,** and **dictation**.)

9. I will spell each word.
   Put an **X** next to any word you missed and write that word correctly.

   (Write each word on the board as you spell it.)

EXERCISE 4

Morphograph Analysis

Note. Pronounce the morphograph **gin** with a "hard" **g** sound.

Everybody, find part **B** on your worksheet.

1. The first word is **providing.**
   What word? (S) *Providing*.
   Tell me the new morphograph in **providing.** (Pause.)
   Get ready. (S) *vide*. Yes, **vide**.

2. (Write on the board: **vid, vide,** and **providing**.)
   We have to figure out which of these spellings of **vide** is correct.

3. Here is how we do that.
   (Point to **d** in **providing**.)
   We see if the **d** is doubled in **providing.**
   Is it? (S) *No*.

4. So can the morphograph **vide** end in **CVC**? (S) *No*.
   So which spelling of **vide** is correct?
   (S) *v - i - d - e.*
   Tell me how to spell **provide.** (Pause.)
   Get ready. (S)
   (Repeat spelling of **provide** until firm.)

5. The next word is **beginner.**
   What word? (S) *Beginner*.
   Tell me the new morphograph in **beginner.** (Pause.)
   Get ready. (S) *gin*.

6. (Write on the board: **gin, gine,** and **beginner**.)
   We have to figure out which of these spellings of **gin** is correct.

7. Here is how we do that.
   (Point to the first **n** in **beginner**.)
   We see if the **n** is doubled in **beginner.**
   Is it? (S) *Yes*.

8. So can the morphograph **gin** end in **CVC**?
   (S) *Yes*.
   So which spelling of **gin** is correct?
   (S) *g - i - n.*
   Tell me how to spell **begin.** (Pause.)
   Get ready. (S)
   (Repeat spelling of **begin** until firm.)

9. Fill in the blanks to show the morphographs in each word.
   Remember to write the morphographs with plus signs between them. (Pause.)

10. (Check and correct.)

━━━━━ **EXERCISE 5** ━━━━━

Word Building

Find part **C** on your worksheet.

Get ready to write some words that have more than one morphograph.

Some of these words follow the rule you have learned about doubling the final **C** in short words.

1. Word one: Write **human** in the first column. (Check.)
   Write **ize** in the second column. (Check.)
   Now write **humanize** in the last column. (Check.)
2. (Repeat step 1 for **begin** + **ing, incur** + **ed,** and **trip** + **ed.**)
3. (Check work and have students rewrite any misspellings.)
4. Everybody, turn your worksheet over and get ready to spell the words from the last column without looking.
5. Word one: **beginning.** (Pause.)
   Spell **beginning.** Get ready. (S)
6. (Repeat step 5 for **tripped, humanize,** and **incurred.**)
7. (Repeat each word until firm. Give individual turns.)

━━━━━ **EXERCISE 6** ━━━━━

Independent Work

1. Complete the rest of the worksheet on your own.
   Be sure to read the instructions carefully.
2. (Check and correct all work.)

EXERCISE 1

Homonyms

1. Everybody, spell the **there** that means: **in that place.** Get ready. (S)
2. Everybody, spell the **their** that means: **they own it.** Get ready. (S)
3. (Repeat steps 1 and 2 until firm. Give individual turns.)

EXERCISE 2

Affix Introduction

1. (Write on the board: **secure, select,** and **seclude.**)
   Each of these words has a morphograph **s-e** at the beginning.
   What morphograph? (S) *se.*
2. Read these words. (Point to **secure.**)
   What word? (S) *Secure.*
   What is the first morphograph in **secure**? (S) *se.*
   What is the next morphograph in **secure**? (S) *cure.*
3. (Point to **select.**)
   What word? (S) *Select.*
   What is the first morphograph in **select**? (S) *se.*
   What is the next morphograph in **select**? (S) *lect.*
4. (Point to **seclude.**)
   What word? (S) *Seclude.*
   What is the first morphograph in **seclude**? (S) *se.*
   What is the next morphograph in **seclude**? (S) *clude.*
5. (Erase the board.)
   Everybody, spell the word **cure.**
   Get ready. (S)
   Now spell the word **secure.** Get ready. (S)
6. Everybody, spell the morphograph **lect.**
   Get ready. (S)
   Now spell the word **select.** Get ready. (S)
7. Everybody, spell the morphograph **clude.**
   Get ready. (S)
   Now spell the word **seclude.** Get ready. (S)
8. (Repeat spelling of **secure, select,** and **seclude** until firm.)

EXERCISE 3

Word and Spelling Introduction

1. (Write on the board: **air, birth, ball,** and **noon.**)
   These words are made up of only one morphograph.
2. (Point to **air.**)
   What word? (S) *Air.*
   Spell **air.** Get ready. (S)
   (Repeat this procedure for each word.)
3. (Erase the words.)
   Spell the words again.
   First word: **ball.** Get ready. (S)
   (Repeat until firm.)
4. (Repeat step 3 for **birth, noon,** and **air.**)
5. Find part **A** on your worksheet.
   Get ready to write the words you just spelled.
6. First word: **noon.**
   What word? (S) *Noon.*
   Write **noon.**
   (Repeat for **ball, birth,** and **air.**)
7. You'll find the spellings of the words we're going to check in appendix **M,** section **B.**
8. (Call on a student.)
   Look up the spelling of the word **noon.**
9. (Assign each of the remaining words to different students.)
10. Get ready to check part **A.**
    Put an **X** next to any word you missed and write that word correctly.
11. (Call on the student who looked up **noon.**)
    Spell **noon.**
    (Write **noon** on the board.)
12. (Repeat step 11 for each remaining word.)

Nonword Base

1. (Write on the board: **pense.**)
Here is a new morphograph that cannot stand alone.
It is pronounced **pense.**
What morphograph? (S) *pense.*

2. Everybody, spell **pense.** Get ready. (S)
(Repeat until firm.)

3. Get ready to spell words that have the morphograph **pense.**
First word: **expense.**
What is the first morphograph in **expense**? (S) *ex.*
What is the next morphograph in **expense**? (S) *pense.*
Spell **expense.** Get ready. (S)

4. Next word: **compensate.**
What is the first morphograph in **compensate**? (S) *com.*
What is the next morphograph in **compensate**? (S) *pense.*
What is the next morphograph in **compensate**? (S) *ate.*
Spell **compensate.** Be careful. Get ready. (S)

5. (Repeat step 4 for **dispense** and **propensity.**)

Spelling Review

1. I'll spell some words quickly.
See if you can figure out each word.

2. Listen: **m - e - d - i - c.**
Everybody, what word? (S) *Medic.*

3. Listen: **f - o - r - m - a - l - i - z - e.**
What word? (S) *Formalize.*

4. (Repeat step 3 for **humanism, begin, process, wives, expel, wonderful, condense, dictator, prepare,** and **conspire.**)

5. Find part **B** on your worksheet.
Get ready to write some of those words.

6. First word: **process.**
Write it.

7. Next word: **prepare.**
Write it.

8. (Repeat step 7 for **formalize, dictator, wonderful, begin, medic,** and **wives.**)

9. I will spell each word.
Put an **X** next to any word you missed and write that word correctly.
(Write each word on the board as you spell it.)

Word Building

Find part **C** on your worksheet.

Get ready to write some words that have more than one morphograph.

Some of these words follow the rule you have learned about doubling the final **C** in short words.

1. Word one: Write **permit** in the first column. (Check.)
Write **e-d** in the second column. (Check.)
Now write **permitted** in the last column. (Check.)

2. (Repeat step 1 for **civil + ize, tract + or,** and **expel + ed.**)
(Check work and have students rewrite any misspellings.)

3. Everybody, turn your worksheet over and get ready to spell the words from the last column without looking.

4. Word one: **civilize.** (Pause.)
Spell **civilize.** Get ready. (S)

5. (Repeat step 4 for **expelled, permitted,** and **tractor.**)

6. (Repeat each word until firm. Give individual turns.)

Morphograph Analysis

Everybody, find part **D** on your worksheet.

1. Each word in part **D** has a morphograph that you have not been taught.
   Here is how to find those morphographs.
   You identify all the morphographs in the word that you know.
   The part that is left over is the new morphograph.
2. The first word is **medicine.**
   What is the first morphograph you know in that word? (S) *Medic.*
   Underline it.
3. What is the morphograph in **medicine** that you have **not** been taught? (S) *ine.*
4. Write the two morphographs in **medicine** with a plus sign between them.
5. Everybody, spell the new morphograph in **medicine.** Get ready. (S)
   (Repeat spelling of **ine** until firm.)
6. Do the next word on your own. Underline the morphographs that you know.
   Then write the morphographs in **backward** with a plus sign between them.
7. (Pause while students write the morphographs in **backward.**)
   Everybody, what is the new morphograph in **backward**? (S) *ward.*
   Spell **ward.** Get ready. (S)
   (Repeat spelling of **ward** until firm.)

Independent Work

1. Complete the rest of the worksheet on your own.
   Be sure to read the instructions carefully.
2. (Check and correct all work.)

Lesson 134

EXERCISE 1

Word and Spelling Introduction

1. (Write on the board: **teen, stand,** and **stood.**)
   These words are made up of only one morphograph.
2. (Point to **teen.**)
   What word? (S) *Teen.*
   Spell **teen.** Get ready. (S)
   (Repeat this procedure for each word.)
3. (Erase the words.)
   Spell the words again.
   First word: **stand.** Get ready. (S)
   (Repeat until firm.)
4. (Repeat step 3 for **stood** and **teen.**)
5. Find part **A** on your worksheet.
   Get ready to write the words you just spelled.
6. First word: **stood.**
   What word? (S) *Stood.*
   Write **stood.**
   (Repeat for **teen** and **stand.**)
7. You'll find the spellings of the words we're going to check in appendix **M,** section **B.**
8. (Call on a student.)
   Look up the spelling of the word **stood.**
9. (Assign each of the remaining words to different students.)
10. Get ready to check part **A.**
    Put an **X** next to any word you missed and write that word correctly.
11. (Call on the student who looked up **stood.**)
    Spell **stood.**
    (Write **stood** on the board.)
12. (Repeat step 11 for each remaining word.)

EXERCISE 2

Nonword Base

1. (Write on the board: **pute.**)
   Here is a new morphograph that cannot stand alone.
   It is pronounced **pute.**
   What morphograph? (S) *pute.*

2. Everybody, spell **pute.** Get ready. (S)
   (Repeat until firm.)
3. Get ready to spell some words that have the morphograph **pute.**
   First word: **dispute.**
   What is the first morphograph in **dispute?** (S) *dis.*
   What is the next morphograph in **dispute?** (S) *pute.*
   Spell **dispute.** Get ready. (S)
4. Next word: **compute.**
   What is the first morphograph in **compute?** (S) *com.*
   What is the next morphograph in **compute?** (S) *pute.*
   Spell **compute.** Get ready. (S)
5. (Repeat step 4 for **repute.**)

EXERCISE 3

Spelling Review

Find part **B** on your worksheet.

You are going to write some words made up of morphographs you have spelled before.

1. First word: **gravity.**
   What word? (S) *Gravity.*
   Write **gravity.**
2. Next word: **criticism.**
   What word? (S) *Criticism.*
   Write **criticism.**
3. (Repeat step 2 for **hoping, strength, changing, civilized, weren't,** and **because.**)
4. I'll spell each word.
   Put an **X** next to any word you missed and write that word correctly.
   (Write each word on the board as you spell it.)

Word Building

Get ready to spell some words that have more than one morphograph.

1. First word: **secure.**
   What is the first morphograph in **secure**?
   (S) *se.*
   What is the next morphograph in **secure**?
   (S) *cure.*
   Spell **secure.** Get ready. (S)

2. Next word: **realize.**
   What is the first morphograph in **realize**?
   (S) *real.*
   What is the next morphograph in **realize**?
   (S) *ize.*
   Spell **realize.** Get ready. (S)

3. (For **criticism, service, interchange, composite, partially,** and **divide,** have students identify each morphograph and spell each entire word.)

4. Find part **C** on your worksheet.
   You are going to write the words you just spelled.

5. First word: **realize.** Write it.

6. Next word: **partially.** Write it.

7. (Repeat step 6 for **secure, divide, criticism, composite, service,** and **interchange.**)

8. (Check spellings and have students rewrite any missed words.)

Morphograph Analysis

Everybody, find part **D** on your worksheet.

1. The word is **forbidden.**
   What word? (S) *Forbidden.*
   Tell me the second morphograph in **forbidden.** (Pause.)
   Get ready. (S) *bid.* Yes, **bid.**

2. (Write on the board: **bid, bide,** and **forbidden.**)
   We have to figure out which one of these spellings of **bid** is correct.

3. Here is how we do that.
   (Point to the first **d** in **forbidden.**)
   We see if the **d** is doubled in **forbidden.**
   Is it? (S) *Yes.*

4. So can the morphograph **bid** end in **CVC**?
   (S) *Yes.*
   So which spelling of **bid** is correct?
   (S) *b - i - d.*
   Tell me how to spell **forbid.** (Pause.)
   Get ready. (S)
   (Repeat spelling of **forbid** until firm.)

5. Fill in the blanks to show the morphographs.
   Remember to write the morphographs with plus signs between them. (Pause.)

6. (Check and correct.)

Independent Work

1. Complete the rest of the worksheet on your own.
   Be sure to read the instructions carefully.

2. (Check and correct all work.)

Lesson 135

EXERCISE 1

Word and Spelling Introduction

1. (Write on the board: **ever, nine,** and **seven.**)
   These words are made up of only one morphograph.
2. (Point to **ever.**)
   What word? (S) *Ever.*
   Spell **ever.** Get ready. (S)
   (Repeat this procedure for each word.)
3. (Erase the words.)
   Spell the words again.
   First word: **seven.** Get ready. (S)
   (Repeat until firm.)
4. (Repeat step 3 for **nine** and **ever.**)
5. Find part **A** on your worksheet.
   Get ready to write the words you just spelled.
6. First word: **nine.**
   What word? (S) *Nine.*
   Write **nine.**
   (Repeat for **ever** and **seven.**)
7. You'll find the spellings of the words we're going to check in appendix **M,** section **B.**
8. (Call on a student.)
   Look up the spelling of the word **nine.**
9. (Assign each of the remaining words to different students.)
10. Get ready to check part **A.**
    Put an **X** next to any word you missed and write that word correctly.
11. (Call on a student who looked up **nine.**)
    Spell **nine.**
    (Write **nine** on the board.)
12. (Repeat step 11 for each remaining word.)

EXERCISE 2

Spelling Review

1. I'll spell some words quickly.
   Then I'll call on different people to spell each word.
   When I call on you, spell the word quickly.

2. My turn: **f - o - r - b - i - d.**
   Everybody, what word? (S) *Forbid.*
3. Next word: **c - o - m - p - l - e - t - e.**
   What word? (S) *Complete.*
4. (Repeat step 3 for **beginner, afternoon, secure, separate, authorize, election, controlled, expensive, straighten,** and **length.**)
5. Your turn.
   (Call on a student.)
   Spell **election.** Go.
6. (Praise students who respond correctly.)
7. (Call on a student.)
   Spell **length.** Go.
8. (Repeat step 7 for **secure, controlled, complete, separate, forbid, expensive, beginner, straighten, afternoon,** and **authorize.** A word may be used more than once.)

EXERCISE 3

Nonword Base

1. (Write on the board: **quire.**)
   Here is a new morphograph that cannot stand alone.
   It is pronounced **quire.**
   What morphograph? (S) *quire.*
2. Everybody, spell **quire.** Get ready. (S)
   (Repeat until firm.)
3. Get ready to spell words that have the morphograph **quire.**
   First word: **require.**
   What is the first morphograph in **require**? (S) *re.*
   What is the next morphograph in **require**? (S) *quire.*
   Spell **require.** Get ready. (S)
4. Next word: **inquiring.**
   What is the first morphograph in **inquiring**? (S) *in.*
   What is the next morphograph in **inquiring**? (S) *quire.*

What is the next morphograph in
inquiring? (S) *ing.*
Spell **inquiring.** Be careful. Get ready. (S)

5. (Repeat step 4 for **acquired.**)

EXERCISE 4

Morphograph Analysis

Everybody, find part **B** on your worksheet.

1. The first word is **forgotten.**
   What word? (S) *Forgotten.*
   Tell me the new morphograph in
   forgotten. (Pause.)
   Get ready. (S) *got.* Yes, **got.**

2. (Write on the board: **got, gote,** and
   forgotten.)
   We have to figure out which of these
   spellings of **got** is correct.

3. Here is how we do that.
   (Point to the first **t** in **forgotten.**)
   We see if the **t** is doubled in **forgotten.**
   Is it? (S) *Yes.*

4. So can the morphograph **got** end in **CVC**?
   (S) *Yes.*
   So which spelling of **got** is correct?
   (S) *g - o - t.*
   Tell me how to spell **forgot.** (Pause.)
   Get ready. (S)
   (Repeat spelling of **forgot** until firm.)

5. The next word is **desirous.**
   What word? (S) *Desirous.*
   Tell me the new morphograph in
   desirous. (Pause.)
   Get ready. (S) *sire.* Yes, **sire.**

6. (Write on the board: **sir, sire,** and
   desirous.)
   We have to figure out which of these
   spellings of **sire** is correct.

7. Here is how we do that.
   (Point to the **r** in **desirous.**)
   We see if the **r** is doubled in **desirous.**
   Is it? (S) *No.*

8. So can the morphograph **sire** end in
   CVC? (S) *No.*
   So which spelling of **sire** is correct?
   (S) *s - i - r - e.*

Tell me how to spell **desire.** (Pause.)
Get ready. (S)
(Repeat spelling of **desire** until firm.)

9. Fill in the blanks to show the
   morphographs that go in each word.
   Remember to write the morphographs
   with plus signs between them. (Pause.)

10. (Check and correct.)

EXERCISE 5

Independent Work

1. Complete the rest of the worksheet on
   your own.
   Be sure to read the instructions carefully.

2. (Check and correct all work.)

┌─ **Answer Key** ──────────────

Part D
authorize, construction, medical
wasn't, very, realistic, planning
elections, majority

└───────────────────────────

Morphograph Analysis

Everybody, find part **A** on your worksheet.

1. Each word in part **A** has a morphograph that you have not been taught.
   Here is how to find those morphographs.
   You identify all the morphographs in the word that you know.
   The part that is left over is the new morphograph.
2. The first word is **sociable.**
   What is the first morphograph you know in that word? (S) *able.*
   Underline it.
3. What is the morphograph in **sociable** that you have **not** been taught? (S) *soci.*
4. Write the two morphographs in **sociable** with a plus sign between them.
5. Everybody, spell the new morphograph in **sociable.**
   Get ready. (S)
   (Repeat spelling of **soci** until firm.)
6. Do the next word on your own. Underline the morphographs that you know.
   Then write the morphographs in **exhilarate** with a plus sign between each one.
7. (Pause while students write the morphographs in **exhilarate.**)
   Everybody, what is the new morphograph in **exhilarate**? (S) *hilar.*
   Spell **hilar.** Get ready. (S)
   (Repeat spelling of **hilar** until firm.)

Word and Spelling Introduction

1. (Write on the board: **image** and **collar.**)
   These words are made up of only one morphograph.

2. (Point to **image.**)
   What word? (S) *Image.*
   Spell **image.** Get ready. (S)
   (Repeat this procedure for **collar.**)
3. (Erase the words.)
   Spell the words again.
   First word: **collar.** Get ready. (S)
   (Repeat until firm.)
4. (Repeat step 3 for **image.**)
5. Find part **B** on your worksheet.
   Get ready to write the words you just spelled.
6. First word: **image.**
   What word? (S) *Image.*
   Write **image.**
   (Repeat for **collar.**)
7. You'll find the spellings of the words we're going to check in appendix **M**, section **B.**
8. (Call on a student.)
   Look up the spelling of the word **image.**
9. (Assign the remaining word to another student.)
10. Get ready to check part **A.**
    Put an **X** next to any word you missed and write that word correctly.
11. (Call on the student who looked up **image.**)
    Spell **image.**
    (Write **image** on the board.)
12. (Repeat step 11 for **collar.**)

Homonyms

1. Everybody, spell the **their** that means: **they own it.** Get ready. (S)
2. Everybody, spell the **there** that means: **in that place.** Get ready. (S)
3. (Repeat steps 1 and 2 until firm. Give individual turns.)

EXERCISE 4

Sentence Dictation

Find part **C** on your worksheet.
Get ready to write sentences made of words you know.

1. Remember, the first letter of the sentence is capitalized, and you put a period at the end of the sentence.
2. Listen. We obtained authorization <u>to</u> tour <u>the</u> redesigned building.
   Everybody, say that sentence.
   Get ready. (S) *We obtained authorization to tour the redesigned building.*
   (Repeat until firm.)
3. Write that sentence by number one on your worksheet.
   Remember to spell every word correctly.
   (Repeat the sentence as students write.)
4. Listen: <u>You</u> <u>are</u> receiving intensive spelling instruction.
   Everybody, say that sentence.
   Get ready. (S) *You are receiving intensive spelling instruction.*
   (Repeat until firm.)
5. Write that sentence by number two on your worksheet.
   Remember to spell every word correctly.
   (Repeat the sentence as students write.)
6. (Check and correct misspellings. Underlined words—<u>the</u>, <u>to</u>, <u>you</u>, and <u>are</u>—have not been taught.)

EXERCISE 5

Word Building

Get ready to spell some words that have more than one morphograph.

1. First word: **exhilarate.**
   What is the first morphograph in **exhilarate**? (S) *ex.*
   What is the next morphograph in **exhilarate**? (S) *hilar.*
   What is the next morphograph in **exhilarate**? (S) *ate.*
   Spell **exhilarate.** Get ready. (S)

2. Next word: **sociable.**
   What is the first morphograph in **sociable**? (S) *soci.*
   What is the next morphograph in **sociable**? (S) *able.*
   Spell **sociable.** Get ready. (S)
3. (For **partial, medicine, election, divide, acquire,** and **prepare,** have students identify each morphograph and spell each word.)
4. Find part **D** on your worksheet.
   You are going to write some of the words you just spelled.
5. First word: **acquire.** Write it.
6. Next word: **partial.** Write it.
7. (Repeat step 6 for **election, medicine, prepare,** and **divide.**)
8. (Check spellings and have students rewrite any missed words.)

EXERCISE 6

Independent Work

1. Complete the rest of the worksheet on your own.
   Be sure to read the instructions carefully.
2. (Check and correct all work.)

Supplemental Blackline Masters

Supplemental blackline masters 53 and 54 provide additional practice on material covered in Lessons 131 through 135. You may assign any or all of the activities, and you may award bonus points.

Spelling Review

1. I'll spell some words quickly.
   See if you can figure out each word.
2. Listen: **e - x - h - i - l - a - r - a - t - e.**
   Everybody, what word? (S) *Exhilarate.*
3. Listen: **i - m - a - g - e.**
   What word? (S) *Image.*
4. (Repeat step 3 for **collar, social, seventeen, civilized, separate, poisonous, requirement, computer, medicine,** and **compromise.**)
5. Find part **A** on your worksheet.
   Get ready to write some of those words.
6. First word: **social.**
   Write it.
7. Next word: **poisonous.**
   Write it.
8. (Repeat step 7 for **separate, medicine, collar, computer, image,** and **requirement.**)
9. I will spell each word.
   Put an **X** next to any word you missed and write that word correctly.
   (Write each word on the board as you spell it.)

Word Building

Get ready to spell some words that have more than one morphograph.

1. First word: **expensive.**
   What is the first morphograph in **expensive**? (S) *ex.*
   What is the next morphograph in **expensive**? (S) *pense.*
   What is the next morphograph in **expensive**? (S) *ive.*
   Spell **expensive.** Get ready. (S)

2. Next word: **revision.**
   What is the first morphograph in **revision**? (S) *re.*
   What is the next morphograph in **revision**? (S) *vise.*
   What is the next morphograph in **revision**? (S) *i-o-n.*
   Spell **revision.** Get ready. (S)
3. (For **transferred, likelihood, medical, usefully, beautiful, idealism, secluded,** and **notice,** have students identify each morphograph and spell each word.)
4. Find part **B** on your worksheet.
   You are going to write some of the words you just spelled.
5. First word: **medical.** Write it.
6. Next word: **idealism.** Write it.
7. (Repeat step 6 for **beautiful, notice, likelihood,** and **usefully.**)
8. (Check spellings and have students rewrite any missed words.)

Independent Work

1. Complete the rest of the worksheet on your own.
   Be sure to read the instructions carefully.
2. (Check and correct all work.)

Lesson 138

Many of the words in today's lesson are very important. They are words that college students often misspell. Let's see how you do on these words.

EXERCISE 1

Spelling Review

1. I'll spell some words quickly.
   See if you can figure out each word.
2. Listen: f - r - i - e - n - d - l - i - n - e - s - s.
   Everybody, what word? (S) *Friendliness*.
3. Listen: s - t - u - d - y - i - n - g.
   What word? (S) *Studying*.
4. (Repeat step 3 for **receive, doesn't, careless, hoping, strength, applied, definite, using, separate,** and **realize.**)
5. Find part **A** on your worksheet.
   Get ready to write some of those words.
6. First word: **strength.**
   Write it.
7. Next word: **careless.**
   Write it.
8. (Repeat step 7 for **realize, friendliness, using, studying, separate,** and **receive.**)
9. I will spell each word.
   Put an **X** next to any word you missed and write that word correctly.
   (Write each word on the board as you spell it.)

EXERCISE 2

Word Building

Get ready to spell some words that have more than one morphograph.

1. First word: **shining.**
   What is the first morphograph in **shining**?
   (S) *shine*.
   What is the next morphograph in **shining**?
   (S) *ing*.
   Spell **shining.** Get ready. (S)

2. Next word: **loosen.**
   What is the first morphograph in **loosen**?
   (S) *loose*.
   What is the next morphograph in **loosen**?
   (S) *en*.
   Spell **loosen.** Get ready. (S)
3. (For **magician, quietly, marriage, surround, success, prepare, disease,** and **business,** have students identify each morphograph and spell each word.)
4. Find part **B** on your worksheet.
   You are going to write some of the words you just spelled.
5. First word: **quietly.**
   Write it.
6. Next word: **surround.**
   Write it.
7. (Repeat step 6 for **shining, business, marriage,** and **prepare.**)
8. (Check spellings and have students rewrite any missed words.)

EXERCISE 3

Study for Spelling Test

Find appendix **M,** section **B.**

1. During Lesson 140, we're going to have a spelling test.
2. Many of the test words will come from appendix **M,** section **B.**
3. When you've completed your worksheet, study the words.

Note. Students may study in pairs or independently.

EXERCISE 4

Independent Work

1. Complete the rest of the worksheet on your own.
   Be sure to read the instructions carefully.
2. (Check and correct all work.)

Most of the words in today's lesson are often misspelled by college students.

EXERCISE 1

Spelling Review

1. I'll spell some words quickly.
   Then I'll call on different people to spell each word.
   When I call on you, spell the word quickly.
2. My turn: **b - u - s - i - n - e - s - s.**
   Everybody, what word? (S) *Business.*
3. Next word: **l - i - n - e - s.**
   What word? (S) *Lines.*
4. (Repeat step 3 for **except, usual, perform, controlled, decision, preferred, conceive, profession, separation,** and **athlete.**)
5. Your turn.
   (Call on a student.)
   Spell **athlete.** Go.
6. (Praise students who respond correctly.)
7. (Call on a student.)
   Spell **usual.** Go.
8. (Repeat step 7 for **conceive, separation, decision, except, business, lines, perform, preferred, separation,** and **controlled.**)

EXERCISE 2

Word Building

Get ready to spell some words that have more than one morphograph.

1. First word: **really.**
   What is the first morphograph in **really**? (S) *real.*
   What is the next morphograph in **really**? (S) *ly.*
   Spell **really.** Get ready. (S)

2. Next word: **describe.**
   What is the first morphograph in **describe**? (S) *de.*
   What is the next morphograph in **describe**? (S) *scribe.*
   Spell **describe.** Get ready. (S)
3. (For **completely, stretcher, destructive, disappoint, accurately, various, recommend, loneliness, government,** and **marriage,** have students identify each morphograph and spell each word.)
4. Find part **A** on your worksheet.
   You are going to write some of the words you just spelled.
5. First word: **stretcher.** Write it.
6. Next word: **loneliness.** Write it.
7. (Repeat step 6 for **various, marriage, really, government, completely,** and **recommend.**)
8. (Check spellings and have students rewrite any missed words.)

EXERCISE 3

Study for Spelling Test

Find appendix **M,** section **B.**

1. During Lesson 140, we're going to have a spelling test.
2. Many of the test words will come from appendix **M,** section **B.**
3. When you've completed your worksheet, study the words.

Note. Students may study in pairs or independently.

Independent Work

1. Complete the rest of the worksheet on your own.
   Be sure to read the instructions carefully.
2. (Check and correct all work.)

Answer Key

Part B
professor, business, separate
inexpensive, transferred

Note. There is no student worksheet for Lesson 140.

═══════ **EXERCISE 1** ═══════

Spelling Test

1. Everybody, take out a sheet of lined paper for the spelling test.
2. I'll dictate 50 words.
   Some of them you haven't spelled before. But you have spelled all the morphographs.
   If you get 45 words or more correct, you earn 12 worksheet points.
3. Word one: **actor.**
   What word? (S) *Actor.*
   Write **actor.**
4. Word two: **realize.**
   What word? (S) *Realize.*
   Write **realize.**
5. (Repeat step 4 for the following list of words.)

3.	social	21.	indirectly
4.	expensive	22.	control
5.	compromise	23.	requirement
6.	uncivilized	24.	exhilarate
7.	supervise	25.	stretcher
8.	introduce	26.	unfriendly
9.	direction	27.	wonderful
10.	divide	28.	shopper
11.	referred	29.	contraction
12.	production	30.	action
13.	instantly	31.	straighten
14.	election	32.	weren't
15.	compare	33.	physical
16.	medicine	34.	heroic
17.	prepare	35.	happiness
18.	substantial	36.	question
19.	understand	37.	statement
20.	majority	38.	poisonous

39.	interview	45.	athletic
40.	unplanned	46.	intermission
41.	selective	47.	instruction
42.	insecure	48.	professor
43.	visual	49.	basically
44.	tourists	50.	strengthen

6. I'll spell each word. Put an **X** next to any word you missed and write that word correctly.
   (Write each word on the board as you spell it.)
7. (Award points: 45–50 . . . . 12 points
   43–44 . . . . 10 points
   41–42 . . . . 7 points
   39–40 . . . . 5 points
   37–38 . . . . 3 points)

Crossword Puzzles

The crossword puzzles are made up exclusively of the words presented in the review lessons. Every word in these lessons has been used. For each review lesson, there are two or three sets of puzzles, depending on how many words are in the lesson. A set is made up of two puzzles—an original and an alternate. The alternate uses the same words and clues as the original, but in a different arrangement. This gives you a good deal of flexibility in how you use the puzzles.

The crossword puzzle blackline masters are located at the back of this Teacher Presentation Book.

Crossword Puzzles

Name _____ Date _____

ACROSS

1 To gain again
2 The act of injecting
4 Not proven
7 To hold within a container
9 A picture taken with a camera
10 The act of progressing
12 To protect, in the past
14 Not protected
16 To store again
17 Please + ure
19. Fame + ous
20 Sure + ly

DOWN

1 Having the qualities of rain
3 The act of excepting
5 Every night
6 The most shiny
8 That which is painful
11 Take the *phono* from *phonograph*
12 Press + ure
13 One who wins
15 Having the qualities of a cloud
18 Certain

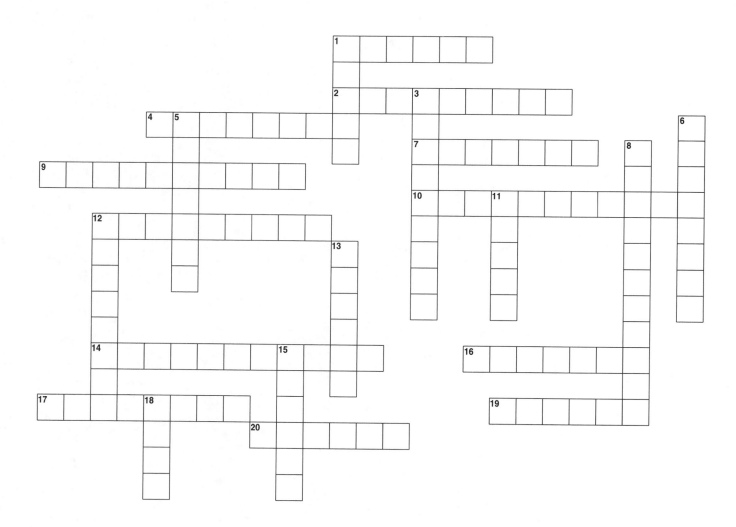

Name _____   Date _____

ACROSS

2 Not protected
6 The act of excepting
10 Having the qualities of a cloud
11 The most shiny
13 To store again
14 Not proven
16 Take the *phono* from *phonograph*
18 The act of progressing
22 Having the qualities of rain

DOWN

1 Press + ure
3 Please + ure
4 That which is painful
5 The act of injecting
7 A picture taken with a camera
8 Fame + ous
9 One who wins
12 To protect, in the past
15 Every night
17 To hold within a container
19 To gain again
20. Sure + ly
21 Certain

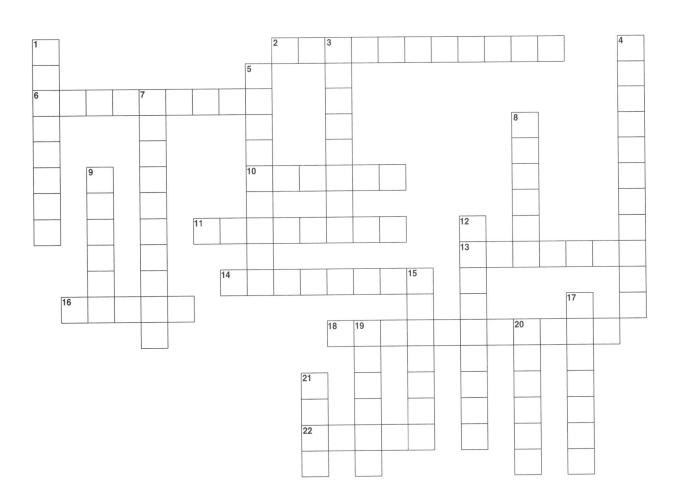

Name _____ Date _____

ACROSS

1 To make stronger
3 A substance that can kill; arsenic
5 Having glory
6 Not crooked
7 Take the *astro* from *astrophysics*
9 Snap + y
14 The act of retaining; re + tent + ion
15 Pre + side
18 Full of wonder
19 How something is gainful
20 The act of receiving; re + cept + ion

DOWN

2 Without thought
4 Able to deceive; de + cept + ive
8 Having fury
10 How something is pure
11 When you trace
12 The most rich
13 Having length
16 One who blows
17 A person who writes books

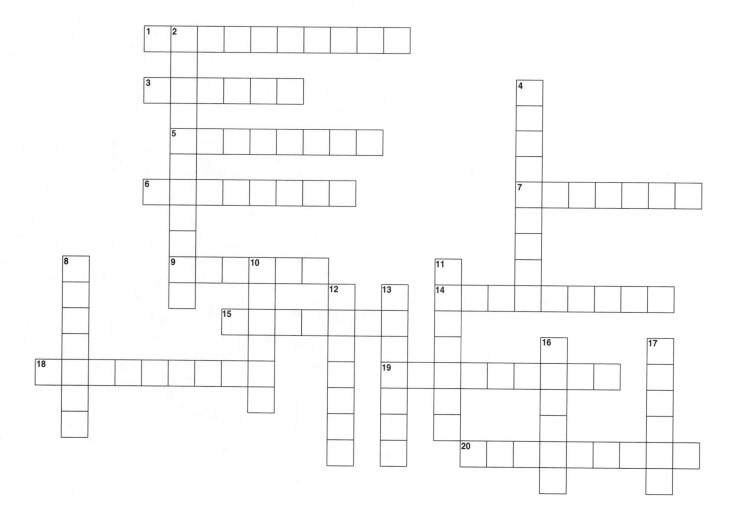

Name _____ Date _____

ACROSS

2 Having length
4 The most rich
5 Able to deceive; de + cept + ive
6 Snap + y
8 One who blows
10 Not crooked
14 The act of retaining; re + tent + ion
15 Having glory
17 To make stronger
18 How something is gainful
19 How something is pure
20 A substance that can kill; arsenic

DOWN

1 Pre + side
3 The act of receiving; re + cept + ion
7 A person who writes books
9 Full of wonder
11 Without thought
12 Take the *astro* from *astrophysics*
13 Having fury
16 When you trace

Name _____ Date _____

ACROSS

3 Plural of basic
4 Related to physics
7 To make smaller; to lose weight
9 Real + ist
10 Not heroic
14 Able to be quoted
15 Sounds like *hope*, starts with *sc*
17 Before second
19 To ask for; to _____ a song
21 To plant, in the past
22 State + ly
23 The person in charge; _____ of police

DOWN

1 That which fails
2 With + out
5 When you induce
6 Having thirst
8 Con + quest
11 Went straight to
12 What you answer; ask a _____
13 Plural of duty
16 Opposite of liked
17 How something is flat
18 To ship, in the past
19 To change, re + vise
20 To push forward; pro + pel

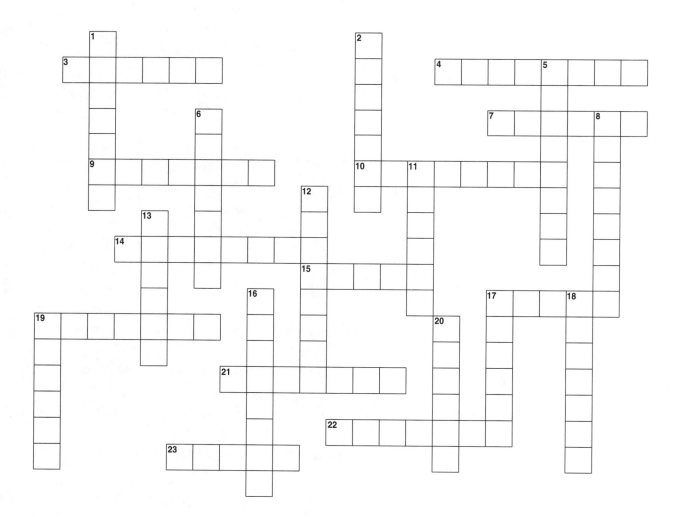

Name _____ Date _____

ACROSS

2 To ask for; to ____ a song
4 Not heroic
6 To change, re + vise
7 What you answer; ask a ____
9 Plural of duty
10 Before second
12 The person in charge; ____ of police
13 To push forward; pro + pel
17 Related to physics
19 To make smaller; to lose weight
20 Able to be quoted
21 State + ly
22 Having thirst

DOWN

1 Went straight to
2 Real + ist
3 To ship, in the past
5 Con + quest
8 With + out
10 That which fails
11 Sounds like *hope*, starts with *sc*
13 To plant, in the past
14 When you induce
15 How something is flat
16 Opposite of liked
18 Plural of basic

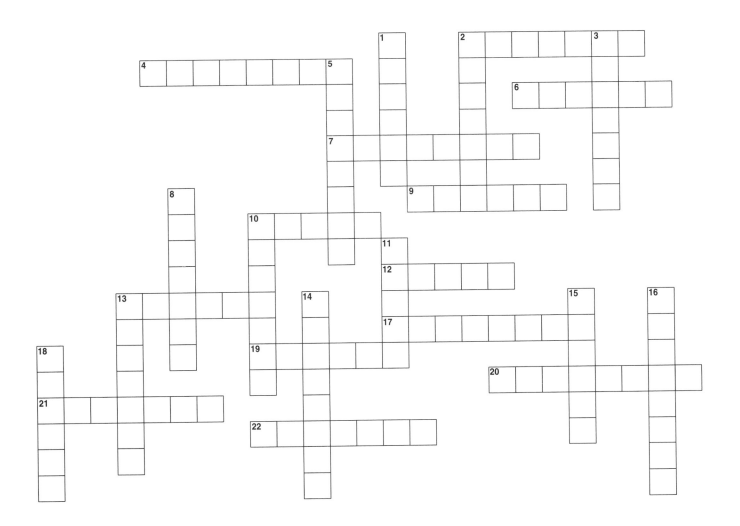

Name _____ Date _____

ACROSS

1 How something is plain
4 Dis + count
6 To express, in the past
10 Stated wrong
12 Swiftly; fast
15 Where trains stop; a train ____
16 A train wheel runs on this; sounds like *fail*
18 To make longer
19 Without breath
22 Re + late + ive
23 How something is brief

DOWN

1 Add *ous* to *poison*
2 Nephews and ____
3 When you hop
5 To make; to manufacture
7 Sickness
8 Not human
9 One who drives a car; motor + ist
11 Opposite of displeasure
12 One fourth of a gallon
13 Not friendly
14 Silently
17 Heavy + ly
20 Plural of herb
21 The life force within a body

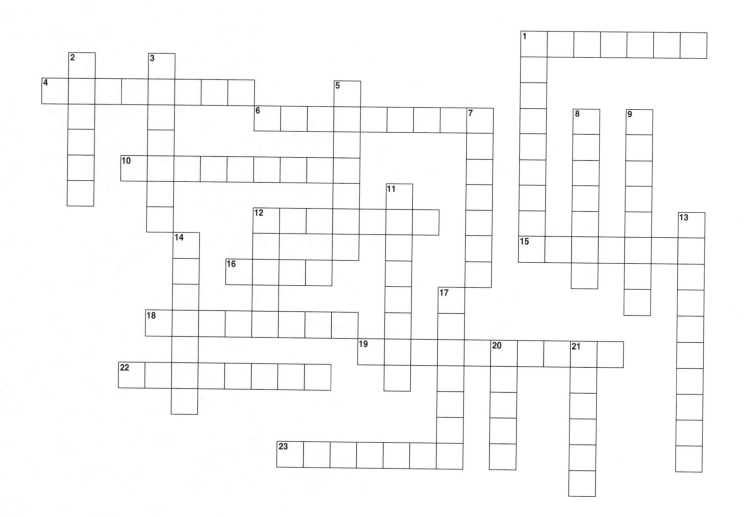

Name _____ Date _____

ACROSS

1 Stated wrong
6 Not human
8 To make; to manufacture
9 To express, in the past
11 Re + late + ive
17 Where trains stop; a train ____
19 The life force within a body
20 Silently
22 Not friendly
23 Opposite of displeasure
24 Swiftly; fast
25 How something is plain

DOWN

2 Sickness
3 When you hop
4 Without breath
5 One fourth of a gallon
7 Nephews and ____
10 Heavy + ly
12 A train wheel runs on this; sounds like *fail*
13 One who drives a car; motor + ist
14 To make longer
15 Add *ous* to *poison*
16 How something is brief
18 Dis + count
21 Plural of herb

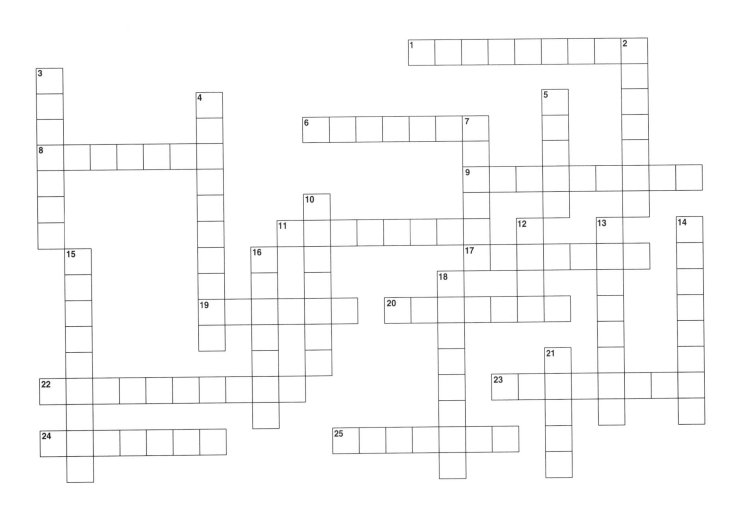

Name _____   Date _____

ACROSS

1 1000s
4 A possibility; sounds like *dance*
8 Over + coat
10 Plural of one who votes
11 Able to be in fashion
14 Having the quality of danger
15 That which is huge
16 Tossed; sounds like *grown*
17 Lid; top; sounds like *lover*
18 Plural of class

DOWN

2 One who takes part in athletics
3 Trans + fuse + ion
5 A turnaround; re + verse + al
6 Familiar; sounds like *phone*
7 In + vert + ion
9 That which is shaky
11 To make a rule against; to not allow
12 To make mention of; re + fer
13 Push + y

Name _____ Date _____

ACROSS

1 Plural of one who votes
6 That which is shaky
7 To make a rule against; to not allow
8 Having the quality of danger
9 That which is huge
12 In + vert + ion
14 Over + coat
15 Familiar; sounds like *phone*
16 A possibility; sounds like *dance*
18 A turnaround; re + verse + al

DOWN

2 Trans + fuse + ion
3 To make mention of; re + fer
4 Tossed; sounds like *grown*
5 1000s
7 Able to be in fashion
10 Lid; top; sounds like *lover*
11 One who takes part in athletics
13 Plural of class
17 Push + y

Name _____ Date _____

ACROSS

3 Able to be questioned
7 Not mental; related to physics
8 One who folds
10 The life force within a body
11 Con + struct + ive
13 Having length
14 To ground, in the past
16 Not structured
17 Forgive + en
18 The act of expressing

DOWN

1 Not above ground
2 The most old
4 To transform, in the past
5 That which is bold
6 When something sheds
8 Add *ous* to *fame*
9 Related to music
12 The act of instructing
15 To change; sounds like *be wise*

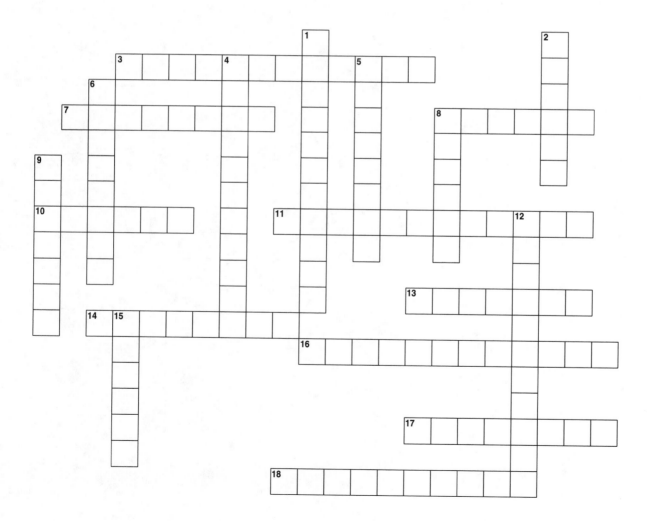

Name _____ Date _____

ACROSS

3 Forgive + en
5 The most old
7 Related to music
9 When something sheds
12 Not structured
14 The life force within a body
15 To change; sounds like *be wise*
17 Not mental; related to physics
18 The act of expressing

DOWN

1 Not above ground
2 Con + struct + ive
3 One who folds
4 That which is bold
6 To transform, in the past
8 The act of instructing
10 To ground, in the past
11 Able to be questioned
13 Having length
16 Add *ous* to *fame*

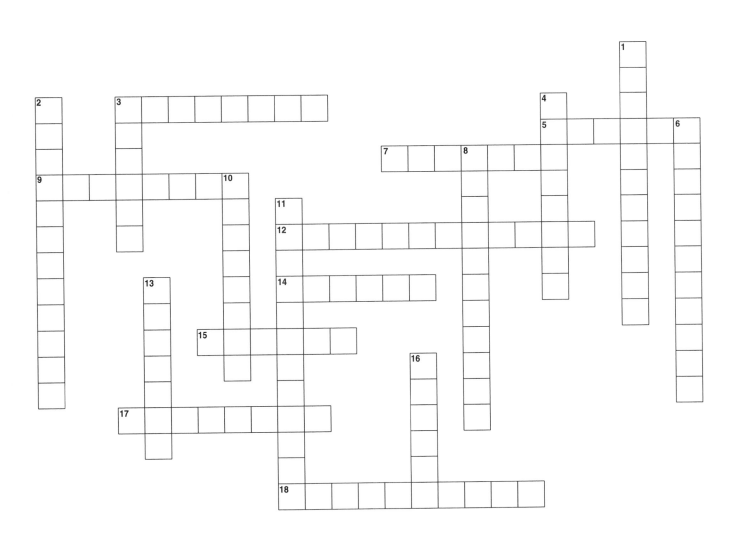

Name _____ Date _____

ACROSS

1 Having to do with citizens; the _____ War
2 Able to be noted
3 One who writes books
6 How something is quiet
12 When something snaps
13 To move again
14 To spell wrong, in the past
15 Full of wonder
16 Where trains stop; a train _____

DOWN

1 A signed agreement
4 Not equal
5 One who designs
7 That which does not follow the rule; ex + cept + ion
8 An error; to take wrong
9 Having the qualities of poison
10 Related to a sign
11 Able to be used

Name _____ Date _____

ACROSS

1 Full of wonder
3 One who designs
5 An error; to take wrong
9 Having the qualities of poison
11 When something snaps
14 One who writes books
15 Having to do with citizens; the _____ War
16 To move again

DOWN

2 Able to be used
4 That which does not follow the rule;
ex + cept + ion
5 To spell wrong, in the past
6 Related to a sign
7 A signed agreement
8 Not equal
10 Where trains stop; a train _____
12 Able to be noted
13 How something is quiet

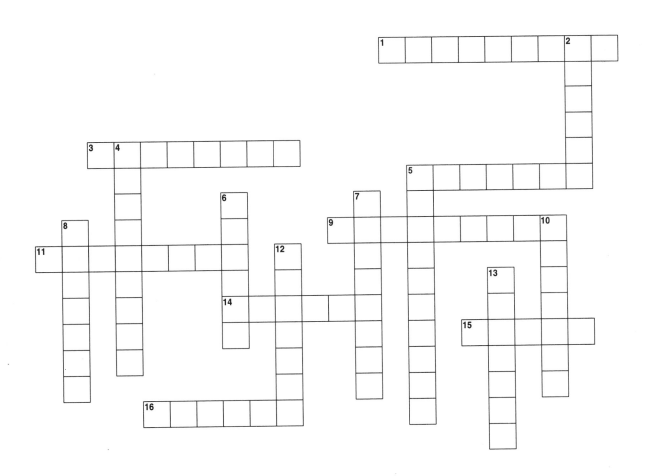

Name _____ Date _____

ACROSS

1 To watch closely; ob + serve
5 To cover again; to get back
8 Not reasonable
9 Related to acting; act + ual
12 Wanting everything for oneself; greedy
13 *Fashionable* minus *able*
14 How something is basic
15 One who performs
16 Having the qualities of danger

DOWN

2 The most sweet
3 To stretch out your arm; sounds like *beach*
4 One who speaks
6 Related to instruction
7 Opposite of minor; sounds like *wager*
9 On the other side; _____ the ocean
10 To make stronger; re + in + force
11 1000

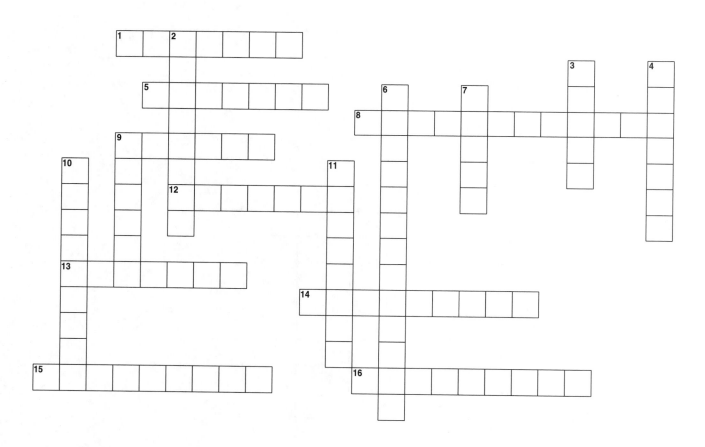

Name _____ Date _____

ACROSS

2 How something is basic
5 Not reasonable
7 On the other side; ____ the ocean
10 Related to instruction
13 Wanting everything for oneself; greedy
14 One who performs
15 Related to acting; act + ual
16 To cover again; to get back

DOWN

1 Having the qualities of danger
3 One who speaks
4 Opposite of minor; sounds like *wager*
6 To stretch out your arm; sounds like *beach*
8 To make stronger; re + in + force
9 *Fashionable* minus *able*
11 1000
12 To watch closely; ob + serve
13 The most sweet

Name _____ Date _____

ACROSS

1 Take the *ion* from *objection*
4 Having the qualities of poison
7 A robber; one who steals
8 To spoil; in the past
9 Related to the spirit
12 To make up (especially music)
13 That which equips
16 The act of expressing
17 Feelings for another's sorrow; com + pass + ion

DOWN

2 A box; a carton; that which contains
3 In between; beginning, _____, and end
5 That which states
6 Full of thought
10 A + round
11 That which amuses
14 All right; nothing wrong
15 Plural of berry

Name _____ Date _____

ACROSS

3 The act of expressing
6 Feelings for another's sorrow;
com + pass + ion
8 In between; beginning, _____, and end
9 A + round
10 Take the *ion* from *objection*
12 Full of thought
14 All right; nothing wrong
15 Plural of berry
16 That which equips

DOWN

1 That which states
2 To spoil; in the past
4 That which amuses
5 Having the qualities of poison
6 A box; a carton; that which contains
7 Related to the spirit
11 To make up (especially music)
13 A robber; one who steals

Name _____ Date _____

ACROSS

2 How someone is civil
5 To get
6 That which governs
9 One who swims
11 Opposite of crooked
12 To change from one to another; trans + fer
13 I *study*, you *study*, she _____
14 Like a realist
15 Opposite of different; the same

DOWN

1 A polite word to use when you ask for something
3 To join, in the past
4 That which is lifeless
6 Little by little
7 To make believe
8 Opposite of remember
10 Not mental; related to physics

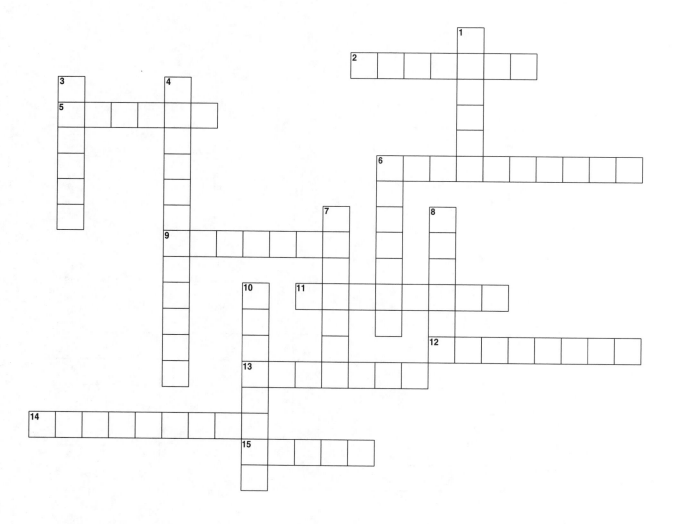

Name _____ Date _____

ACROSS

1 Opposite of remember
4 Not mental; related to physics
6 Little by little
8 Opposite of crooked
9 Like a realist
12 To join, in the past
13 I *study*, you *study*, she _____
14 That which governs
15 To change from one to another; trans + fer

DOWN

2 To get
3 How someone is civil
4 A polite word to use when you ask for something
5 Opposite of different; the same
7 That which is lifeless
10 One who swims
11 To make believe

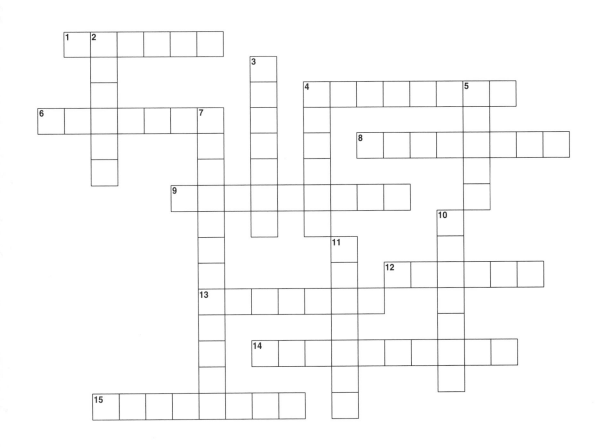

181

Name _____ Date _____

ACROSS

2 A part; a portion; sect + ion
5 Friend + ship
7 Something hard to solve; a crossword _____
9 A round shape forms a _____
10 To view again
14 Worth
15 The state of being depressed
16 The cause
17 To see or learn of for the first time

DOWN

1 Related to a graph
3 Plural of thief
4 Opposite of amateur
6 To act (especially on the stage)
8 How something is equal
11 Not complete
12 A person who acts
13 The state of being weak

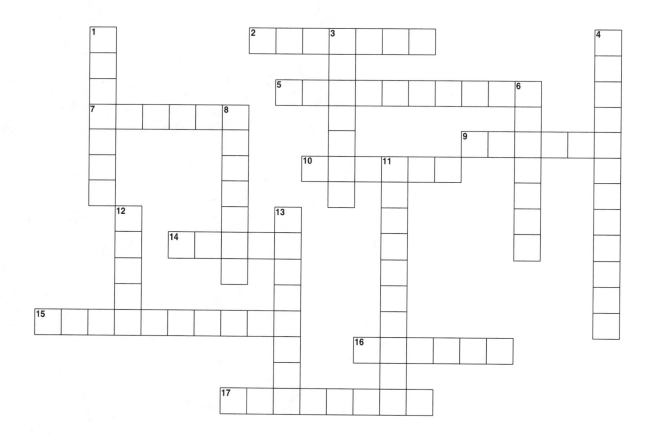

Name _____ Date _____

ACROSS

1 To act (especially on the stage)
3 To view again
7 A round shape forms a _____
10 That which is weak
11 Related to a graph
12 The cause
14 How something is equal
15 Friend + ship
16 A person who acts

DOWN

1 Opposite of amateur
2 Something hard to solve; a crossword _____
4 Worth
5 Plural of thief
6 To see or learn of for the first time
8 Not complete
9 The state of being depressed
13 A part; a portion; sect + ion

Name _____   Date _____

ACROSS

1 A forecast; pre + dict + ion
7 Plural of half
9 To be there; at + tend
10 Opposite of usual
15 A box; a carton; something that contains
16 How something is done in a complete way
17 1000

DOWN

2 Something that can be seen or touched; a thing
3 A part of speech; a word that describes a verb
4 To answer
5 How something is done in a physical way
6 Not supported
8 An order for a magazine
11 Opposite of multiply
12 Opposite of sour
13 In + stance
14 Opposite of give

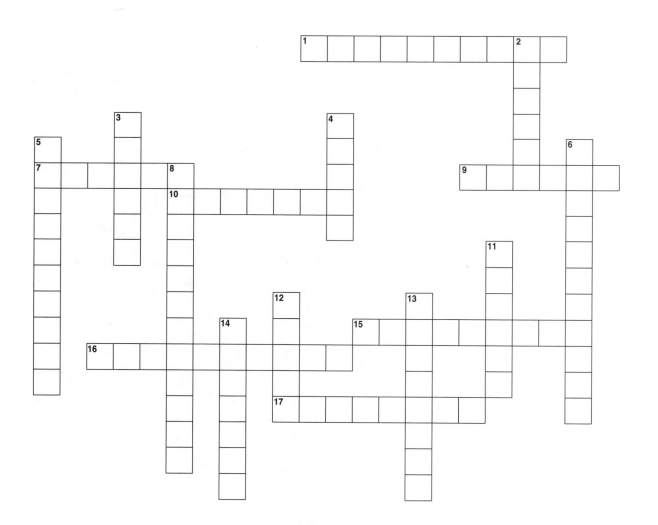

Name _____ Date _____

ACROSS

1 1000
4 Opposite of usual
6 Opposite of sour
7 An order for a magazine
12 Something that can be seen or touched; a thing
13 To be there; at + tend
14 How something is done in a complete way
15 Opposite of multiply
16 A part of speech; ad + verb
17 To answer

DOWN

2 Not supported
3 A forecast; pre + dict + ion
5 In + stance
8 A box; a carton; something that contains
9 How something is done in a physical way
10 Opposite of give
11 Plural of half

Name _____ Date _____

ACROSS

2 The top layer; the ____ of the water
7 Movement
8 Author + ship
10 To get well after an illness
12 Having the qualities of poison
13 To keep something from falling; sup + port
14 A person who takes part in athletics
15 Out of breath

DOWN

1 To view before
2 A school subject; the study of plants and animals
3 An unusual and exciting experience
4 The act of expressing
5 Good looks; opposite of ugliness
6 The act of instructing
9 A picture taken with a camera
11 To use up; con + sume

Copyright © by SRA/McGraw-Hill. Permission is granted to reproduce this page for classroom use.

Name _____ Date _____

ACROSS

2 To view before
5 To use up; con + sume
7 To keep something from falling; sup + port
9 Author + ship
12 The act of instructing
13 Having the qualities of poison
14 The act of expressing

DOWN

1 Good looks; opposite of ugliness
3 To get well after an illness
4 A picture taken with a camera
6 Movement
7 A school subject; the study of plants and animals
8 Out of breath
9 A person who takes part in athletics
10 An unusual and exciting experience
11 The top layer; the _____ of the water

Name _____ Date _____

ACROSS

1 To refer, in the past
5 To see how two things are the same; com + pare
6 The act of directing
9 Not civilized
11 Opposite of multiply
13 One who acts
14 To watch over workers; super + vise
15 The act of producing
16 The act of electing
17 You take this when you are sick

DOWN

2 Opposite of cheap
3 Related to society
4 How something is done in an instant
7 To make known; intro + duce
8 To know what is real; sounds like *seal eyes*
10 To give a little and take a little; com + pro + mise
12 To get ready

Name _____   Date _____

ACROSS

1 To give a little and take a little; com + pro + mise
5 The act of directing
6 To watch over workers; super + vise
11 To make known; intro + duce
15 The act of electing
16 To refer, in the past
17 Opposite of cheap

DOWN

2 You take this when you are sick
3 Not civilized
4 The act of producing
7 How something is done in an instant
8 Related to society
9 Opposite of multiply
10 To get ready
12 To know what is real; sounds like *seal eyes*
13 To see how two things are the same; com + pare
14 One who acts

Name _____ Date _____

ACROSS

1 One who shops
3 Opposite of minority
4 People on a tour
10 Take the *ness* from *selectiveness*
13 To know what something means
14 Related to substance
15 To ask a person questions; The reporter will _____ the movie star.
16 Not planned

DOWN

1 That which stretches
2 To regulate; con + trol
5 Related to vision
6 Not directly
7 That which requires
8 Full of wonder
9 Not friendly
11 Not secure
12 To make lively; ex + hilar + ate

Name _____ Date _____

ACROSS

1 Related to substance
4 To regulate; con + trol
5 That which requires
8 People on a tour
10 Not directly
11 To make lively; ex + hilar + ate
13 One who shops
14 To know what something means
15 Not friendly
16 Not secure

DOWN

1 Take the *ness* from *selectiveness*
2 Related to vision
3 To ask a person questions; The reporter will _____ the movie star.
6 Opposite of minority
7 That which stretches
9 Not planned
12 Full of wonder

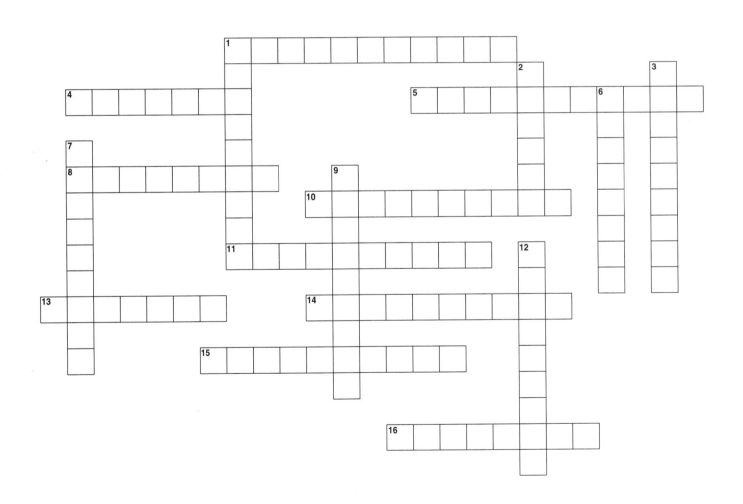

Name _____ Date _____

ACROSS

3 Having the qualities of poison
8 That which states
10 A teacher (usually at a university)
12 Like a hero
13 The act of acting
14 To make straight
15 The act of contracting

DOWN

1 An interruption (usually during a movie or play)
2 Opposite of answer
4 To make stronger
5 How something is basic
6 Like an athlete
7 Happy + ness
9 The act of instructing
11 Related to physics

Name _____ Date _____

ACROSS

2 Having the qualities of poison
6 An interruption (usually during a movie or play)
7 The act of contracting
10 Related to physics
12 The act of instructing
13 Like a hero
14 That which states
15 Happy + ness

DOWN

1 A teacher (usually at a university)
3 To make straight
4 How something is basic
5 To make stronger
8 Opposite of answer
9 The act of acting
11 Like an athlete

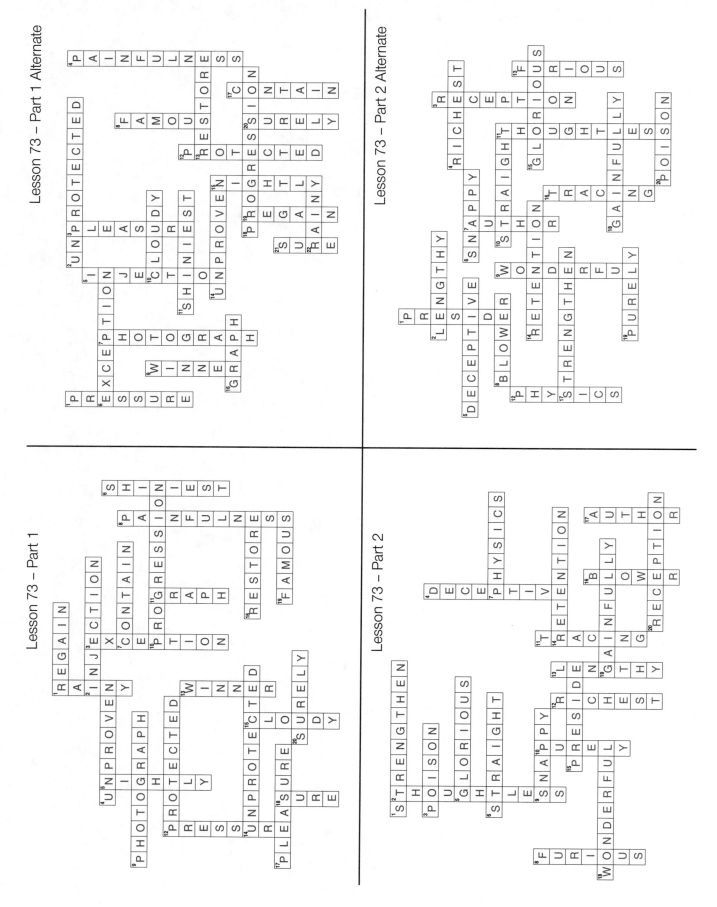

Lesson 73 – Part 1 Alternate

Lesson 73 – Part 2 Alternate

Lesson 73 – Part 1

Lesson 73 – Part 2

194

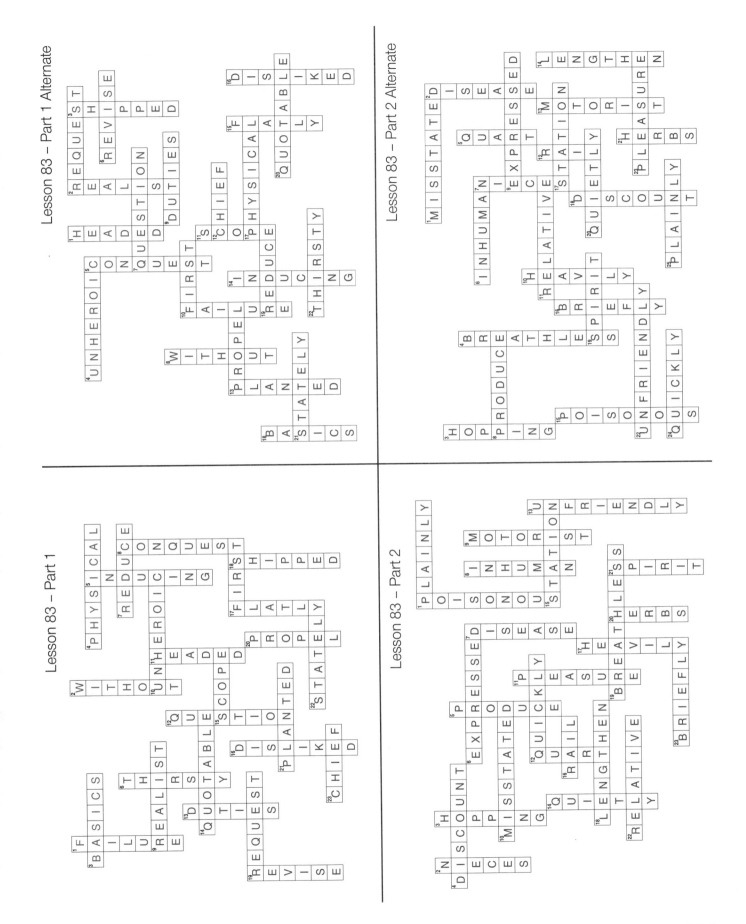

195

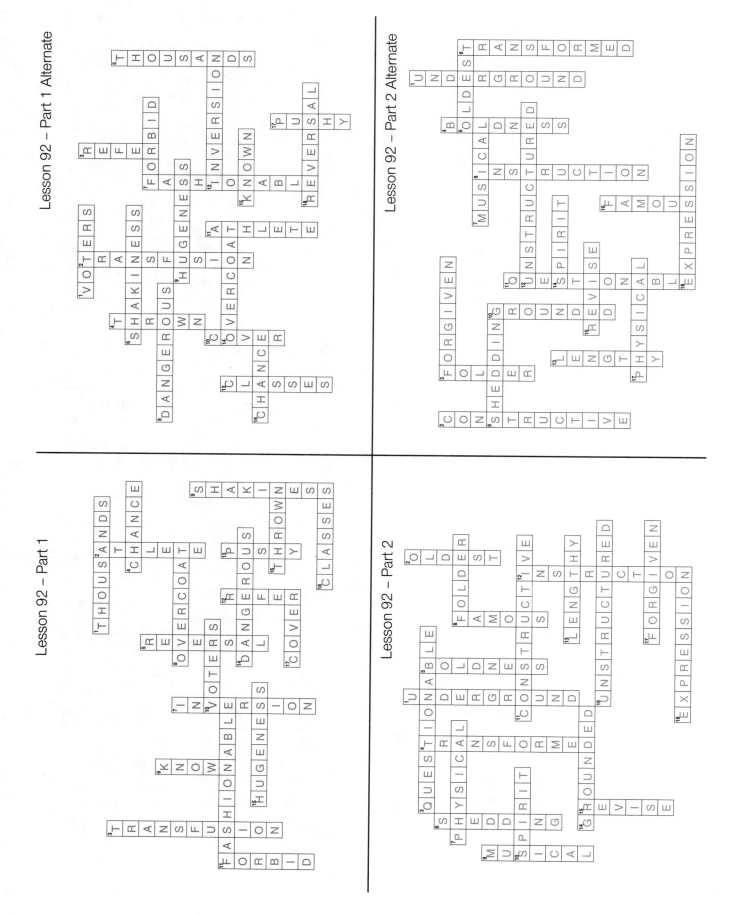

Lesson 92 – Part 1 Alternate

Lesson 92 – Part 2 Alternate

Lesson 92 – Part 1

Lesson 92 – Part 2

196

Lesson 92 – Part 3 Alternate

Lesson 102 – Part 1 Alternate

Lesson 92 – Part 3

Lesson 102 – Part 1

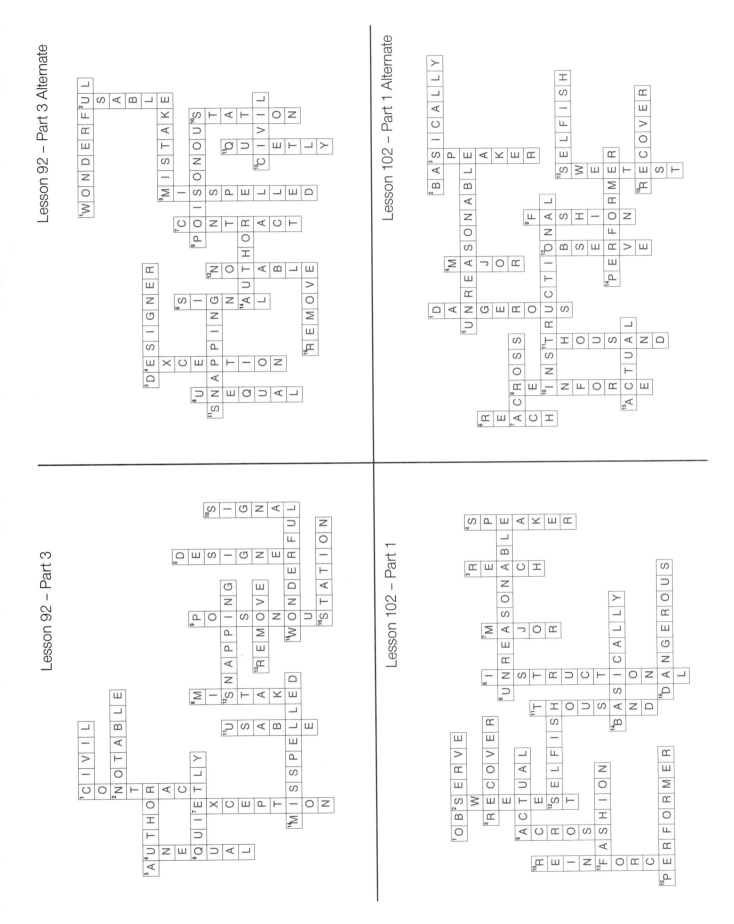

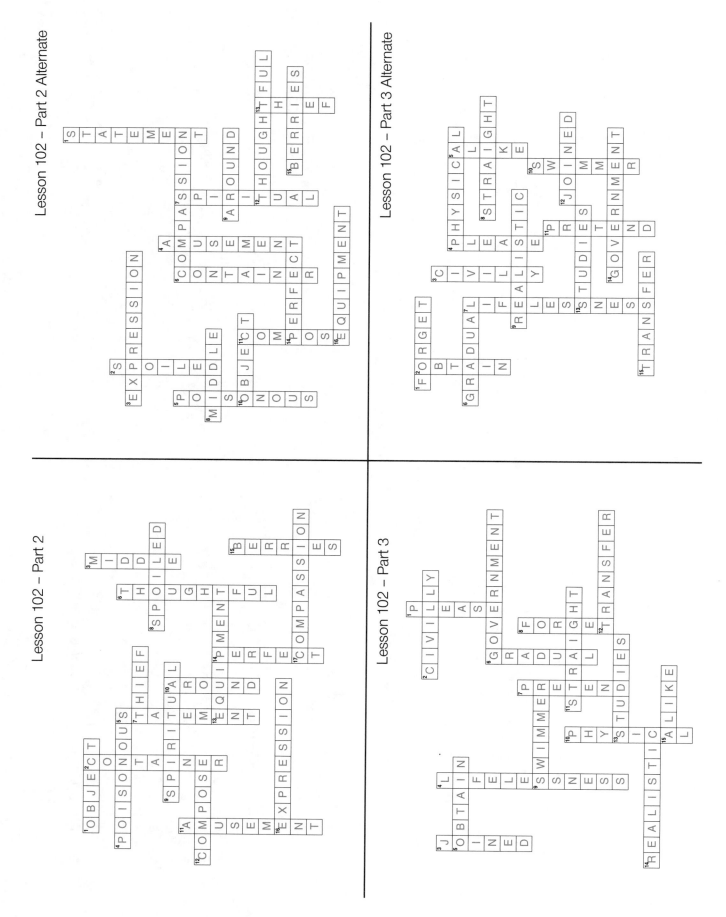

Lesson 102 – Part 2

Lesson 102 – Part 2 Alternate

Lesson 102 – Part 3

Lesson 102 – Part 3 Alternate

198

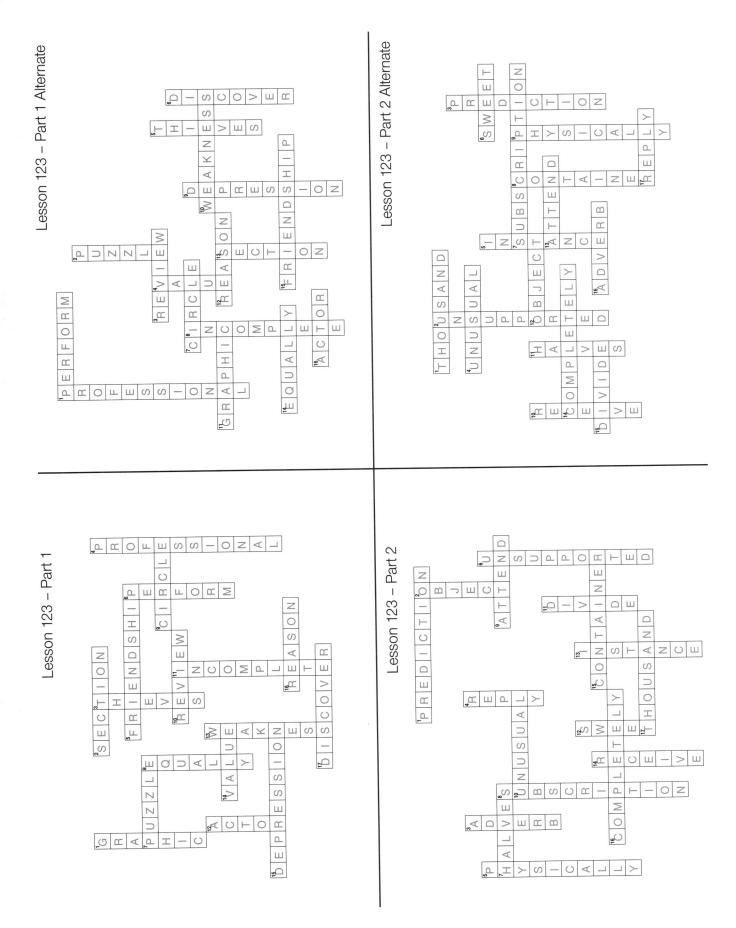

Lesson 123 – Part 1 Alternate

Lesson 123 – Part 2 Alternate

Lesson 123 – Part 1

Lesson 123 – Part 2

199

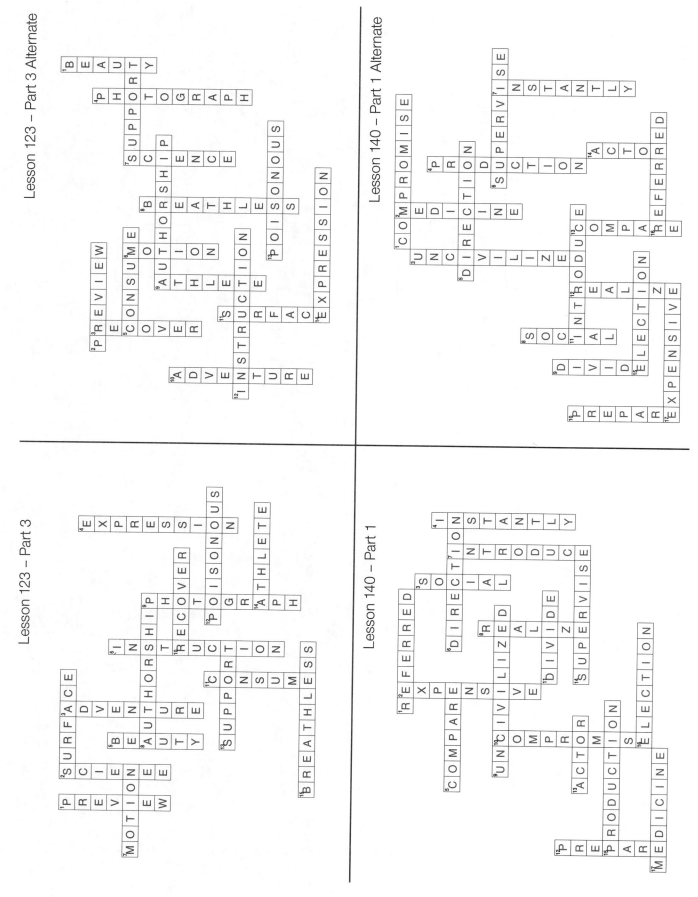

Lesson 123 – Part 3 Alternate

Lesson 140 – Part 1 Alternate

Lesson 123 – Part 3

Lesson 140 – Part 1

200

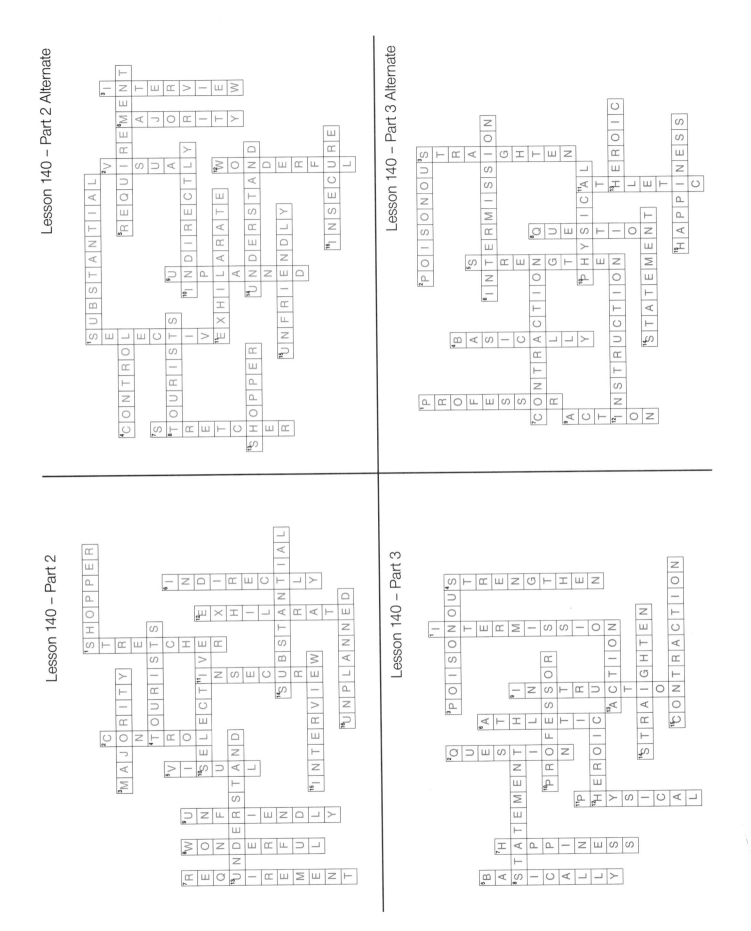

Lesson 140 – Part 2 Alternate

Lesson 140 – Part 3 Alternate

Lesson 140 – Part 2

Lesson 140 – Part 3

Supplemental Blackline Masters

Name _____ Date _____

Part A

Word Building
Write a new word in the blank.

1. danger + ous   = _____
2. seize + ure   = _____
3. quest + ion + able = _____
4. poison + ous   = _____
5. con + tent   = _____
6. re + sent + ment   = _____
7. shine + y   = _____
8. fail + ure   = _____

Part B

Proofreading
Fill in the bubble below the misspelled word. Write the word correctly in the blank.

1. <u>Could</u> you speak a little <u>lowder, please</u> ?
   ○   ○   ○   _____

2. <u>Where</u> are all the <u>fameous</u> <u>people</u>?
   ○   ○   ○   _____

3. <u>Thier</u> was no <u>reason</u> for the <u>rejection</u>.
   ○   ○   ○   _____

4. The <u>gloryous</u> <u>cities</u> were <u>surprising</u>.
   ○   ○   ○   _____

5. They <u>expressed</u> <u>delite</u> over the <u>outcome</u>.
   ○   ○   ○   _____

6. Everyone who was on <u>duty</u> felt <u>frightened</u> and <u>edgey</u>.
   ○   ○   ○

Name _____ Date _____

Part C

Morphograph Analysis
Fill in the blanks to show the morphographs in each word.

1. _____ + _____ = feature

2. _____ + _____ + _____ = repressive

3. _____ + _____ + _____ = defeated

4. _____ + _____ = profound

5. _____ + _____ = valuable

Part D

Vocabulary
Write the contraction.

1. _____ we are

2. _____ cannot

3. _____ they will

4. _____ do not

5. _____ he is

Part E

Writing
Write two or three sentences about the picture. The sentences must contain the words **compete**, **athlete**, and **progress**.

_____

_____

_____

_____

_____

Name _____ Date _____

Part A

Word Building
Write a new word in the blank.

1. hope + ful   = _____   4. con + tent + ment = _____

2. dis + ease   = _____   5. fame + ous   = _____

3. re + tain + ing   = _____

Part B

Proofreading
Fill in the bubble beside the the word that goes in the blank. Write the word in the blank.

1. The _____ has been great.   ○ weather   ○ wether

2. They found _____ things in the garage.   ○ their   ○ there

3. We _____ rocks into the lake.   ○ through   ○ threw

4. Pete ate _____ much.   ○ to   ○ too

5. Please bring those books _____.   ○ hear   ○ here

6. I've never heard such a strange _____.   ○ tail   ○ tale

Part C

Word Building
Make 9 real words from the morphographs in the box. Additional words are possible.

est	mad	happy	ly	wide	ness	fine

1. _____   6. _____

2. _____   7. _____

3. _____   8. _____

4. _____   9. _____

5. _____

Name _____ Date _____

Part C

Morphograph Analysis
Fill in the blanks to show the morphographs in each word.

1. _____ + _____ = texture

2. _____ + _____ + _____ = protective

3. _____ + _____ + _____ = discharged

4. _____ + _____ = stories

5. _____ + _____ = pleasure

Part D

Vocabulary
Write the contraction.

1. _____ that is

2. _____ should not

3. _____ they have

4. _____ who is

5. _____ she will

Part E

Writing
Write two or three sentences about the picture. The sentences must contain the words **distance, weather,** and **cloud.**

_____

_____

_____

_____

_____

Name _____ Date _____

Part A

Word Building
Write the new word in the blank.

1. dis + please + ing   = _____   4. danger + ous + ly   = _____

2. speed + y + est   = _____   5. in + crease + ing + ly = _____

3. re + spect + ful   = _____

Part B

Proofreading
Fill in the bubble beside the the word that goes in the blank. Write the word in the blank.

1. I poked a _____ in my worksheet.   ○ hole   ○ whole

2. Would you care for a _____ of pie?   ○ peace   ○ piece

3. Robin didn't _____ the question.   ○ hear   ○ here

4. _____ police officers visited our school.   ○ Too   ○ Two

5. Our house became _____ warm.   ○ vary   ○ very

6. The dog's _____ is short.   ○ tail   ○ tale

Part C

Word Building
Make 9 real words from the morphographs in the box.

ed	cover	un	re	dis	solve

1. _____   6. _____

2. _____   7. _____

3. _____   8. _____

4. _____   9. _____

5. _____

Name _____ Date _____

Part D

Morphograph Analysis
Fill in the blanks to show the morphographs in each word.

1. _____ + _____ = expel

2. _____ + _____ + _____ = refusal

3. _____ + _____ + _____ = respectable

4. _____ + _____ = chiefly

5. _____ + _____ = complain

Part E

Vocabulary
Write the word for each meaning.

1. _____ one who types

2. _____ fourth of a dollar

3. _____ the quality of fury

4. _____ do not like

5. _____ really famous

Part F

Writing
Write two or three sentences about the picture. The sentences must contain the words **recreation, afternoon,** and **winner.**

_____

_____

_____

_____

_____

Name _____ Date _____

Part A

Word Building
Write a new word in the blank.

1. create + ive   = _____

2. dis + courage   = _____

3. re + gard + less   = _____

4. niece + es   = _____

5. in + tense + ive + ly = _____

Part B

Proofreading
Fill in the bubble below the misspelled word. Write the word correctly in the blank.

1. Mom <u>agreed</u> that <u>we'er</u> getting new <u>glasses</u> today.   _____
   ○   ○   ○

2. The <u>tourists</u> traveled <u>joyusly</u> <u>together</u>.   _____
   ○   ○   ○

3. The <u>clowdiness</u> and <u>temperature</u> made us <u>unhappy</u>.   _____
   ○   ○   ○

Part C

Proofreading
Circle the letter beside the misspelled word in each group.
Then write the word correctly on the line.

1. **A** breakable
   B dowbt
   C pleasure
   D peaceful
   _____

2. **A** increase
   B changing
   C noisily
   D ejucate
   _____

3. **A** exchange
   B chance
   C wreckage
   D sturdyness
   _____

4. **A** honesty
   B tomorow
   C inspect
   D product
   _____

5. **A** revursal
   B compound
   C chance
   D vision
   _____

6. **A** basic
   B transeport
   C incident
   D refuse
   _____

Name _____ Date _____

Part D

Morphograph Analysis

Fill in the blanks to show the morphographs in each word.

1. _____ + _____ = infer

2. _____ + _____ + _____ = transformed

3. _____ + _____ + _____ = explainable

4. _____ + _____ = poundage

5. _____ + _____ = resign

Part E

Vocabulary

Write the word for each meaning.

1. _____ one who explores

2. _____ one who produces art

3. _____ the quality of joy

4. _____ more than one watch

5. _____ not pleasing

Part F

Writing

Write two or three sentences about the
picture. The sentences must contain the
words **danger, poison,** and **reach.**

_____

_____

_____

_____

_____

Name _____ Date _____

Part A

Word Building
Write the new word in the blank.

1. dis + pose + al   = _____
2. a + muse + ment   = _____
3. for + got + en   = _____
4. photo + graph + y   = _____
5. mis + in + struct + ed = _____

Part B

Proofreading
Fill in the bubble beside the word that goes in the blank. Write the word in the blank.

1. Martin always hangs up his _____.   ○ close   ○ clothes

2. I don't _____ the answer.   ○ know   ○ no

3. Our club _____ after school.   ○ meats   ○ meets

4. There is a _____ tree growing in our yard. ○ loan   ○ lone

5. The tickets go on _____ in the morning. ○ sail   ○ sale

6. We can't _____ the music.   ○ hear   ○ here

Part C

Morphograph Analysis
Fill in the blanks to show the morphographs in each word.

1. _____ + _____ = expel

2. _____ + _____ + _____ = refusal

3. _____ + _____ + _____ = respectable

4. _____ + _____ = chiefly

5. _____ + _____ = complain

Name _____ Date _____

Part D

Word Building
Make 18 real words from the morphographs in the box. Additional words are possible.

ing	serve	tain	con	re	fine	form	de

1. _____   10. _____

2. _____   11. _____

3. _____   12. _____

4. _____   13. _____

5. _____   14. _____

6. _____   15. _____

7. _____   16. _____

8. _____   17. _____

9. _____   18. _____

Part E

Writing
Write two or three sentences about the picture. The sentences must contain the words **swim, island,** and **worry.**

_____

_____

_____

_____

_____

Name _____ Date _____

Part A

Word Building
Write the new word in the blank.

1. fail + ure = _____

2. trans + plant = _____

3. wake + en + ing = _____

4. con + struct + ion = _____

5. ex + cept + ion + al = _____

Part B

Proofreading
Circle the letter beside the misspelled word in each group.
Then write the word correctly on the line.

1. **A** reqwest
   B revision
   C while
   D feature
   _____

2. **A** basic
   B quoteable
   C dangerous
   D reverse
   _____

3. **A** breifly
   B physical
   C spinning
   D tomorrow
   _____

4. **A** transfer
   B photograph
   C straight
   D heavyest
   _____

5. **A** science
   B committee
   C interested
   D duties
   _____

6. **A** worried
   B showen
   C cloudiness
   D pleasure
   _____

Part C

Morphograph Analysis
Fill in the blanks to show the morphographs in each word.

1. _____ + _____ = denial

2. _____ + _____ + _____ = shamefully

3. _____ + _____ + _____ = extension

4. _____ + _____ + _____ = appointment

5. _____ + _____ = worthy

Name _____ Date _____

Part D

Word Building
Make 9 real words from the morphographs in the box.

tract	con	ject	in	ion	duct	re

1. _____ 6. _____
2. _____ 7. _____
3. _____ 8. _____
4. _____ 9. _____
5. _____

Part E

Vocabulary
Write the word for each meaning.

1. _____ not typical
2. _____ full of hate
3. _____ most light
4. _____ place back

Part F

Writing
Write two or three sentences about the picture. The sentences must contain the words **pretend, explore,** and **discover.**

_____
_____
_____
_____
_____

Name _____ Date _____

Part A

Word Building
Write the new word in the blank.

1. graph + ic + ly   = _____

2. mother + hood   = _____

3. fact + ual   = _____

4. per + form + ing   = _____

5. per + fect + ion   = _____

Part B

Proofreading
Circle the letter beside the misspelled word in each group.
Then write the word correctly on the line.

1. **A** useless

   B realy

   C changing

   D strength

   _____

2. **A** sleepyness

   B athletic

   C furious

   D basic

   _____

3. **A** nineteen

   B fashion

   C version

   D cheif

   _____

4. **A** photograph

   B vizion

   C breathless

   D spirit

   _____

5. **A** sieze

   B duties

   C request

   D settle

   _____

6. **A** straight

   B explain

   C hopefully

   D thrown

   _____

Part C

Morphograph Analysis
Fill in the blanks to show the morphographs in each word.

1. _____ + _____ = spiritual

2. _____ + _____ + _____ = likelihood

3. _____ + _____ + _____ = performer

4. _____ + _____ + _____ = contraction

5. _____ + _____ = recur

Name _____ Date _____

Part D

Word Search
These words are in the puzzle.
Circle 9 or more of the words.

tend	alike	wonder
thousand	shine	cement
sort	graphic	ground
danger	heroic	voters
spend	government	

```
g t t w c s h i n e
g h t g o e p g t c
g o v e r n m e n t
r u c o n a d e n e
o s o r t d p e n d
u a l i k e r h r t
n n c c h e r o i c
d d a n g e r s m c
```

Part E

Vocabulary
Write the contraction.

1. _____ does not

2. _____ you are

3. _____ they have

4. _____ she is

Part F

Writing
Write two or three sentences about the
picture. The sentences must contain the
words **construct, danger,** and **gradual.**

_____

_____

_____

_____

_____

Name _____ Date _____

Part A

Word Building
Write the new word in the blank.

1. hero + ic + ly   = _____

2. class + ic + ly   = _____

3. act + ive + ate   = _____

4. sign + ate + ure   = _____

5. ex + plore + er   = _____

Part B

Proofreading
Circle the letter beside the misspelled word in each group.
Then write the word correctly on the line.

1. **A** winner

   B veried

   C searches

   D rhythmically

   _____

2. **A** soften

   B should'nt

   C reduction

   D misplaced

   _____

3. **A** trophys

   B stepping

   C restriction

   D committee

   _____

4. **A** cheif

   B activate

   C vision

   D extent

   _____

5. **A** translate

   B stretchs

   C falsehood

   D delightful

   _____

6. **A** scenic

   B guiding

   C lighten

   D feetured

   _____

Part C

Morphograph Analysis
Fill in the blanks to show the morphographs in each word.

1. _____ + _____ + _____ = belongs

2. _____ + _____ + _____ = designate

3. _____ + _____ + _____ = replied

4. _____ + _____ + _____ = confusing

5. _____ + _____ + _____ = transmitted

Name _____   Date _____

Part D

Proofreading
Rewrite the letter, spelling each
word correctly.

_____

_____

_____

_____

_____

_____

_____

_____

_____

_____

_____

Dear Pat,

    Thank you vary much for the pet lzard you sent
me. Wood you blieve that the little fellow has begun
snaping at people? My aunt was playing with him
last nite. Suddenly, the lizard jumped up and bit
her write on the knows. Lukyly, the bite wasn't bad.

    Thanks again for the unuseual pet.

                    Your firend,

                    Chris

Part E

Writing
Write two or three sentences about the
picture. The sentences must contain the
words **forgotten**, **likelihood**, and **apartment**.

_____

_____

_____

_____

_____

Name _____ Date _____

Part A

Word Building
Write the new word in the blank.

1. im + prove + ment　　= _____
2. con + vert + ed　　　= _____
3. be + lief + s　　　　= _____
4. ob + serve + ate + ion = _____
5. sign + ate + ure　　　= _____

Part B

Proofreading
Fill in the bubble below the misspelled word. Write the word correctly in the blank.

1. Scientists proclame that the new medication will improve the condition. _____
　　○　　　○　　　　　　　○

2. The childhood belief in elves fasinates many writers. _____
　　　○　　○　　　　○

3. The endless search for my beautiful bracelet was depresing. _____
　　○　　　　　　　　　○　　　○

4. The commisioner obtained permission to reduce our taxes. _____
　　○　　　○　　　○

Part C

Morphograph Analysis
Fill in the blanks to show the morphographs in each word.

1. _____ + _____ + _____ = incurable
2. _____ + _____ + _____ = signature
3. _____ + _____ + _____ = perfection
4. _____ + _____ + _____ = subtraction
5. _____ + _____ + _____ = improvement

Name _____ Date _____

Part D

Word Search
These words are in the puzzle.
Circle 6 or more of the words.

today	draw	duty
tough	false	agree
over	grief	after
style		

```
t o u g h s
a o v e r t
f g d u t y
t r r a l l
e i a e y e
r e w g e e
d f a l s e
```

Part E

Vocabulary
Write the plural for each word.

1. _____ life

2. _____ wolf

3. _____ knife

4. _____ leaf

5. _____ half

Part F

Writing
Write two or three sentences about the
picture. The sentences must contain the
words **photograph**, **prevent**, and **because.**

_____

_____

_____

_____

_____

_____

Name _____ Date _____

Part A

Word Building
Write the new word in the blank.

1. de + ceive   = _____

2. ad + vise + ment   = _____

3. e + value + ate   = _____

4. ob + serve + ate + ion = _____

5. de + pend + ing   = _____

Part B

Proofreading
Rewrite the letter, spelling each
word correctly.

_____

_____

_____

_____

_____

_____

_____

_____

_____

_____

_____

_____

_____

_____

Dear Customer:
    Are you spending more time than you need to
on jobs arround the house? I am righting to inform
you that we are now produsing the most usefull
tool ever made for the home. The E-Z Tool can do
thousans of jobs. It waters plants. It washs
windows, serves you dinner, and cures bad breth,
to. The E-Z Tool can be put together easyly using
instrucshuns that come with each order.
    Please send us your order tomorow.
            Sincrely,
            I. M. Selling

Name _____ Date _____

Part C

Morphograph Analysis
Fill in the blanks to show the morphographs in each word.

1. _____ + _____ + _____ = adjustment

2. _____ + _____ + _____ = emerged

3. _____ + _____ + _____ = destruction

4. _____ + _____ + _____ = implied

5. _____ + _____ + _____ = basically

Part D

Writing
Write a story about the picture. Use as many of these words as you can: **instruction, students, skills, concept, sketches, image, simple, draw, brushes, show, class, doggy, book, realistic, describe,** and **form.**

_____

_____

_____

_____

_____

_____

_____

_____

_____

_____

_____

_____

Name _____ Date _____

Part A

Word Building

Write the new word in the blank.

1. e + duce + ate   = _____

2. inter + act + ion   = _____

3. sup + press + ion   = _____

4. e + mote + ion + al   = _____

5. family + **es**   = _____

Part B

Proofreading

Fill in the bubble below the misspelled word. Write the word correctly in the blank.

1. <u>Describing</u> the robber's <u>voise</u> to the <u>detective</u> was a challenge.   _____
   ○   ○   ○

2. The <u>flawwed</u> signature was a trick to <u>deceive</u> my <u>assistant</u>.   _____
   ○   ○   ○

3. To <u>adequeately</u> <u>evaluate</u> the foxes, we will have to <u>observe</u> them.   _____
   ○   ○   ○

4. To our <u>disbelief</u>, the <u>supplies</u> were shipped to a <u>dishonist</u> customer.   _____
   ○   ○   ○

Part C

Morphograph Analysis

Fill in the blanks to show the morphographs in each word.

1. _____ + _____ + _____ = medication

2. _____ + _____ + _____ = prediction

3. _____ + _____ + _____ = attractive

4. _____ + _____ + _____ = intersection

5. _____ + _____ + _____ = instantly

Name _____ Date _____

Part D

Word Building
Make 8 real words from the morphographs in the box.

verse	con	sign	re	serve	ion	ate

1. _____   5. _____

2. _____   6. _____

3. _____   7. _____

4. _____   8. _____

Part E

Writing
Write a story about the picture. Use as many of these words as you can: **elephant, photographer, relentless, heroically, rope, heavy, hardships, river, bridge, insects, guide, adventurous, exploration,** and **hike.**

_____

_____

_____

_____

_____

_____

_____

_____

_____

_____

_____

_____

Name _____ Date _____

Part A

Word Building
Write the new word in the blank.

1. re + fer + ing   = _____
2. hot + est   = _____
3. dis + arm + ed   = _____
4. ship + ing   = _____
5. de + tect + ive   = _____

Part B

Proofreading
Fill in the bubble below the misspelled word. Write the word correctly in the blank.

1. The <u>study</u> of <u>insects</u> <u>facinates</u> me.   _____
   ○   ○   ○

2. Some forms of <u>energy</u> are <u>destructive</u> to the <u>enviroment</u>.   _____
                  ○   ○   ○

3. My doctor won't <u>write</u> a <u>persription</u> unless it is really <u>necessary</u>.   _____
                   ○   ○   ○

4. Our <u>friends</u> just <u>bougth</u> a new <u>automobile</u>.   _____
       ○   ○   ○

Part C

Morphograph Analysis
Fill in the blanks to show the morphographs in each word.

1. _____ + _____ + _____ = precisely
2. _____ + _____ + _____ = remoteness
3. _____ + _____ + _____ = inquiry
4. _____ + _____ + _____ = commotion
5. _____ + _____ + _____ = attraction

Name _____ Date _____

Part D

Word Building
Make 11 real words from the morphographs in the box.

ex	ion	com	press	re	sup	ive

1. _____   7. _____

2. _____   8. _____

3. _____   9. _____

4. _____   10. _____

5. _____   11. _____

6. _____

Part E

Writing
Write a story about the picture. Use as many of these words as you can: **dismiss, court, emotional, detective, tear, denies, contempt, reporter, crying, confession, prove, benches, objection, comical, challenge,** and **honesty.**

_____

_____

_____

_____

_____

_____

_____

_____

_____

_____

Name _____ Date _____

Part A

Vocabulary
Write the plural for each word.

1. _____ worry   4. _____ chief

2. _____ thief   5. _____ wife

3. _____ scratch 6. _____ bush

Part B

Proofreading
Fill in the bubble below the misspelled word. Write the word correctly in the blank.

1. To the <u>relief</u> of the students, the strict <u>professer</u> was <u>dismissed</u>.   _____
   ○   ○   ○

2. <u>Sevral</u> nations provide <u>protection</u> to <u>foreign</u> citizens.   _____
   ○   ○   ○

3. The <u>gradual</u> increase in <u>temperature</u> <u>improoved</u> everyone's mood.   _____
   ○   ○   ○

4. The <u>photographs</u> of the <u>island</u> were <u>remarkible</u>.   _____
   ○   ○   ○

Part C

Morphograph Analysis
Fill in the blanks to show the morphographs in each word.

1. _____ + _____ + _____ = dictionary

2. _____ + _____ + _____ = partially

3. _____ + _____ + _____ = precisely

4. _____ + _____ + _____ = basically

5. _____ + _____ + _____ = unlikely

Name _____ Date _____

Part D

Word Building

If there is an **i-o-n** form of the word, write it in the second column.
If there is no **i-o-n** form of the word, leave the second column blank.
In the last column, write the word with the morphograph **o-r** or **e-r**.

	ion form	**or** or **er** form
1. profess	_____	_____
2. instruct	_____	_____
3. custom	_____	_____
4. invent	_____	_____
5. inspect	_____	_____

Part E

Writing

Write a story about the picture. Use as many of these words as you can: **progress, division, instructor, educate, perform, likelihood, incomplete, approval, introduce,** and **constant.**

_____

_____

_____

_____

_____

_____

_____

_____

_____

_____

_____

Name _____ Date _____

Part A

Vocabulary
Write the plural for each word.

1. _____ match   4. _____ photograph

2. _____ calf   5. _____ supply

3. _____ leaf   6. _____ bush

Part B

Proofreading
Fill in the bubble below the misspelled word. Write the word correctly in the blank.

1. The student's <u>notebook</u> was <u>tradgically</u> <u>submerged</u> in the lake.   _____
   ○   ○   ○

2. A cold <u>compress</u> <u>basically</u> can help an <u>infecsion</u>.   _____
         ○   ○   ○

3. This <u>oblong</u> shape makes a <u>perfect</u> <u>struture</u>.   _____
        ○   ○   ○

4. The <u>shopper</u> <u>nervousley</u> asked the <u>assistants</u> for help.   _____
       ○   ○   ○

Part C

Morphograph Analysis
Fill in the blanks to show the morphographs in each word.

1. _____ + _____ + _____ = likelihood

2. _____ + _____ + _____ = disgraceful

3. _____ + _____ + _____ = imperfect

4. _____ + _____ + _____ = commission

5. _____ + _____ + _____ = observer

Name _____ Date _____

Part D

Word Building

If there is an **i-o-n** form of the word, write it in the second column.
If there is no **i-o-n** form of the word, leave the second column blank.
In the last column, write the word with the morphograph **o-r** or **e-r.**

	ion form	**or** or **er** form
1. conduct	_____	_____
2. supply	_____	_____
3. inject	_____	_____
4. act	_____	_____
5. light	_____	_____

Part E

Writing

Write a story about the picture. Use as many of these words as you can: **protection, construction, paint, boat, investment, alongside, artist, transform, because, became, convert, relationship, expensive, include, tourism,** and **compare.**

_____
_____
_____
_____
_____
_____
_____
_____
_____
_____

Name _____ Date _____

Part A

Word Building
Write a new word in the blank.

1. danger + ous = _____dangerous_____
2. seize + ure = _____seizure_____
3. quest + ion + able = _____questionable_____
4. poison + ous = _____poisonous_____
5. con + tent = _____content_____
6. re + sent + ment = _____resentment_____
7. shine + y = _____shiny_____
8. fail + ure = _____failure_____

Part B

Proofreading
Fill in the bubble below the misspelled word. Write the word correctly in the blank.

1. Could you speak a little lowder, please ?   _____louder_____
   ○   ●   ○
2. Where are all the fameous people?   _____famous_____
   ○   ○   ○
3. Thier was no reason for the rejection.   _____There_____
   ●   ○   ○
4. The gloryous cities were surprising.   _____glorious_____
   ●   ○   ○
5. They expressed delite over the outcome.   _____delight_____
        ○   ●   ○
6. Everyone who was on duty felt frightened and edgey.   _____edgy_____
                        ○   ○   ●

204   Copyright © 2001 SRA/McGraw-Hill. Permission is granted to reproduce for classroom use.

Name _____ Date _____

Part C

Morphograph Analysis
Fill in the blanks to show the morphographs in each word.

1. ___feat___ + ___ure___ = feature
2. ___re___ + ___press___ + ___ive___ = repressive
3. ___de___ + ___feat___ + ___ed___ = defeated
4. ___pro___ + ___found___ = profound
5. ___value___ + ___able___ = valuable

Part D

Vocabulary
Write the contraction.

1. ___we're___ we are
2. ___can't___ cannot
3. ___they'll___ they will
4. ___don't___ do not
5. ___he's___ he is

Part E

Writing
Write two or three sentences about the picture. The sentences must contain the words **compete**, **athlete**, and **progress**.

_____
_____
_____
_____
_____

Copyright © 2001 SRA/McGraw-Hill. Permission is granted to reproduce for classroom use.   205

Name _____ Date _____

Part A

Word Building
Write a new word in the blank.

1. hope + ful = ___hopeful___   4. con + tent + ment = ___contentment___
2. dis + ease = ___disease___   5. fame + ous = ___famous___
3. re + tain + ing = ___retaining___

Part B

Proofreading
Fill in the bubble beside the the word that goes in the blank. Write the word in the blank.

1. The ___weather___ has been great.   ● weather   ○ wether
2. They found ___their___ things in the garage.   ● their   ○ there
3. We ___threw___ rocks into the lake.   ○ through   ● threw
4. Pete ate ___too___ much.   ○ to   ● too
5. Please bring those books ___here___.   ○ hear   ● here
6. I've never heard such a strange ___tale___.   ○ tail   ● tale

Part C

Word Building
Make 9 real words from the morphographs in the box. Additional words are possible.

est	mad	happy	ly	wide	ness	fine

1. ___maddest___   6. ___widest___
2. ___madly___   7. ___widely___
3. ___madness___   8. ___wideness___
4. ___happiest___   9. ___finest___
5. ___happily___

206   Copyright © 2001 SRA/McGraw-Hill. Permission is granted to reproduce for classroom use.

Name _____ Date _____

Part C

Morphograph Analysis
Fill in the blanks to show the morphographs in each word.

1. ___text___ + ___ure___ = texture
2. ___pro___ + ___tect___ + ___ive___ = protective
3. ___dis___ + ___charge___ + ___ed___ = discharged
4. ___story___ + ___es___ = stories
5. ___please___ + ___ure___ = pleasure

Part D

Vocabulary
Write the contraction.

1. ___that's___ that is
2. ___shouldn't___ should not
3. ___they've___ they have
4. ___who's___ who is
5. ___she'll___ she will

Part E

Writing
Write two or three sentences about the picture. The sentences must contain the words **distance**, **weather**, and **cloud**.

_____
_____
_____
_____
_____

Copyright © 2001 SRA/McGraw-Hill. Permission is granted to reproduce for classroom use.   207

Name _____ Date _____

Part A

Word Building
Write the new word in the blank.

1. dis + please + ing = _displeasing_
2. speed + y + est = _speediest_
3. re + spect + ful = _respectful_
4. danger + ous + ly = _dangerously_
5. in + crease + ing + ly = _increasingly_

Part B

Proofreading
Fill in the bubble beside the the word that goes in the blank. Write the word in the blank.

1. I poked a _hole_ in my worksheet. ● hole ○ whole
2. Would you care for a _piece_ of pie? ○ peace ● piece
3. Robin didn't _hear_ the question. ● hear ○ here
4. _Two_ police officers visited our school. ○ Too ● Two
5. Our house became _very_ warm. ○ vary ● very
6. The dog's _tail_ is short. ● tail ○ tale

Part C

Word Building
Make 9 real words from the morphographs in the box.

ed	cover	un	re	dis	solve

1. _covered_
2. _uncover_
3. _uncovered_
4. _recover_
5. _recovered_
6. _discover_
7. _discovered_
8. _dissolve_
9. _dissolved_

208 Copyright © 2001 SRA/McGraw-Hill. Permission is granted to reproduce for classroom use.

Name _____ Date _____

Part D

Morphograph Analysis
Fill in the blanks to show the morphographs in each word.

1. _ex_ + _pel_ = expel
2. _re_ + _fuse_ + _al_ = refusal
3. _re_ + _spect_ + _able_ = respectable
4. _chief_ + _ly_ = chiefly
5. _com_ + _plain_ = complain

Part E

Vocabulary
Write the word for each meaning.

1. _typist_ one who types
2. _quarter_ fourth of a dollar
3. _furious_ the quality of fury
4. _dislike_ do not like
5. _infamous_ really famous

Part F

Writing
Write two or three sentences about the picture. The sentences must contain the words **recreation**, **afternoon**, and **winner**.

_____
_____
_____
_____
_____
_____

Copyright © 2001 SRA/McGraw-Hill. Permission is granted to reproduce for classroom use. 209

Name _____ Date _____

Part A

Word Building
Write a new word in the blank.

1. create + ive = _creative_
2. dis + courage = _discourage_
3. re + gard + less = _regardless_
4. niece + es = _nieces_
5. in + tense + ive + ly = _intensively_

Part B

Proofreading
Fill in the bubble below the misspelled word. Write the word correctly in the blank.

1. Mom agreed that we'er getting new glasses today. _we're_
   ○   ●   ○
2. The tourists traveled joyusly together. _joyously_
   ○   ●   ○
3. The clowdiness and temperature made us unhappy. _cloudiness_
   ●   ○   ○

Part C

Proofreading
Circle the letter beside the misspelled word in each group.
Then write the word correctly on the line.

1. A breakable
   Ⓑ dowbt
   C pleasure
   D peaceful
   doubt
2. A increase
   B changing
   C noisily
   Ⓓ ejucate
   educate
3. A exchange
   B chance
   C wreckage
   Ⓓ sturdyness
   sturdiness
4. A honesty
   Ⓑ tomorow
   C inspect
   D product
   tomorrow
5. Ⓐ revursal
   B compound
   C chance
   D vision
   reversal
6. A basic
   Ⓑ transeport
   C incident
   D refuse
   transport

210 Copyright © 2001 SRA/McGraw-Hill. Permission is granted to reproduce for classroom use.

Name _____ Date _____

Part D

Morphograph Analysis
Fill in the blanks to show the morphographs in each word.

1. _in_ + _fer_ = infer
2. _trans_ + _form_ + _ed_ = transformed
3. _ex_ + _plain_ + _able_ = explainable
4. _pound_ + _age_ = poundage
5. _re_ + _sign_ = resign

Part E

Vocabulary
Write the word for each meaning.

1. _explorer_ one who explores
2. _artist_ one who produces art
3. _joyous_ the quality of joy
4. _watches_ more than one watch
5. _displeasing_ not pleasing

Part F

Writing
Write two or three sentences about the picture. The sentences must contain the words **danger**, **poison**, and **reach**.

_____
_____
_____
_____
_____

Copyright © 2001 SRA/McGraw-Hill. Permission is granted to reproduce for classroom use. 211

Copyright © 2001 SRA/McGraw-Hill. Permission is granted to reproduce for classroom use.

233

Name _____ Date _____

Part A

Word Building
Write the new word in the blank.

1. dis + pose + al = _disposal_
2. a + muse + ment = _amusement_
3. for + got + en = _forgotten_
4. photo + graph + y = _photography_
5. mis + in + struct + ed = _misinstructed_

Part B

Proofreading
Fill in the bubble beside the word that goes in the blank. Write the word in the blank.

1. Martin always hangs up his _clothes_ ○ close ● clothes
2. I don't _know_ the answer. ● know ○ no
3. Our club _meets_ after school. ○ meats ● meets
4. There is a _lone_ tree growing in our yard. ○ loan ● lone
5. The tickets go on _sale_ in the morning. ○ sail ● sale
6. We can't _hear_ the music. ● hear ○ here

Part C

Morphograph Analysis
Fill in the blanks to show the morphographs in each word.

1. _ex_ + _pel_ = expel
2. _re_ + _fuse_ + _al_ = refusal
3. _re_ + _spect_ + _able_ = respectable
4. _chief_ + _ly_ = chiefly
5. _com_ + _plain_ = complain

Name _____ Date _____

Part D

Word Building
Make 18 real words from the morphographs in the box. Additional words are possible.

ing	serve	tain	con	re	fine	form	de

1. _serving_
2. _conserve_
3. _conserving_
4. _contain_
5. _containing_
6. _fining_
7. _confine_
8. _confining_
9. _define_
10. _defining_
11. _detain_
12. _detaining_
13. _retain_
14. _retaining_
15. _forming_
16. _conform_
17. _conforming_
18. _reform_

Part E

Writing
Write two or three sentences about the picture. The sentences must contain the words **swim**, **island**, and **worry**.

_____
_____
_____
_____
_____

Name _____ Date _____

Part A

Word Building
Write the new word in the blank.

1. fail + ure = _failure_
2. trans + plant = _transplant_
3. wake + en + ing = _wakening_
4. con + struct + ion = _construction_
5. ex + cept + ion + al = _exceptional_

Part B

Proofreading
Circle the letter beside the misspelled word in each group.
Then write the word correctly on the line.

1. **A** reqwest
   B revision
   C while
   D feature
   request

2. **A** basic
   B quoteable
   C dangerous
   D reverse
   quotable

3. **A** breifly
   B physical
   C spinning
   D tomorrow
   briefly

4. **A** transfer
   B photograph
   C straight
   D heavyest
   heaviest

5. **A** science
   B committee
   C interested
   D duties
   interested

6. **A** worried
   B showen
   C cloudiness
   D pleasure
   shown

Part C

Morphograph Analysis
Fill in the blanks to show the morphographs in each word.

1. _deny_ + _al_ = denial
2. _shame_ + _ful_ + _ly_ = shamefully
3. _ex_ + _tend_ + _ion_ = extension
4. _ap_ + _point_ + _ment_ = appointment
5. _worth_ + _y_ = worthy

38

Name _____ Date _____

Part D

Word Building
Make 9 real words from the morphographs in the box.

tract	con	ject	in	ion	duct	re

1. _contract_
2. _contraction_
3. _inject_
4. _injection_
5. _induct_
6. _induction_
7. _reject_
8. _rejection_
9. _traction_

Part E

Vocabulary
Write the word for each meaning.

1. _atypical_ not typical
2. _hateful_ full of hate
3. _lightest_ most light
4. _replace_ place back

Part F

Writing
Write two or three sentences about the picture. The sentences must contain the words **pretend**, **explore**, and **discover**.

_____
_____
_____
_____

Name _____ Date _____

Part A

Word Building
Write the new word in the blank.

1. graph + ic + ly = graphically
2. mother + hood = motherhood
3. fact + ual = factual
4. per + form + ing = performing
5. per + fect + ion = perfection

Part B

Proofreading
Circle the letter beside the misspelled word in each group.
Then write the word correctly on the line.

1. A useless
   B realy
   C changing
   D strength
   _____ really

2. **A** sleepyness
   B athletic
   C furious
   D basic
   _____ sleepiness

3. A nineteen
   B fashion
   C version
   D cheif
   _____ chief

4. A photograph
   B vizion
   C breathless
   D spirit
   _____ vision

5. **A** sieze
   B duties
   C request
   D settle
   _____ seize

6. A straight
   B explain
   C hopefully
   D throwen
   _____ thrown

Part C

Morphograph Analysis
Fill in the blanks to show the morphographs in each word.

1. spirit + ual = spiritual
2. like + ly + hood = likelihood
3. per + form + er = performer
4. con + tract + ion = contraction
5. re + cur = recur

Copyright © 2001 SRA/McGraw-Hill. Permission is granted to reproduce for classroom use.

Name _____ Date _____

Part D

Word Search
These words are in the puzzle.
Circle 9 or more of the words.

tend   alike   wonder
thousand   shine   cement
sort   graphic   ground
danger   heroic   voters
spend   government

```
g t t w c s h i n e
g h t g o e p g t c
g o v e r n m e n t
r u c o n a d e n e
o s o r t d p e n d
u a l i k e r h r t
n n c c h e r o i c
d d a n g e r s m c
```

Part E

Vocabulary
Write the contraction.

1. doesn't   does not
2. you're   you are
3. they've   they have
4. she's   she is

Part F

Writing
Write two or three sentences about the
picture. The sentences must contain the
words **construct, danger,** and **gradual.**

_____
_____
_____
_____
_____
_____

Copyright © 2001 SRA/McGraw-Hill. Permission is granted to reproduce for classroom use.

Name _____ Date _____

Part A

Word Building
Write the new word in the blank.

1. hero + ic + ly = heroically
2. class + ic + ly = classically
3. act + ive + ate = activate
4. sign + ate + ure = signature
5. ex + plore + er = explorer

Part B

Proofreading
Circle the letter beside the misspelled word in each group.
Then write the word correctly on the line.

1. A winner
   B veried
   C searches
   D rhythmically
   _____ varied

2. A soften
   B should'nt
   C reduction
   D misplaced
   _____ shouldn't

3. **A** trophys
   B stepping
   C restriction
   D committee
   _____ trophies

4. **A** cheif
   B activate
   C vision
   D extent
   _____ chief

5. A translate
   B stretchs
   C falsehood
   D delightful
   _____ stretches

6. A scenic
   B guiding
   C lighten
   D feetured
   _____ featured

Part C

Morphograph Analysis
Fill in the blanks to show the morphographs in each word.

1. be + long + s = belongs
2. de + sign + ate = designate
3. re + ply + ed = replied
4. con + fuse + ing = confusing
5. trans + mit + ed = transmitted

Copyright © 2001 SRA/McGraw-Hill. Permission is granted to reproduce for classroom use.

Name _____ Date _____

Part D

Proofreading
Rewrite the letter, spelling each
word correctly.

Dear Pat,
    Thank you vary much for the pet lizard you sent
me. Wood you blieve that the little fellow has begun
snaping at people? My aunt was playing with him
last nite. Suddenly, the lizard jumped up and bit
her write on the knows. Lukyly, the bite wasn't bad.
    Thanks again for the unuseual pet.
                                    Your firend,
                                    Chris

Dear Pat,
_____ Thank you very much for the pet lizard
you sent me. Would you believe that the
little fellow has begun snapping at people?
My aunt was playing with him last night.
Suddenly, the lizard jumped up and bit her
right on the nose. Luckily, the bite wasn't
bad.
_____ Thanks again for the unusual pet.
_____ Your friend,
_____ Chris

Part E

Writing
Write two or three sentences about the
picture. The sentences must contain the
words **forgotten, likelihood,** and **apartment.**

_____
_____
_____
_____
_____

Copyright © 2001 SRA/McGraw-Hill. Permission is granted to reproduce for classroom use.

43

Name _____ Date _____

Part A

Word Building
Write the new word in the blank.

1. im + prove + ment = _improvement_
2. con + vert + ed = _converted_
3. be + lief + s = _beliefs_
4. ob + serve + ate + ion = _observation_
5. sign + ate + ure = _signature_

Part B

Proofreading
Fill in the bubble below the misspelled word. Write the word correctly in the blank.

1. Scientists proclame that the new medication will improve the condition. _proclaim_
   ○ ● ○

2. The childhood belief in elves fasinates many writers. _fascinates_
   ○ ○ ●

3. The endless search for my beautiful bracelet was depresing. _depressing_
   ○ ○ ●

4. The commisioner obtained permission to reduce our taxes. _commissioner_
   ● ○ ○

Part C

Morphograph Analysis
Fill in the blanks to show the morphographs in each word.

1. _in_ + _cure_ + _able_ = incurable
2. _sign_ + _ate_ + _ure_ = signature
3. _per_ + _fect_ + _ion_ = perfection
4. _sub_ + _tract_ + _ion_ = subtraction
5. _im_ + _prove_ + _ment_ = improvement

220   Copyright © 2001 SRA/McGraw-Hill. Permission is granted to reproduce for classroom use.

44

Name _____ Date _____

Part D

Word Search
These words are in the puzzle.
Circle 6 or more of the words.

today   draw   duty
tough   false   agree
over   grief   after
style

t o u g h	s
a o v e r	t
f g d u t	y
t r r a l	l
e i a e y	e
r e w g e	e
d f a l s e

Part E

Vocabulary
Write the plural for each word.

1. _lives_   life
2. _wolves_ wolf
3. _knives_ knife
4. _leaves_ leaf
5. _halves_ half

Part F

Writing
Write two or three sentences about the picture. The sentences must contain the words **photograph**, **prevent**, and **because**.

_____
_____
_____
_____
_____

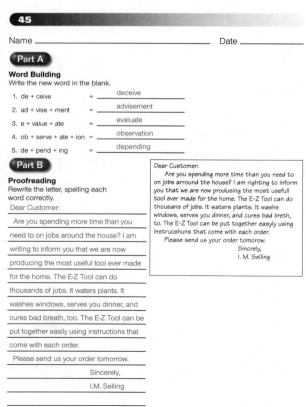

Copyright © 2001 SRA/McGraw-Hill. Permission is granted to reproduce for classroom use.   221

45

Name _____ Date _____

Part A

Word Building
Write the new word in the blank.

1. de + ceive = _deceive_
2. ad + vise + ment = _advisement_
3. e + value + ate = _evaluate_
4. ob + serve + ate + ion = _observation_
5. de + pend + ing = _depending_

Part B

Proofreading
Rewrite the letter, spelling each word correctly.

> Dear Customer:
>   Are you spending more time than you need to on jobs arround the house? I am righting to inform you that we are now produsing the most usefull tool ever made for the home. The E-Z Tool can do thousans of jobs. It waters plants. It washs windows, serves you dinner, and cures bad breth, to. The E-Z Tool can be put together easyly using instrucshuns that come with each order.
>   Please send us your order tomorrow.
>   Sincerely,
>   I. M. Selling

Dear Customer:

Are you spending more time than you

need to on jobs around the house? I am

writing to inform you that we are now

producing the most useful tool ever made

for the home. The E-Z Tool can do

thousands of jobs. It waters plants. It

washes windows, serves you dinner, and

cures bad breath, too. The E-Z Tool can be

put together easily using instructions that

come with each order.

Please send us your order tomorrow.

Sincerely,

I.M. Selling

222   Copyright © 2001 SRA/McGraw-Hill. Permission is granted to reproduce for classroom use.

46

Name _____ Date _____

Part C

Morphograph Analysis
Fill in the blanks to show the morphographs in each word.

1. _ad_ + _just_ + _ment_ = adjustment
2. _e_ + _merge_ + _ed_ = emerged
3. _de_ + _struct_ + _ion_ = destruction
4. _im_ + _ply_ + _ed_ = implied
5. _base_ + _ic_ + _ly_ = basically

Part D

Writing
Write a story about the picture. Use as many of these words as you can: **instruction, students, skills, concept, sketches, image, simple, draw, brushes, show, class, doggy, book, realistic, describe,** and **form.**

_____
_____
_____
_____
_____
_____
_____
_____
_____
_____
_____

Copyright © 2001 SRA/McGraw-Hill. Permission is granted to reproduce for classroom use.   223

---

236   Copyright © 2001 SRA/McGraw-Hill. Permission is granted to reproduce for classroom use.

47

Name _____ Date _____

Part A

Word Building
Write the new word in the blank.

1. e + duce + ate = educate
2. inter + act + ion = interaction
3. sup + press + ion = suppression
4. e + mote + ion + al = emotional
5. family + es = families

Part B

Proofreading
Fill in the bubble below the misspelled word. Write the word correctly in the blank.

1. Describing the robber's voise to the detective was a challenge.   voice
2. The flawwed signature was a trick to deceive my assistant.   flawed
3. To adequeately evaluate the foxes, we will have to observe them.   adequately
4. To our disbelief, the supplies were shipped to a dishonist customer.   dishonest

Part C

Morphograph Analysis
Fill in the blanks to show the morphographs in each word.

1. medic + ate + ion = medication
2. pre + dict + ion = prediction
3. at + tract + ive = attractive
4. inter + sect + ion = intersection
5. in + stant + ly = instantly

48

Name _____ Date _____

Part D

Word Building
Make 8 real words from the morphographs in the box.

verse	con	sign	re	serve	ion	ate

1. converse
2. reverse
3. conversation
4. resign
5. reservation
6. conservation
7. conserve
8. reserve

Part E

Writing
Write a story about the picture. Use as many of these words as you can: **elephant, photographer, relentless, heroically, rope, heavy, hardships, river, bridge, insects, guide, adventurous, exploration,** and **hike.**

49

Name _____ Date _____

Part A

Word Building
Write the new word in the blank.

1. re + fer + ing = referring
2. hot + est = hottest
3. dis + arm + ed = disarmed
4. ship + ing = shipping
5. de + tect + ive = detective

Part B

Proofreading
Fill in the bubble below the misspelled word. Write the word correctly in the blank.

1. The study of insects facinates me.   fascinates
2. Some forms of energy are destructive to the enviroment.   environment
3. My doctor won't write a persription unless it is really necessary.   prescription
4. Our friends just bought a new automobile.   bought

Part C

Morphograph Analysis
Fill in the blanks to show the morphographs in each word.

1. pre + cise + ly = precisely
2. re + mote + ness = remoteness
3. in + quire + y = inquiry
4. com + mote + ion = commotion
5. at + tract + ion = attraction

50

Name _____ Date _____

Part D

Word Building
Make 11 real words from the morphographs in the box.

ex	ion	com	press	re	sup	ive

1. express
2. expression
3. expressive
4. compress
5. compression
6. repress
7. repressive
8. repression
9. suppress
10. suppressive
11. suppression

Part E

Writing
Write a story about the picture. Use as many of these words as you can: **dismiss, court, emotional, detective, tear, denies, contempt, reporter, crying, confession, prove, benches, objection, comical, challenge,** and **honesty.**

Name _____ Date _____

Part A

Vocabulary
Write the plural for each word.

1. worries   worry   4. chiefs   chief
2. thieves   thief   5. wives   wife
3. scratches   scratch   6. bushes   bush

Part B

Proofreading
Fill in the bubble below the misspelled word. Write the word correctly in the blank.

1. To the relief of the students, the strict professer was dismissed.   professor
2. Sevral nations provide protection to foreign citizens.   Several
3. The gradual increase in temperature improoved everyone's mood.   improved
4. The photographs of the island were remarkible.   remarkable

Part C

Morphograph Analysis
Fill in the blanks to show the morphographs in each word.

1. dict + ion + ary = dictionary
2. part + ial + ly = partially
3. re + cise + ly = precisely
4. base + ic + ly = basically
5. un + like + ly = unlikely

Name _____ Date _____

Part D

Word Building
If there is an **i-o-n** form of the word, write it in the second column.
If there is no **i-o-n** form of the word, leave the second column blank.
In the last column, write the word with the morphograph **o-r** or **e-r.**

	ion form	**or** or **er** form
1. profess	profession	professor
2. instruct	instruction	instructor
3. custom		customer
4. invent	invention	inventor
5. inspect	inspection	inspector

Part E

Writing
Write a story about the picture. Use as many of these words as you can: **progress, division, instructor, educate, perform, likelihood, incomplete, approval, introduce,** and **constant.**

_____
_____
_____
_____
_____
_____
_____
_____
_____
_____
_____
_____

Name _____ Date _____

Part A

Vocabulary
Write the plural for each word.

1. matches   match   4. photographs   photograph
2. calves   calf   5. supplies   supply
3. leaves   leaf   6. bushes   bush

Part B

Proofreading
Fill in the bubble below the misspelled word. Write the word correctly in the blank.

1. The student's notebook was tradgically submerged in the lake.   tragically
2. A cold compress basically can help an infecsion.   infection
3. This oblong shape makes a perfect struture.   structure
4. The shopper nervousley asked the assistants for help.   nervously

Part C

Morphograph Analysis
Fill in the blanks to show the morphographs in each word.

1. like + ly + hood = likelihood
2. dis + grace + ful = disgraceful
3. im + per + fect = imperfect
4. com + miss + ion = commission
5. ob + serve + er = observer

Name _____ Date _____

Part D

Word Building
If there is an **i-o-n** form of the word, write it in the second column.
If there is no **i-o-n** form of the word, leave the second column blank.
In the last column, write the word with the morphograph **o-r** or **e-r.**

	ion form	**or** or **er** form
1. conduct	conduction	conductor
2. supply		supplier
3. inject	injection	injector
4. act	action	actor
5. light		lighter

Part E

Writing
Write a story about the picture. Use as many of these words as you can: **protection, construction, paint, boat, investment, alongside, artist, transform, because, became, convert, relationship, expensive, include, tourism,** and **compare.**

_____
_____
_____
_____
_____
_____
_____
_____
_____
_____
_____
_____